Programming Series

Focus on
Data Structures

Ninth Edition

Richard L. Stegman

Focus on Data Structures
Ninth Edition

Copyright © 2020, Richard L. Stegman

1000-10-00010100-1001-11000010-11001100

ISBN: 9781700775597

Table of Contents

Chapter 1. Introduction

Introduction to Data Structures
Analysis of Algorithms

Introduction to Data Structures

One important area of computer science deals with the study of algorithms. An algorithm is a step-by-step process for solving a problem. There are typically three important features of an algorithm:

1. The algorithm must have a finite number of instructions or steps.

2. Each instruction in the algorithm is well defined (not ambiguous).

3. The algorithm eventually halts.

The oldest known arithmetic algorithm was reported around 300 B.C. by Euclid and is a method for computing the greatest common divisor of two whole numbers. The greatest common divisor is the largest whole number that divides both numbers without remainders.

If the two numbers are A and B, Euclid's algorithm is as follows:

```
1. Compute the remainder of the division of A and B.

2. Replace A by B.

3. Replace B by the remainder computed in step 1.

4. Repeat steps 1 - 3 until B is zero.

5. The greatest common divisor is the final value of A.
```

For example, find the greatest common divisor of A = 24 and B = 9:

```
1. The remainder of 24 / 9 = 6.
2. A = 9.
3. B = 6.
4. Repeat steps 1 - 3.

1. The remainder of 9 / 6 = 3.
2. A = 6.
3. B = 3.
4. Repeat steps 1 - 3.

1. The remainder of 6 / 3 = 0.
2. A = 3.
3. B = 0.
5. The greatest common divisor is 3.
```

Computer programs are also examples of algorithms. Here's a Java method that computes the greatest common divisor of two numbers following Euclid's algorithm:

```java
// Calculates the greatest common divisor of two numbers

public int gcd(int A, int B) {
    int remainder;

    while (B != 0) {
        remainder = A % B;
        A = B;
        B = remainder;
    }
    return A;
}
```

Whether we realize it or not, algorithms are at the very center of our lives and their impact is broad and far-reaching. Here are a few of the most important algorithms today:

• **Google Page Rank.** Page rank determines how important a website is during a search based upon the number and quality of links to a page as well as the frequency and location of keywords within the page.

• **NAS Data Collection, Interpretation, and Encryption.** NSA algorithms have been spying upon millions of unsuspecting citizens by monitoring phone calls, emails, webcam images, and geographic locations.

• **MP3 Compression.** The MP3 compression algorithm reduces the number of bits required to represent the audio recording and still sound like a true reproduction of the original uncompressed audio.

Additional algorithms that impact our lives deal with e-commerce security, HDTV, JPEG, face recognition, social network news feeds and recommendations, particle collision simulations, and the human genome project.

Implementing Algorithms

Our study of algorithms will make us more proficient programmers as understanding the basics of algorithms and their relation to data structures is important for all branches of computer science. We utilize various programming languages to help us implement algorithms. Programming languages can be placed on a continuum. At one end are the languages that are closest to the physical machine (low-level languages such as machine language and assembler language). At the other end are languages designed for sophisticated problem solving (high-level languages such as C, Java, Objective-C, C++, Swift).

Below is an example of a high-level mathematical language developed at the NYU Courant Institute of Mathematical Sciences in the late 1960s called SETL (Set Language) that outputs all prime numbers from 2 – 100.

```
print({n ∈ [2..100] | ∄ j ∈ [2..n-1] | n mod j = 0})
```

If it's not obvious ☺, this outputs the set of all numbers, n, which are elements of the range of numbers from 2 to 100, such that there does not exist a number j, which is an element of the range of numbers from 2 to n-1, such that n modulus j = 0.

The Study of Data Structures

We study data structures so that we can learn to write more efficient algorithms or programs. One of the central focuses of data structures will be the way in which we organize our data. The means by which we structure our data will determine the types of algorithms we can develop. A data structure and its associated algorithm are closely intertwined, neither one making sense without the other. Linus Torvalds, designer of Linux, has said, "Bad programmers worry about the code. Good programmers worry about data structures and their relationships."

How we organize our data will determine the algorithms we may employ to manipulate the data. For example, suppose we have a collection of n pairs of names and telephone numbers:

$$(n_1, p_1), (n_2, p_2), (n_3, p_3), ..., (n_n, p_n)$$

We want to develop an algorithm that can search and find a telephone number when provided with a name. But the type of algorithm that we can produce is very much dependent upon how the telephone numbers and names are stored or organized.

For example, if there is no order or organization to the name-telephone number pairs, the best algorithm we could devise would be one in which we looked at name after name, n_1, n_2, n_3, ..., n_n, until either the correct name was found or until we realized that the name was not present in our collection. If the correct name is found, we can simply read and output the corresponding telephone number. This *linear search* algorithm might work well for a small collection of name-telephone number pairs, but it will not be efficient for name-telephone number pairs that number in the millions.

We could do better if we knew the data was structured in some way, perhaps alphabetical order. Then we could create a second list which would tell us for each letter in the alphabet, where the last name with that letter appeared. For names beginning with d, we could avoid having to look at names beginning with other letters and we could end our search when we reach a name beginning with the letter e. So because of this new organization of our data, it is possible to structure a different, perhaps more efficient, algorithm. Of course the tradeoff here is that this new algorithm will require additional storage for the second list. But the utilization of this additional storage will make our algorithm much faster. This tradeoff of *time vs. space* (speed vs. memory) will become a major theme of our study of data structures.

Definition and Goals

We can define data structures as a study of organizing information and data efficiently, which considers not only the items being stored but also their relationship to each other.

The goal of this data structures course will be to explore many different kinds of data objects or structures. For each structure, we will consider:

- the class of operations to be performed

- the way to represent this structure so that these operations may be efficiently carried out

Specifically, we will study arrays, stacks, recursion, queues, linear and non-linear linked lists, binary trees, splay trees, priority queues, binary heaps, memory management, searching and sorting algorithms.

Analysis of Algorithms

Order of Magnitude Analysis

What does it mean to compare one algorithm with another? Suppose we have two algorithms for performing the same task. What does it mean to compare the algorithms and conclude that one is more efficient (faster) than the other? We can code up the two algorithms and run the programs and see which one finishes first. But there are three fundamental problems with this approach.

1. If algorithm A runs faster than algorithm B, it could be the result of a more efficient coding job on algorithm A. In this case we are really comparing how efficiently we implemented algorithm A over algorithm B rather than comparing the algorithms themselves. Another implementation of each of the algorithms might show algorithm B running faster than algorithm A. We want to avoid this.

2. Perhaps due to the types of the operations required by the algorithms, algorithm A runs faster than algorithm B on one computer architecture, while the opposite might be true when the algorithms are run on a different computer architecture. We would like to compare the efficiencies of the algorithms independent of a particular computer architecture.

3. Finally, there is a danger that we will select data on which one of the algorithms run uncharacteristically fast or slow. Therefore, we would like to perform our analysis independent of specific data.

To overcome these problems, we employ mathematical techniques to analyze algorithms independent of a specific implementation of an algorithm, independent of a particular computer architecture, and independent of the type of data that the algorithm utilizes. *Our approach will be to consider the time requirement of an algorithm as a function of problem size*, i.e., the number of items in a table, the size of an array, the number of nodes in a list or tree, etc.

We want to determine how quickly the algorithm's time requirement grows as a function of the problem size. We characterize this growth rate as a proportion of the problem size. For example, an algorithm might require time proportional to n or proportional to n^2 where n is the size of the problem.

Consider the following two statements:

Algorithm A requires time proportional to n.

Algorithm B requires time proportional to n^2.

Although we cannot determine the exact amount of time required by either algorithm A or B, we can determine that for large problems, algorithm A will require significantly less time than algorithm B. The amount of time required by algorithm A increases at a slower rate than the amount of time required by algorithm B.

Big-O Notation

Big-O notation (or *order-of* notation) is the primary analysis tool we use to characterize the running times of algorithms. It allows us to characterize an algorithm's running time as a function of its input size and is concerned with what happens for very large values of n.

◆ Constant Time: O(1)

O(1) represents operations that run in constant time regardless of the size of the input data. The amount of work is not dependent upon the size of the problem. Accessing an array element takes the same amount of time no matter how many items are in the array and would be said to run in constant time.

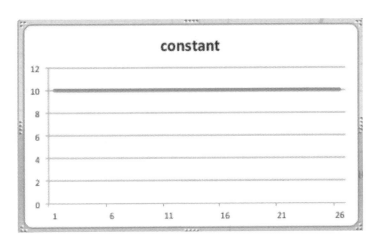

♦ Logarithm Time: $O(\log_2 n)$

In logarithmic time, the amount of work depends on the logarithm of the size of the problem. The key thing to note is that $O(\log_2 n)$ algorithms grow slowly. Doubling n has a relatively small effect as logarithmic curves flatten out nicely. Algorithms that successively cut the amount of data to be processed in half at each step typically fall into this category. An example of an $O(\log_2 n)$ or logarithmic algorithm is finding an item in a sorted list using binary search or finding an item in a balanced binary search tree.

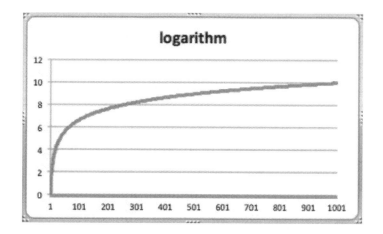

♦ Linear Time: $O(n)$

Linear time describes an algorithm whose performance will grow linearly and in direct proportion to the size of the input data. The larger the input, the longer it takes, in an even tradeoff. Every time you double n, the operation will take twice as long. Iterating through an array or linked list to find an item takes $O(n)$ time. Printing all the elements in a list of n elements is also $O(n)$.

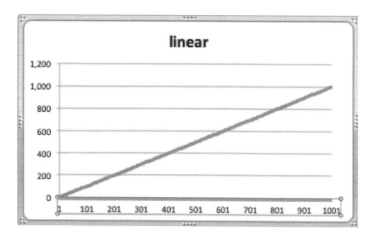

◆ **n log₂ n Time:** $O(n \ \log_2 \ n)$

Algorithms of this type typically involve performing an $O(\log \ n)$ operation for each item n in your input. Most efficient sort algorithms, such as quicksort, heapsort, and mergesort, have n-log-n complexity. That is, these algorithms can transform an unsorted array of size n into a sorted array in $O(n \ \log_2 \ n)$ time.

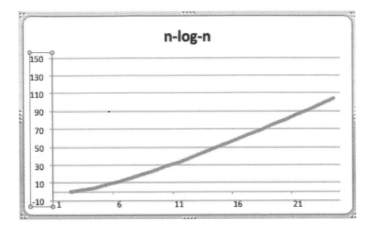

◆ **Quadratic Time:** $O(n^2)$

The algorithm's performance is proportional to the square of the input data. This means that whenever you increase the size of the input data by a factor of n, the running time of the algorithm will increase by a factor of n^2. Algorithms of this type typically involve applying a linear algorithm n times, such as in a sorting algorithm where every element in an array is compared to every other element. Quadratic operations are only really practical up to a certain input size as every time n doubles, the operation takes four times as long. Most simple sorting algorithms, such as bubblesort and quicksort (in the worst case), are $O(n^2)$ algorithms.

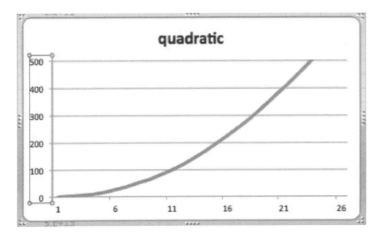

◆ Cubic Time: $O(n^3)$

The algorithm's performance is proportional to the cube of the input data. This means that whenever you increase the size of the input data by a factor of n, the running time of the algorithm will increase by a factor of n^3. Algorithms that utilize triple-nested loops will typically require cubic time.

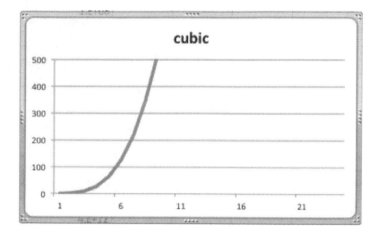

◆ Exponential Time: $O(2^n)$

Exponential time algorithms are extremely slow as $O(2^n)$ means that the execution time taken will double with each additional element n added to the input data. Exponential time increases dramatically in relation to the size of n and such algorithms are impractical for any reasonably large input size n.

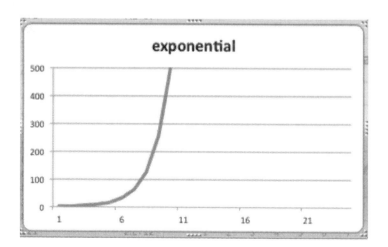

Note that our functions above are ordered by increasing growth rate. We can summarize our functions in the tables and graphs below.

constant	logarithm	linear	n-log-n	quadratic	cubic	exponential
1	$\log_2 n$	n	$n \log_2 n$	n^2	n^3	2^n

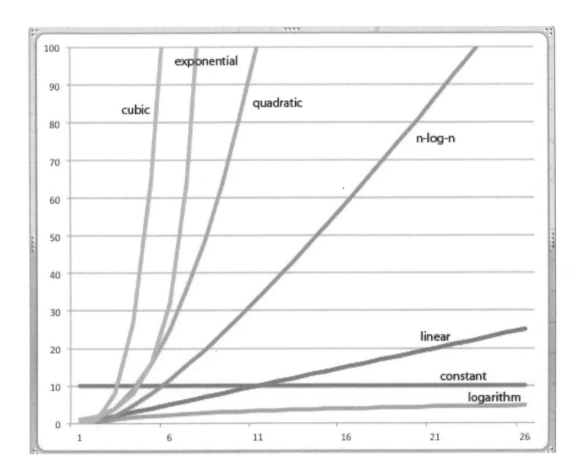

n	constant	logarithm	linear	n-log-n	quadratic	cubic	exponential
1	10	0	1	0	1	1	2
2	10	1	2	2	4	8	4
3	10	2	3	5	9	27	8
4	10	2	4	8	16	64	16
5	10	2	5	12	25	125	32
6	10	3	6	16	36	216	64
7	10	3	7	20	49	343	128
8	10	3	8	24	64	512	256
9	10	3	9	29	81	729	512
10	10	3	10	33	100	1,000	1,024
11	10	3	11	38	121	1,331	2,048
12	10	4	12	43	144	1,728	4,096
13	10	4	13	48	169	2,197	8,192
14	10	4	14	53	196	2,744	16,384
15	10	4	15	59	225	3,375	32,768
16	10	4	16	64	256	4,096	65,536
17	10	4	17	69	289	4,913	131,072
18	10	4	18	75	324	5,832	262,144
19	10	4	19	81	361	6,859	524,288
20	10	4	20	86	400	8,000	1,048,576
21	10	4	21	92	441	9,261	2,097,152
22	10	4	22	98	484	10,648	4,194,304
23	10	5	23	104	529	12,167	8,388,608
24	10	5	24	110	576	13,824	16,777,216
25	10	5	25	116	625	15,625	33,554,432

Note above that as $n \geq 10$, the range of values for the exponential function exceed those of the cubic function. This is not shown on the preceding graph. The graph below shows the exponential and cubic functions for larger values of $n \geq 10$.

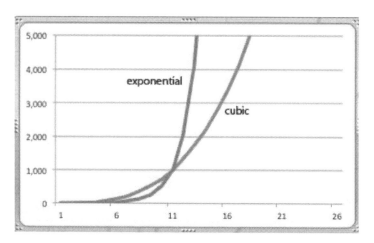

In summary, algorithms that run in $O(n\ \log\ n)$ time or faster are considered efficient. Algorithms with exponential running time are infeasible for all but the smallest sized input and should almost never be considered efficient. In the region between $n-\log-n$ and exponential time, the usefulness of an algorithm depends on the typical input sizes.

One Final Example

Assume a computer can execute 1,000,000 instructions per second. If the computer executes n = 1,000,000 instructions, how long will it take for the computer to execute $O(n\ \log_2\ n)$ instructions? $O(n^2)$ instructions? $O(n^3)$ instructions?

$O(n\ \log_2\ n)$ instructions: 20 seconds

$O(n^2)$ instructions: 11.5 days

$O(n^3)$ instructions: 317 centuries

Chapter 2. Array Mapping Functions

One-Dimensional Arrays
Two-Dimensional Arrays
❖ Written Homework: Array Mapping Functions

One-Dimensional Arrays

The array is often the only means for structuring data that is provided for us in a programming language. If we were to ask a programmer to define an array, the response might be, *"a consecutive set of memory locations."* Unfortunately, the programmer would be confusing the distinction between a data structure and its representation.

It's true that arrays are almost always implemented by using consecutive memory locations but not always. Intuitively, an array is a set of pairs, *index* and *value*. For each index that is defined, there is a value associated with that index. In other words, there is a correspondence or mapping between the index and value.

The simplest form of an array is a one-dimensional array. We might define a one-dimensional array as a *finite, ordered set of homogenous elements.*

- **finite** – specific number of elements in the array

- **ordered** – elements are arranged so that there is a first, second, third, etc.

- **homogenous** – all the elements of the array must be of the same type (integer, character, etc.)

There are typically two operations that one may perform on an array, `store` and `extract`:

- `Store (array, integer, value)` – causes the value of the $integer^{th}$ element of the array to take the value of the variable.

```
list[i] = x
```

- `Extract(array, integer)` – returns the $integer^{th}$ element of the array.

```
x = list[i]
```

But what if arrays were not primitive to a programming language? How do compilers deal with structures such as arrays? How do compilers implement arrays in a programming language? We'll take a look at these issues.

Given the following array declaration in our mythical programming language:

```
integer list[3];
```

Assume that the array uses zero-based indexing and that each integer requires four bytes of storage. Our memory organization might look like this:

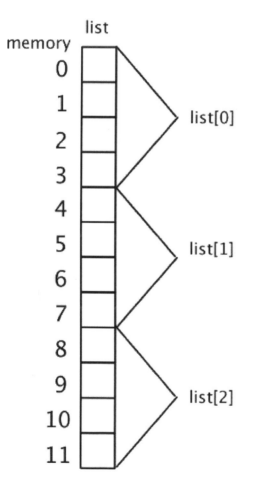

Suppose we want to perform a *store* or an *extract* operation on the third element of the array, `list[2]`. How can we get to the starting memory location that is used to store the third element of the array? How can we map an element of a one-dimensional array to a specific memory location?

Looking at the location of the third element of the array, we see that if we're able to skip the first two elements of the array, we can get to the third element. But each element of the array requires four bytes of storage. That is, the element size of the array equals four (`esize = 4`). Therefore, it's necessary to skip 2 * 4 or 8 bytes in memory to get to the starting memory location of the third element of the array.

```
location (list[2]) = 2 * 4 = 8
```

To generalize:

```
location(list[n]) = n * esize

location(list[2]) = 2 * 4 = 8
```

So the third element of the array begins at memory location 8, as can be seen by the diagram above.

However, we have made an assumption that is typically not valid. We assumed that the start of the array in memory is at location 0. But this is hardly ever the case. We must generalize our diagram and mapping function to take this into account. We will assume an arbitrary starting base address in memory for our array.

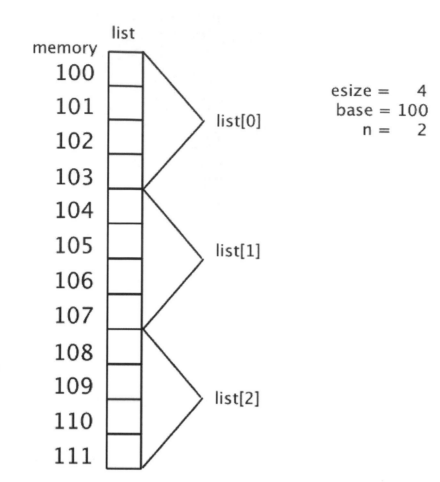

memory / list

100	
101	
102	list[0]
103	
104	
105	list[1]
106	
107	
108	
109	list[2]
110	
111	

esize = 4
base = 100
n = 2

Our new mapping function becomes:

```
location(list[n]) = base + n * esize

location (list[2]) = 100 + 2 * 4 = 108
```

However, we have made one more invalid assumption. While it's true that an array declared in Java uses zero based indexing, we may wish to implement an array whose lower bound can take on any value as long as it is less than or equal to the upper bound.

Our new array declaration might look like this:

```
integer list[3..5];
```

We want an array with three elements whose lower bound is 3 and whose upper bound is 5.

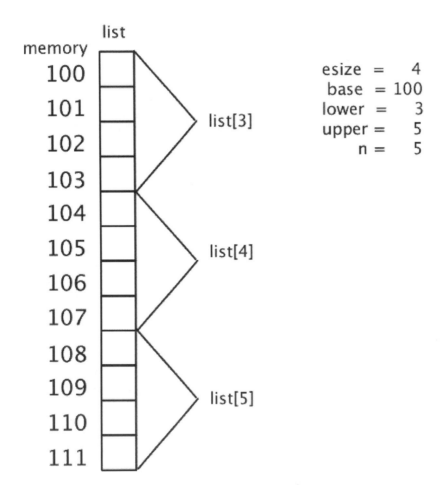

esize =   4
base   = 100
lower =   3
upper =   5
    n =   5

Suppose, once again, that we're interested in performing a *store* or an *extract* operation on the third element of the array. How do we know how many elements to skip to get to the correct memory location for the third element? What new mapping function must we use to allow declarations of this type?

```
location (list[n]) = base + (n - lower) * esize

location (list[5]) = 100 + (5 - 3) * 4 = 108
```

Once again, the starting address in memory of the third element of the array maps to memory location 108!

We now have a general purpose mapping function which allows us to map an element of a one-dimensional array to a specific memory location for an array that can have an arbitrary base address and an arbitrary upper and lower bound.

```
location (list[n]) = base + (n - lower) * esize
```

We can add functionality to the array such that:

- each element of the array can be of a different `esize`
- the elements of the array do not have to be contiguous in memory

It's obvious that we must modify our mapping function because the previous mapping function required a fixed `esize` for each element of the array. Our new array implementation will require a separate contiguous set of memory locations that will hold the addresses in memory of each varying length element of our array. We call this additional data structure a *pointer array*.

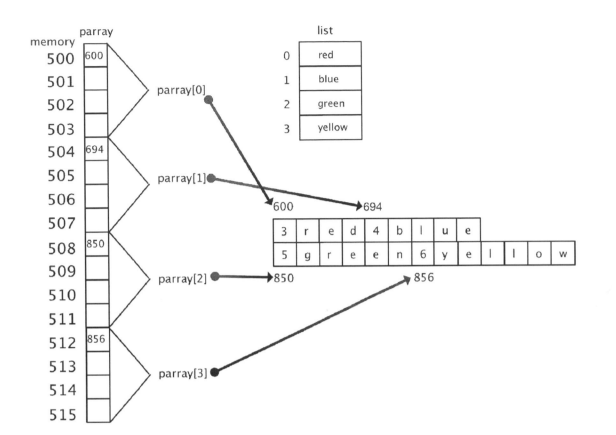

Now we have an array, the pointer array, with a fixed length. Therefore, the location of the address of a particular element of the pointer array can be calculated as before. Once this location is determined, its contents can be used to determine the location of the actual array element.

```
Location(list[n])    = content (base  + (n - lower) * esize)

Location (list[3])   = content (500 + (3 - 0) * 4)

                     = content (512) = 856
```

Note that this method adds an extra level of indirection to referencing an array element by involving an extra memory reference, thereby decreasing efficiency. At the same time, more storage is required for the pointer array. However, this extra overhead gives us the convenience of being able to maintain such an array.

Time Complexity for Unordered Arrays

	Average Case	Worst Case
Insert:	O(1)	O(n)
Delete:	O(1)	O(1)
Search:	O(n)	O(n)

Time Complexity for Ordered Arrays

	Average Case	Worst Case
Insert:	O(n)	O(n)
Delete:	O(n)	O(n)
Search:	O(log n)	O(log n)

Two Dimensional Arrays

A two-dimensional array illustrates the difference between a logical view of data and a physical view or physical representation of the data. Although it is convenient for the programmer to think in terms of a two-dimensional array, the array must be stored in the memory of a computer that is usually linear. In fact, we can consider the memory of a computer as being represented as a one-dimensional array.

How do we transform our logical view of a two-dimensional array into its physical representation in the computer's one-dimensional array memory representation?

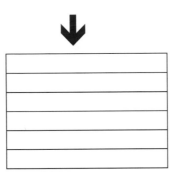

One method used for storing elements of a two-dimensional array in a linear memory representation is called *row-major order*. In row-major order, the first row of the array occupies the first set of memory locations reserved for the array; the second row of the array occupies the second set of memory locations, etc.

Given the following two-dimensional array representation for two rows and three columns:

```
integer list[0..1, 0..2];
```

The array created is shown below:

list[0,0]	list[0,1]	list[0,2]
list[1,0]	list[1,1]	list[1,2]

The array is stored in row-major memory as shown below:

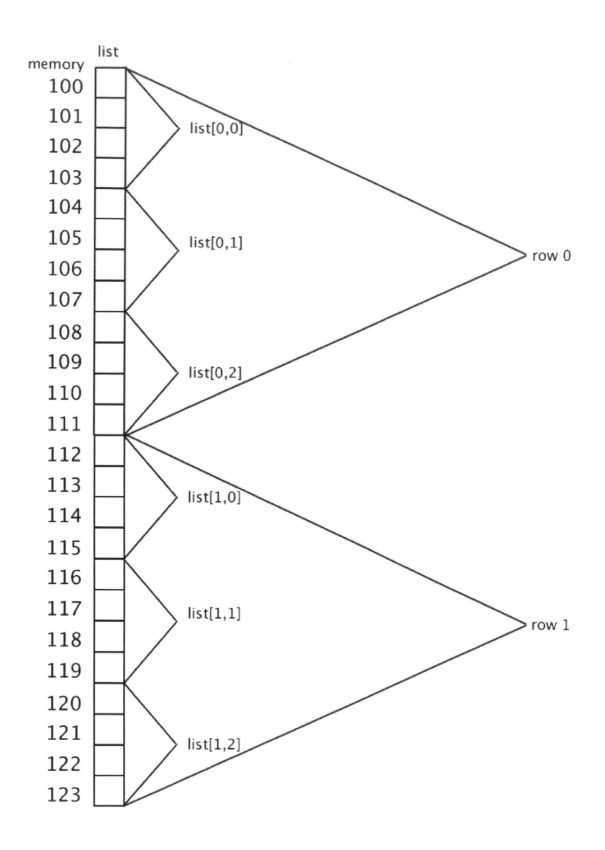

We're going to derive a mapping function to take us from an element of a two-dimensional array to its physical representation in memory. In this example, we're going to determine the starting memory location of list[1, 1]. Let's first analyze our array declaration:

```
integer list[0..1, 0..2];

L1    = lower bound of row
U1    = upper bound of row
L2    = lower bound of column
U2    = upper bound of column
i1    = row of element to map
i2    = column of element to map
base  = base address of array
esize = size of each array element
```

Now it's time to map list[1, 1] to its location in memory. We must determine the following:

a) How many rows do we skip to get to the correct row in which our element is to be found?

b) How many array elements are in each row?

c) How many bytes does each row occupy in memory?

d) How many bytes do we skip in memory to get to the first memory location of the row in which our element is to be found?

e) What is the starting location in memory for the row in which our element is to be found?

f) How many elements do we skip in the correct row to get to the element whose memory location we're trying to locate?

g) How many bytes do these elements occupy in memory?

h) What is the memory location our element be found at?

a) How many rows do we skip to get to the correct row in which our element is to be found?

```
i1 - L1
```

b) How many array elements are in each row?

```
U2 - L2 + 1
```

c) How many bytes does each row occupy in memory?

```
(U2 - L2 + 1 ) * esize
```

d) How many bytes do we skip in memory to get to the first memory location of the row in which our element is to be found?

```
(i1 - L1) * (U2 - L2 + 1) * esize
```

e) What is the starting location in memory for the row in which our element is to be found?

```
base + (i1 - L1) * (U2 - L2 + 1) * esize
```

f) How many elements do we skip in the correct row to get to the element whose memory location we're trying to locate?

```
i2 - L2
```

g) How many bytes do these elements occupy in memory?

```
(i2 - L2) * esize
```

h) What is the memory location our element will be found at?

```
base + (i1 - L1) * (U2 - L2 + 1) * esize + (i2 - L2) * esize
```

Simplifying the expression above produces the following two-dimensional array mapping function:

```
location (list[i1, i2]) =

                base + [(i1 - L1) * (U2 - L2 + 1) + (i2 - L2)] * esize
```

So in our example:

```
        L1    = lower bound of row        = 0
        U1    = upper bound of row        = 1
        L2    = lower bound of column     = 0
        U2    = upper bound of column     = 2
        i1    = row of element to map     = 1
        i2    = column of element to map  = 1
        base  = base address of array     = 100
        esize = size of each array element = 4
```

```
location (list[i1, i2])

  =  base + [(i1 - L1) * (U2 - L2 + 1) + (i2 - L2)] * esize
  = 100 + [(1 - 0)     * (2 - 0 + 1)    + (1 - 0)]    * 4
  = 100 + [1 * 3 + 1] * 4
  = 100 + 16
  = 116
```

❖ Written Homework: Array Mapping Functions

1. Assume each element of an array list, stored in row-major order, occupies four bytes of storage. If array list is declared by each of the following, and the base address of the array is 100, find the address of the indicated array element. Please show all work.

Declaration   **Address**

```
integer list[1..50];            list[23]

integer list[0..20, 0..15];     list[8, 12]

integer list[-8..9, -11..22];   list[7, 16]
```

2. Develop a formula, as in our class discussion, to access an array element if the two-dimensional array is stored in column-major order, i.e., array elements are stored in memory column-by-column rather than row-by-row. Please show all work.

a) How many columns do we skip to get to the correct column in which our element is to be found?

b) How many array elements are in each column?

c) How many bytes does each column occupy in memory?

d) How many bytes do we skip in memory to get to the first memory location of the column in which our element is to be found?

e) What is the starting location in memory for the column in which our element is to be found?

f) How many elements do we skip in the correct column to get to the element whose memory location we're trying to locate?

g) How many bytes do these elements occupy in memory?

h) What is the memory location our element will be found at?

i) Simplifying the expression produces the following mapping function:

Chapter 3. Number Systems

Decimal: Base 10
Binary: Base 2
Hexadecimal: Base 16
Negative Numbers
❖ Written Homework: Number Systems
❖ Computer Lab: Number Systems

Decimal: Base 10

A decimal base 10 integer uses 10 digits (0, 1, 2, 3, 4, 5, 6, 7, 8, 9) to represent values. But what does it mean to represent a decimal base 10 integer as, say, 739? In a base 10 integer, each digit represents a unique power of 10. The rightmost digit represents 10^0, moving left one position, the digit represents 10^1, then 10^2, etc.

```
10⁰  =    1
10¹  =   10
10²  =  100
```

To understand the value represented by 739, we can break it down into its components:

```
9 * 10⁰  =  9 *    1  =    9
3 * 10¹  =  3 *   10  =   30
7 * 10²  =  7 *  100  =  700
-----------------------------
                          739
```

Binary: Base 2

Just as we use ten digits to represent decimal base 10 integers, we use two digits
(0, 1) to represent binary base 2 values. However, in a binary number, each
digit represents a unique power of 2. The rightmost digit represents 2^0, moving left
one position the digit represents 2^1, then 2^2, then 2^3, etc.

$$
\begin{aligned}
2^0 &= 1 \\
2^1 &= 2 \\
2^2 &= 4 \\
2^3 &= 8 \\
2^4 &= 16 \\
2^5 &= 32 \\
2^6 &= 64 \\
2^7 &= 128
\end{aligned}
$$

Below are the equivalent binary base 2 values of the decimal numbers 0 – 15.

Decimal	Binary
0	0000
1	0001
2	0010
3	0011
4	0100
5	0101
6	0110
7	0111
8	1000
9	1001
10	1010
11	1011
12	1100
13	1101
14	1110
15	1111

Note that we can represent the numbers from 0 to 15 in binary using only four bits
(commonly referred to as a *nibble*).

Binary to Decimal Conversion

In order to determine what the 8-bit binary number below represents in decimal base 10, it's simply a matter of adding the appropriate powers of two:

Binary Number:	1	1	1	0	1	0	1	1
Power of Two:	2^7	2^6	2^5	2^4	2^3	2^2	2^1	2^0
Decimal Equivalent:	128	64	32	16	8	4	2	1

```
1 * 2⁰ = 1 *   1 =   1
1 * 2¹ = 1 *   2 =   2
0 * 2² = 0 *   4 =   0
1 * 2³ = 1 *   8 =   8
0 * 2⁴ = 0 *  16 =   0
1 * 2⁵ = 1 *  32 =  32
1 * 2⁶ = 1 *  64 =  64
1 * 2⁷ = 1 * 128 = 128
----------------------
                   235
```

$$1 * 2^0 = 1 * 1 = 1$$
$$1 * 2^1 = 1 * 2 = 2$$
$$0 * 2^2 = 0 * 4 = 0$$
$$1 * 2^3 = 1 * 8 = 8$$
$$0 * 2^4 = 0 * 16 = 0$$
$$1 * 2^5 = 1 * 32 = 32$$
$$1 * 2^6 = 1 * 64 = 64$$
$$1 * 2^7 = 1 * 128 = 128$$
$$\overline{235}$$

So binary `11101011` is equivalent to `235` decimal.

Decimal to Binary Conversion

Conversion of a decimal number into binary utilizes the following simple algorithm:

```
while num != 0
      divide num by 2
      store the remainder
      assign the quotient to num
output the remainders in reverse order
```

For example, we can convert the decimal integer 147 into binary:

```
147 / 2 = 73    remainder = 1
 73 / 2 = 36    remainder = 1
 36 / 2 = 18    remainder = 0
 18 / 2 =  9    remainder = 0
  9 / 2 =  4    remainder = 1
  4 / 2 =  2    remainder = 0
  2 / 2 =  1    remainder = 0
  1 / 2 =  0    remainder = 1
```

So `147` decimal is equivalent to `10010011` binary, read bottom to top.

Hexadecimal: Base 16

Hexadecimal notation uses 16 digits (0 - 9, A, B, C, D, E, F) to represent base 16 values. Each digit in a *hex* number represents a unique power of 16. The rightmost digit represents 16^0, moving left one position the digit represents 16^1, then 16^2, etc.

$$16^0 = 1$$
$$16^1 = 16$$
$$16^2 = 256$$
$$16^3 = 4096$$

Below are the equivalent hexadecimal base 16 values of the decimal and binary numbers 0 – 15.

Decimal	Binary	Hexadecimal
0	0000	0
1	0001	1
2	0010	2
3	0011	3
4	0100	4
5	0101	5
6	0110	6
7	0111	7
8	1000	8
9	1001	9
10	1010	A
11	1011	B
12	1100	C
13	1101	D
14	1110	E
15	1111	F

Hexadecimal to Decimal Conversion

To convert a hexadecimal value into a decimal value, we simply add the appropriate powers of 16. For example, let's convert `0x1AF` into a decimal number (note that `0x` is typically placed in front of the hexadecimal number to identify the number as hexadecimal):

```
Hexadecimal Number:   1      A      F
                      |      |      |
                      |      |      |
                      |      |      |
Power of 16:          16²    16¹    16⁰
                      |      |      |
                      |      |      |
                      |      |      |
Decimal Equivalent:   256    160    15


F * 16⁰ = 15 *    1 =   15
A * 16¹ = 10 *   16 =  160
1 * 16² =  1 *  256 =  256
-----------------------------
                       431
```

Therefore, hexadecimal `0x1AF` is equivalent to `431` decimal.

Decimal to Hexadecimal Conversion

We use a similar algorithm to convert a decimal value into a hexadecimal number as we used to convert a decimal value into a binary number:

```
while num != 0
      divide num by 16
      store the remainder
      assign the quotient to num
output the remainders in reverse order
```

We can convert decimal 431 into hexadecimal notation:

```
431 / 16 = 26        remainder = F
 26 / 16 =  1        remainder = A
  1 / 16 =  0        remainder = 1
```

So `431` decimal is equivalent to `0x1AF` hexadecimal.

Binary to Hexadecimal Conversion

Conversion of a binary number into hexadecimal is simply a matter of converting each nibble (4 bits) of the binary number into its hex equivalent. For example, let's convert the binary number `0011 0101 1111 1100` into its hexadecimal equivalent:

```
Binary:            0011     0101     1111     1100
                    |        |        |        |
                    |        |        |        |
                    |        |        |        |
Hex Equivalent:     3        5        F        C
```

So `0011 0101 1111 1100` binary is equivalent to `0x35FC` hexadecimal.

Hexadecimal to Binary Conversion

To convert a hexadecimal number into its binary equivalent, we simply convert each hex digit in the number into its decimal equivalent. For example, let's convert hexadecimal `0xB72E` into binary:

```
Hexadecimal:          B        7        2        E
                      |        |        |        |
                      |        |        |        |
                      |        |        |        |
Binary Equivalent:   1011     0111     0010     1110
```

So `0xB72E` hexadecimal is equivalent to `1011 0111 0010 1110` binary. Note that a single hexadecimal digit can be used to represent four bits in a binary number. As a result, it becomes more convenient to represent 16-, 32-, or 64-bit memory addresses in hex notation rather than binary!

Negative Numbers

So far, we've only explored how positive numbers are represented internally in the computer's memory. It's now time to explore how negative numbers can also be represented. For example, if the value 6 is represented in memory as:

```
00000110
```

then how is −6 represented? One common suggestion is to make the high-order bit 1 and leave all other bits unchanged, producing:

```
10000110
```

Unfortunately, this is incorrect. This can be shown by adding the two numbers together (6 + −6) which should produce 0.

```
   00000110      =     6
+  10000110      =    −6
   10001100      =   −12
```

According to this scheme, the sum of 6 + −6 equals −12, and not 0! We must find another representation for negative numbers.

Two's Complement Notation

The technique that computers use to represent negative numbers is referred to as *two's complement notation*. Given any positive number, we can determine its negative internal representation by calculating, or taking, its two's complement. This is performed in two steps:

- flip all bits
- add 1

For example, we can determine the internal representation of -6 by taking the two's complement of 6:

```
00000110      = 6

11111001      flip all bits
+        1    add 1

11111010      = -6
```

According to this scheme, -6 is represented as:

```
11111010
```

We can test this by adding 6 and -6:

```
00000110   =   6
11111010   =  -6
00000000   =   0
```

Note that we are only doing 8-bit arithmetic, so any final carry can be ignored. As another example, let's determine how -25 is represented:

```
00011001   = 25

11100110   flip all bits
+        1    add 1
11100111   = -25
```

Once again we can test this by adding together 25 and -25 and see if it produces zero:

```
00011001   =   25
11100111   =  -25
00000000   =   0
```

Suppose we were given the 8-bit binary number:

```
11010001
```

and were asked to determine its decimal equivalent. We would not be able to do so unless we were told whether the number represented a *signed* or an *unsigned* value. If the number represents an unsigned value, then we use our simple algorithm to convert from binary to decimal by adding each of the appropriate powers of two:

```
1 + 16 + 64 + 128 = 209
```

If the number is representing a signed value, then we look at the leftmost, high-order bit. If it is a 0, then the number is a positive number and we use the algorithm just mentioned and add each of the appropriate powers of two.

However, if the number represents a signed value and the leftmost, high-order bit is a 1, then the number is a negative number being represented in its two's complement notation. To determine what the negative number is, we must take its two's complement by flipping the bits and adding 1:

```
11010001        original number

00101110        flip all bits
+       1        add 1
00101111        two's complement
```

So, the two's complement of 11010001 is 00101111 which equals 47:

```
1 + 2 + 4 + 8 + 32   = 47
```

Therefore if the two's complement of our original number is 47, then our original number must equal -47.

❖ Written Homework: Number Systems

1. Give the 8-bit binary equivalent of the following decimal integers:

a) 121   b) 166

2. Give the unsigned decimal equivalent of the following 8-bit binary integers:

a) 10111110   b) 01111010

3. Give the signed decimal equivalent of the following 8-bit binary integers:

a) 10111110   b) 01111010

4. Translate the following binary digits into hexadecimal notation:

a) 11101100   b) 11111011

5. Convert the following decimal numbers into hexadecimal:

a) 328   b) 819

6. Convert the following hexadecimal numbers into decimal:

a) 0xD7   b) 0x1F5

7. Convert the following hexadecimal numbers into binary:

a) 0x23BA   b) 0x136E

8. Give the two's complement of the following binary numbers:

a) 10001000   d) 00000000
b) 10101111   e) 10000000
c) 10000001

❖ Computer Lab: Number Systems

Construct an object-oriented Java program that performs each of the following conversions. Note that we're only dealing with non-negative numbers.

- Converts a decimal integer into a 32-bit binary number

- Converts a decimal integer into an 8-digit hexadecimal number

- Converts a 32-bit binary number into a decimal integer

- Converts a 32-bit binary number into an 8-digit hexadecimal number

- Converts an 8-digit hexadecimal number into a decimal integer

- Converts an 8-digit hexadecimal number into a 32-bit binary number

Your program should be interactive, requiring the user to select the appropriate option from a menu of options (no GUI required). Note that Java's `Scanner` class will be very helpful reading data from the keyboard.

The conversions you code must be direct. In other words, if you had to convert a base 2 number into base 16, the conversion should be made directly from base 2 to base 16 and not from base 2 to base 10 to base 16. You may not use any methods or utilities from the Java library that do the conversions for you, such as:

```
Integer.toBinaryString()
Integer.toHexString()
```

Your program should send all output to a file called `csis.txt`. This output file will be submitted along with your source code for the lab. All information displayed in the terminal window, including input from the user, should also be sent to the output file.

Be sure to turn in output, in the order provided, for each of the test data shown below. Note that you can omit commas and spaces while inputting the data into the program.

---

1. Decimal to Binary :
a) 65,535
b) 1,000,000
c) 1,234,567,890

2. Decimal to Hexadecimal:
a) 65,535
b) 1,000,000
c) 1,234,567,890

3. Binary to Decimal:
a) 0110 0101 1100 1101 1010 1110 0000 0101
b) 0111 1111 1111 1111 0010 0001 1101 0011
c) 0000 0000 0000 0000 0000 0000 0000 0010

4. Binary to Hexadecimal:
a) 0110 0101 1100 1101 1010 1110 0000 0101
b) 0111 1111 1111 1111 0010 0001 1101 0011
c) 0010 1011 1010 1101 0111 0110 0011 1010

5. Hexadecimal to Decimal:
a) 12345678
b) 2A3DF8A7
c) 00FF00FF

6. Hexadecimal to Binary:
a) 12345678
b) 2A3DF8A7
c) 00FF00FF

For extra credit, perform error checking on the user input displaying appropriate error messages if the user enters invalid data such as a value out of range for a conversion or inappropriate digits for the selected base. Add additional test data to show that your extra credit works properly. Your program should be able to deal with this invalid data in a robust manner without crashing!

★ Number Systems Lab Note 1: A Few Comments:

Each class should be contained within its own source file.

Program output should be captured to a file, `csis.txt`, directly from your program rather than cutting and pasting the output to the file.

All program output displayed in the terminal window should be sent to the output file. This includes the displayed menu, user prompts, as well as any input from the user.

Keep your methods small, usually performing a single task.

Your program should be a complete application including a `main()` method.

Keep `main()` small placing details in the methods of the classes that make up your object-oriented program.

There should be no user-defined `static` methods in your program other than `main()`.

Do not use floats, doubles or scientific notation in your code.

Binary numbers should be output as 32 bits (i.e., display leading zeros) with a space separating nibbles as shown in the input data above.

You may build a GUI for the application although it is not required.

★ Number Systems Lab Note 2: Classes and Methods
Your program should include at least the following classes:

```
Driver, Menu, Decimal, Binary, Hexadecimal
```

Each class must use separate methods to get input, to perform the conversions, and to generate the appropriate output. Shown below are methods for each of the classes that I recommend. The method signatures shown indented represent methods being called from within the unindented methods. You can certainly add more methods than what is shown.

```
Decimal Class                          Binary Class
public void decToBin()                 public void binToDec()
      private void inputDec()                private void inputBin()
      private void toBin()                   private void toDec()
      private void outBin()                  private void outDec()

public void decToHex()                 public void binToHex()
      private void inputDec()                private void inputBin()
      private void toHex()                   private void toHex()
      private void outHex()                  private void outHex()


Hexadecimal Class                      Menu Class
public void hexToDec()                 public void display()
      private void inputHex()          public int getSelection()
      private void toDec()
      private void outDec()

public void hexToBin()
      private void inputHex()
      private void toBin()
      private void outBin()
```

Note that the Menu class will contain a method to display a menu and a method to prompt the user for a menu selection and receive the input from the user. Think Scanner class to capture the input from the keyboard.

★ Number Systems Lab Note 3: Driver Class

Here's a look at my Driver class for the number systems lab. <u>I require that you use this driver class for your lab</u>. No changes to the code below are allowed.

```java
import java.io.*;

public class Driver {
    public static void main(String[] args) throws IOException {
        int choice;

        PrintWriter pw = new PrintWriter(new FileWriter("csis.txt"));
        Decimal dec = new Decimal(pw);
        Binary bin = new Binary(pw);
        Hexadecimal hex = new Hexadecimal(pw);
        Menu menu = new Menu(pw);

        do {
            menu.display();
            choice = menu.getSelection();
            switch (choice) {
                case 1 : dec.decToBin(); break;
                case 2 : dec.decToHex(); break;
                case 3 : bin.binToDec(); break;
                case 4 : bin.binToHex(); break;
                case 5 : hex.hexToDec(); break;
                case 6 : hex.hexToBin(); break;
            }
        } while (choice != 7);
        pw.close();
    }
}
```

That's it! Note that there are no conversions being performed in the `Driver` class (or in the `Menu` class). The conversions are performed within the `Decimal`, `Binary` and `Hexadecimal` classes.

Note that I'm using one-arg constructors to instantiate objects for each of the `Decimal`, `Binary`, `Hexadecimal` and `Menu` classes. The argument that gets passed to each of these constructors is a `PrintWriter` object. This allows each of the classes to have access to the `PrintWriter` object created in the driver. It allows you generate output to the `csis.txt` output file from each of the classes.

The problem that arises is this. An object that is passed as a parameter to a constructor is only visible within the scope of the constructor. Therefore, how can the other methods in each class access the `PrintWriter` object as well?

The solution is to declare a class variable in each class and, within the constructor, assign the `PrintWriter` object passed in as a parameter to the class variable. Once the class variable is assigned the value of the `PrintWriter` object, each of the methods in the class will have access to the `PrintWriter` object.

So we declare a class variable in each of the classes:

```
private PrintWriter pw;
```

Each of the constructors will then need to assign its argument to the class variable. For example:

```
public Decimal(PrintWriter pw) {
    this.pw = pw;
}
```

We use `this` here to distinguish the argument name with the class variable name. If you didn't want to use `this`, you would have to use an argument with a different name than the class variable:

```
public Decimal(PrintWriter p) {
    pw = p;
}
```

★ Number Systems Lab Note 4: PrintWriter Class

Shown below is the use of Java's `PrintWriter` and `FileWriter` classes to open an output file and send output to the output file.

Required declarations:

```
import java.io.*;

public static void main(String[] args) throws IOException {
```

To open a file for output:

```
PrintWriter pw = new PrintWriter(new FileWriter("csis.txt"));
```

To send output to the file:

```
pw.print("Sends to output file.");

pw.println("Sends to output file with linefeed.");
```

To close the output file:

```
pw.close();
```

★ Number Systems Lab Notes 5: Binary to Hexadecimal Conversion

The binary to hex conversion is more of an algorithm that maps one value to another rather than a mathematical conversion algorithm used by the other base conversions.

First, you must read the 32-bit binary number (don't input spaces) into a `String` object, `bin`. Then you must create a `StringBuilder` object, `hex`, perhaps initialized to `"00000000"`, which will hold the resulting hex conversion value. The reason you need to use a `StringBuilder` object to hold the resulting hex value rather than a `String` object is because the value of a `String` object is immutable and cannot be changed once created. The value of a `StringBuilder` object can be modified after creation. Otherwise `String` and `StringBuilder` objects are pretty much the same.

Next you must iterate through `bin`, the `String` object, looking at 4-bits at a time. The `substring` function will allow you to look at 4-bits and will return the resulting 4-bits as a `String`:

```
bin.substring(i, i + 4)
```

The String that the substring function returns can then be compared against a string constant holding a 4-bit value:

```
if (bin.substring(i, i + 4).equals("0000"))
```

If the comparison returns `true`, then you can set the appropriate position in the `String` object, `hex`, to the appropriate hex digit:

```
if (bin.substring(i, i + 4).equals("0000"))
    hex.setCharAt(j, '0');
else if (bin.substring(i, i + 4).equals("0001"))
    hex.setCharAt(j, '1');
```

All of this will take place within a `for` loop that initializes `i` and `j` to 0 and increments `i` by 4 and `j` by 1.

★ Number Systems Lab Note 6: Program Documentation

I've provided a document on the use of Javadoc that can be found in this link on Canvas:

```
Files | Java Review | Javadoc Program Documentation
```

In particular, note the following guidelines:

• Every class must have a Javadoc class comment.

• Every method must have a Javadoc method comment.

• Every method parameter must have an `@param` tag.

• Every method with a return statement must have an `@return` tag.

• Generate the HTML Javadoc documentation for your project and be sure to submit the folder that contains the Javadoc documentation in the zip archive when submitting the lab.

★ Number Systems Lab Note 7: Class Diagram

Shown below is the class diagram for my solution to the number systems lab.

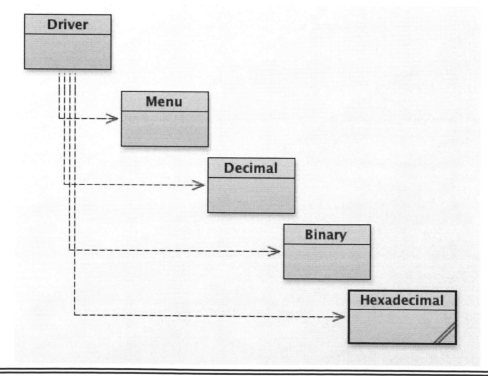

Chapter 4. Stacks

Introduction to Stacks

A stack is an ordered collection of items into which new items may be inserted and from which items may be deleted at one end, called the *top* of the stack.

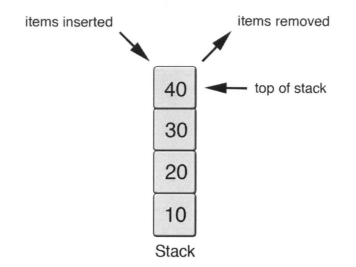

If any new items are to be added to the stack, they will be placed on top of 40, and if any items are to be deleted, 40 will be the first to be deleted.

Actually, a stack is really a dynamic, constantly changing object. The stack above is only a snapshot of the stack at a particular point in its continuing evolution. In order to have a true view of a stack, a motion picture is necessary to see how it expands and shrinks with the passage of time during the course of execution of a program:

• We begin with a stack with no items.

Stack

• Add item 10 to the top of the stack.

Stack

• Add item 20 to the top of the stack.

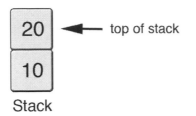

• Add item 30 to the top of the stack.

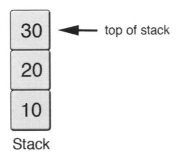

• Add item 40 to the top of the stack.

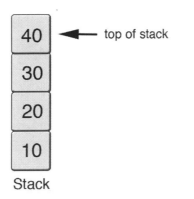

• Remove the top element from the stack.

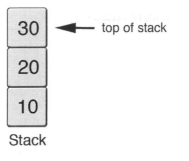

• Remove the top element from the stack.

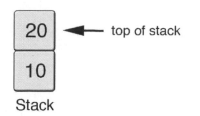

• Add item 40 to the top of the stack.

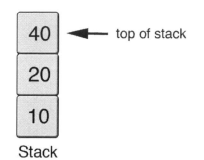

Note that items can only be added at the top of the stack (the last item inserted is at the top of the stack) and deletions can be made only from the top of stack. This illustrates the most important attribute of a stack:

The last element inserted into a stack is the first element deleted from the stack.

In this sense we call the stack a *LIFO* data structure: *Last In First Out*

Note that we cannot distinguish between these two stacks:

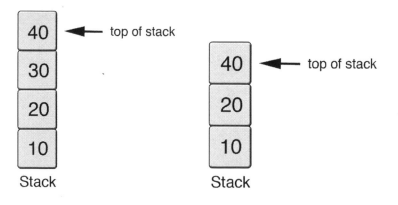

This is because the true picture of a stack is given by a view from the top looking down, rather than from a side looking in. In this sense, there is perceptual difference between the two stacks. In each case the element at the top is 40. While we know that the stacks are not equal, the only way to determine this is to remove all the elements on both stacks and compare them individually. There is really no such provision for taking a picture of the cross section of a stack.

Note that when you click a link on a webpage, your browser opens the new page and inserts the link to the previous page onto a stack. This occurs each time you visit a new page. Clicking the back button on a browser takes you back to the previous webpage that you were visiting. Thus, the browser is exhibiting the last-in-first-out behavior of a stack!

Stack Primitive Operations

In our discussion of arrays, we saw that there were two operations that were used to manipulate arrays, the `store` and the `extract` operations. It was through the use of these operations that we were able to perform various operations, such as sorting and searching, on an array. These fundamental operations are referred to as *primitive operations* and they are defined for each of the data structures that we will look at. Shown below are the primitive operations used to manipulate stacks:

• `s.push(x)` - adds an element `x` to the top of stack `s`. Note that it is illegal to push an element onto a stack that has no more room to hold elements. This condition is called *overflow*.

• `s.pop()` - removes the top element from stack `s` and returns its value. Note that it is illegal to pop a stack that does not contain any elements. This condition is called *underflow*.

• `s.top()` - returns the top element of stack `s` without deleting the element from the stack. Note that it is illegal to top a stack that does not contain any elements. This condition is also called *underflow*. Also note that the `top` operation is really equivalent to a `pop` and a `push` operation:

```
x = s.pop()
s.push(x)
```

Therefore, the `top` operation may not be "officially" considered to be a primitive operation.

• `s.isEmpty()` - determines whether or not stack `s` contains any elements. This primitive operation returns `true` if there are currently no elements on the stack or `false` if the stack contains at least one element.

• `s.isFull()` - determines whether or not stack `s` has reached it maximum capacity for holding elements. This primitive operation returns `true` if the stack is at full capacity or `false` if the stack can still contain more elements.

• `s.clear()` - removes all elements from stack `s`.

Stack Example 1 – Correctly Parenthesized Expressions

Suppose we want to ensure that the parentheses within an algebraic expression are nested correctly. For example:

```
Correct:    (a + b ) * ((c - d) / (f + g))

Incorrect:  (a + b ) * ((c - d) / (f + g)
```

There are two rules we must follow to ensure that the parentheses are nested correctly:

• There must be an equal number of left and right parentheses.

• Every right parenthesis must be preceded by a matching left parenthesis.

For example:

```
) a + b (              violates rule 2

( a + b)) - ( c + d    violates rule 1
```

A way to solve this problem would be to utilize a stack. As the expression is parsed, each time a left parenthesis is encountered it is pushed onto a stack. Each time a right parenthesis is encountered, the stack is popped. If no underflow condition occurs and at the end of parsing the expression the stack is empty, then the expression is correctly parenthesized. Note that as we parse the expression we can ignore any operators, operands, and spaces that we encounter.

Let's determine whether or not the following expression is parenthesized correctly:

```
(a+b)*((c-d)/(f+g))
```

We begin with an empty stack:

Stack

```
(a+b)*((c-d)/(f+g))
^
Push left parenthesis onto stack.
```

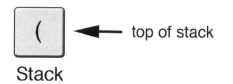

Stack

```
(a+b)*((c-d)/(f+g))
   ^
Matching right parenthesis so we pop the stack.
```

Stack

```
(a+b)*((c-d)/(f+g))
     ^
Push left parenthesis onto stack.
```

Stack

```
(a+b)*((c-d)/(f+g))
       ^
Push left parenthesis onto stack.
```

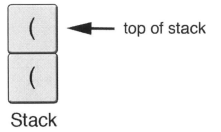

Stack

```
(a+b)*((c-d)/(f+g))
         ^
Matching right parenthesis so we pop the stack.
```

Stack

```
(a+b)*((c-d)/(f+g))
         ^
Push left parenthesis onto stack.
```

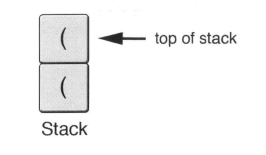

Stack

```
(a+b)*((c-d)/(f+g))
          ^
Matching right parenthesis so we pop the stack.
```

Stack

```
(a+b)*((c-d)/(f+g))
          ^
Matching right parenthesis so we pop the stack.
```

Stack

We have come to the end of the string and the stack is now empty. Therefore, the string is valid. We're now going to extend our example and assume three different types of scopes exist:

- parentheses   ()
- brackets   [ ]
- braces   { }

However, we must now add the following third rule to ensure that the expression is scoped correctly:

- A scope ender must be of the same type as its scope opener.

This rule prevents the following invalid expression:

```
( a + b ]
```

So now we must keep track not only of how many scopes have been opened, but also of their types. Our approach will be to use a stack to hold scope openers.

Whenever a scope opener is encountered, it is pushed onto the stack. Whenever a scope ender is encountered, the stack is examined. If the stack is empty, the scope ender has no matching opener and therefore the string is invalid. If the stack is non empty, we pop the stack and check whether the popped item corresponds to the scope ender. If it does not match, the string is invalid. If it does match, we simply continue. When we come to the end of the string the stack must be empty.

Here is the pseudocode for the above algorithm:

```
while we have not read to the end of the string
    read next symbol (symb) of string
    if symb == '(' or symb == '[' or symb == '{'
        s.push(symb)
    else if symb == ')' or symb == ']' or symb == '}'
        if s.isEmpty()
            return ("Invalid string.")
        else
            i = s.pop()
            if i is not the matching scope opener for symb
                return ("Invalid string.")
if s.isEmpty()
    return ("Valid string.")
else
    return ("Invalid string.")
```

Scope Openers and Scope Enders in HTML

Another application in which matching scopes is important is in the validation of HTML documents. HTML is the standard format for hyperlinked documents on the Internet. In an HTML document, tags delimit portions of the text.

A simple opening HTML tag has the form `<name>` and the corresponding closing tag has the form `</name>`. Commonly used HTML tags include:

`<body>`	document body	`<table>`	table
`<h1>`	section header	`<tr>`	table row
`<center>`	center justify	`<td>`	table data
`<p>`	paragraph	`<ol>`	numbered list
`<strong>`	bold text	`<li>`	list item

Ideally, an HTML document should have matching tags, although most browsers tolerate a certain number of mismatching tags. Here is HTML code taken from the CSIS website. Notice the scope openers (opening tags) and scope enders (closing tags).

```
<table class=Text width="100%" style="border:none;" cellpadding=15 cellspacing=0>
    <tr>
        <td class=TextInHeader  style="padding-top:0px; padding-bottom:0px;
                                                        padding-left:20px;">
            <?php include 'slideshow.php'; ?>
        </td>
        <td colspan="2" style="padding:29px;">
            <div style="vertical-align:top;">
                <span class=Header1Big>Welcome to the Palomar College
                    <br>Computer Science Program<br>
                </span>
                <br>
                We offer degree and certificate programs, as well as coursework and
                preparation for transfer to a four-year program of study. Please take
                a few moments to look through our programs, course listings, and course
                descriptions. We hope you'll find something that will stimulate your
                interest.
                <br><br>
                If we can be of any assistance or guidance in planning your course of
                study or helping you choose a class, please feel free to contact us.
                Once again, welcome to Palomar College and we hope your course of study
                in the Computer Science Program will be a rewarding one.
                <br><br>
            </div>
        </td>
    </tr>
    <tr>
        <td colspan="3">
            <hr size="2" color="#295da9">
        </td>
    </tr>
```

Below is the webpage that get produced from the above HTML code above:

Welcome to the Palomar College Computer Science Program

We offer degree and certificate programs, as well as coursework and preparation for transfer to a four-year program of study. Please take a few moments to look through our programs, course listings, and course descriptions. We hope you'll find something that will stimulate your interest.

If we can be of any assistance or guidance in planning your course of study or helping you choose a class, please feel free to contact us. Once again, welcome to Palomar College and we hope your course of study in the Computer Science Program will be a rewarding one.

Stack Example 2 – Reverse Array Elements

Here's an algorithm to reverse the elements of an array:

```
for i = 1 to 10
    s.push(a[i])

for i = 1 to 10
    a[i] = s.pop()
```

Stack Example 3 – String Format

Here's an algorithm to determine whether an input character string is of the form:

```
x C y
```

where x is a string consisting of the letters 'A' and 'B' and where y is the reverse of x. For example, if:

```
x = "ABABBA"
```

then

```
y = "ABBABA"
```

At each point you may read only the next character of the string.

```
valid = true
read (symb)
while (symb != 'C') and not EOF
    s.push(symb)
    read(symb)
while not EOF and not s.empty() and valid
    read(symb)
    ch = s.pop()
    if (symb != ch)
        valid = false
if not EOF or not s.empty()
    valid = false
if valid
    return ("Valid string.")
else
    return ("Invalid string.")
```

Representing Stacks in Java

A stack is an ordered collection of items. However, Java also contains a data type that also is an ordered collection of items ... the array. But a stack and an array are two different things:

Array: The number of elements in array is fixed and determined by the initial declaration of the array.

Stack: A stack is a dynamic object whose size is constantly changing as items are pushed and popped.

However, although an array cannot be a stack, it can be the home of a stack. The array can be declared with a range that is large enough for the maximum size of the stack. During program execution, the stack will grow and shrink within the space reserved for it. One end of the array will be the fixed bottom of the stack, while the top of the stack will constantly shift as items are pushed and popped.

We implement a Stack class, `IntStack`, containing three instance variables:

* an array to hold the elements of the stack
* an integer to indicate the position of the current top of the stack within the array
* an integer to indicate the size of the array

```
public class IntStack {
    private int[] item;
    private int top;
    private int size;
```

We can declare a default constructor for the `IntStack` class that will initialize an empty `IntStack` to a predetermined size. Note that we initially set the `top` pointer to −1.

```
public IntStack() {
    size = 100;
    item = new int[size];
    top = -1;
}
```

We can also declare a one-argument constructor for the `IntStack` class that will initialize an empty `IntStack` to a size provided in the method argument. Note that once again we initially set the `top` pointer to –1.

```
public IntStack(int max) {
    size = max;
    item = new int[size];
    top = -1;
}
```

We can now create `IntStack` objects by first declaring `IntStack` variables and then instantiating `IntStack` objects:

```
IntStack s1, s2;

s1 = new IntStack();
s2 = new IntStack(500);
```

Note that `IntStack` object `s1` is instantiated using the default constructor and `IntStack` object `s2` is instantiated using the one-argument constructor. Also note that the declaration and instantiation of `IntStack` objects can be performed within the same statement:

```
IntStack s1 = new IntStack();
IntStack s2 = new IntStack(500);
```

The empty stack contains no elements and so we simply check to see if the top pointer is equal to –1.

```
public boolean isEmpty() {
    return top == -1;
}
```

It might seem silly at first to write an `isEmpty()` method that contains only one line of code, but there are two good reasons to *encapsulate* the one line of code into a method.

Firstly, it makes the use of the stack independent of its *implementation*. For example, suppose you used the test for an empty stack directly in your program (assuming that `top` was declared public).

```
if (top == -1)
```

Now suppose that the implementation of the stack changes from an array implementation to a linked list implementation (which we'll soon look at). In the linked list implementation of a stack, the test for an empty stack looks like this:

```
if (list == null)
```

As a result our program breaks down and must be modified to work with the new implementation. Secondly, making the method call:

```
isEmpty()
```

is more meaningful, i.e., easier to read and understand, than the code:

```
if (top == -1)
```

Our method to test for a full stack checks to see if the top pointer has reached the index `item.length-1`. Keep in mind that the array that is being used to house the `IntStack` has been declared to hold `item.length` elements. Therefore the array indexing goes from `0` to `item.length-1`.

```java
public boolean isFull() {
    return top == item.length-1;
}
```

Of course, we could also have made use of the fact that the instance variable `size` holds the number of elements that the `IntStack` has been declared to hold:

```
public boolean isFull() {
    return top == size-1;
}
```

One way to remove all of the elements of an `IntStack` is to set up a loop as follows:

```
while !(s.isEmpty())
    i = s.pop();
```

However, we can use a much simpler approach. All that is necessary is to reset the top pointer to -1. Although there are still data values residing in the array, it effectively removes all elements from the `IntStack`.

```
public void clear() {
    top = -1;
}
```

The process of pushing an item onto a stack requires that we first test for overflow. If the overflow condition occurs, we generate an error message and abort the program. If no overflow occurs, then we must increment the top pointer and then perform a *store* operation on the array at that location:

```
public void push(int x) {
    if (isFull()) {
        System.out.println("Stack Overflow");
        System.exit(1);
    }
    item[++top] = x;
}
```

Likewise, popping a stack requires that we first test for the underflow condition, and if present, we generate an error message and abort the program. If no underflow exists, we must do an `extract` operation on the array at the location of the top pointer and then decrement the top pointer.

```
public int pop() {
    if (isEmpty()) {
        System.out.println("Stack Underflow");
        System.exit(1);
    }
    return item[top--];
}
```

The `top` operation is similar to the `pop` operation. However, when we `top` a stack, the stack remains unchanged:

```
public int top() {
    if (isEmpty()) {
        System.out.println("Stack Underflow");
        System.exit(1);
    }
    return item[top];
}
```

```java
// IntStack.java

public class IntStack {
    private int[] item;
    private int top;
    private int size;

    public IntStack() {
        size = 100;
        item = new int[size];
        top = -1;
    }

    public IntStack(int max) {
        size = max;
        item = new int[size];
        top = -1;
    }

    public boolean isEmpty() {
        return top == -1;
    }

    public boolean isFull() {
        return top == item.length-1;
    }

    public void clear() {
        top = -1;
    }

    public void push(int x) {
        if (isFull()) {
            System.out.println("Stack Overflow");
            System.exit(1);
        }
        item[++top] = x;
    }
```

```java
    public int pop() {
        if (isEmpty()) {
            System.out.println("Stack Underflow");
            System.exit(1);
        }
        return item[top--];
    }


    public int top() {
        if (isEmpty()) {
            System.out.println("Stack Underflow");
            System.exit(1);
        }
        return item[top];
    }
}
```

Our basic array implementation of `IntStack` actually has a defect, in the sense that we require clients to provide us the maximum capacity of the stack ahead of time. However, our stack primitive operations should just be able to create a stack and the stack should be able to grow and shrink to any size. We therefore need to devise a technique for resolving this problem of growing and shrinking the array.

The first thing we might think of is when the client pushes a new item onto the stack we should increase the size of the array by one and when the client pops the stack, we should decrease the array by one. That's easy to code up but it's much too expensive to create a new array size one size larger and copy all the items to that new array.

Our solution, called *repeated doubling*, will be to create a new array of twice the size when the array fills up and copy all the items over to the new array. Then we won't have to create new arrays all that often.

We start with an array of size one.

```
public class ResizeIntStack {
    private int[] item;
    private int top;

    public ResizeIntStack() {
        item = new int[1];
        top = -1;
    }
}
```

If we reach the condition where the stack is full, `top == item.length-1`, then we just resize the array into one of twice the length, and then insert the new item.

```
public void push(int x) {
    if (isFull())
        resize(2 * item.length);
    item[++top] = x;
}
```

Now, how do we resize the array? We create a new array with twice the size and copy our current stack into the first half of the new array and then return it. That will reset our instance variable, `item`, which is the array that houses our stack, to this new larger array.

```
private void resize(int size) {
    int[] temp = new int[size];
    for (int i = 0; i <= top; i++)
        temp[i] = item[i];
    item = temp;
}
```

Now what about the pop operation? What should we do when we remove an item from the stack? We have to think about how to shrink the array. We might think that because we doubled the array when it was full, we halve the array when it gets to be half-full. But we don't want the array to get too empty too quickly. So the efficient solution is to wait until the array gets one quarter full before we halve it. We just test if the array is one quarter full, and, if it is, we resize the array to half full.

```
public int pop() {
    if (isEmpty()) {
        System.out.println("Stack Underflow");
        System.exit(1);
    }
    int temp = item[top--];
    if (top == item.length/4)
        resize(item.length/2);
    return temp;
}
```

There won't be another resizing array operation until the array gets totally full or one-quarter full. Therefore, the array is always between 25% and 100% full. So, array resizing doesn't happen that often. It's a very effective a way of implementing the stack API with an array where the client does not have to provide this maximum capacity of the stack.

Finally, we must also update the `clear()` method:

```
public void clear() {
    item = new int[1];
    top = -1;
}
```

ResizeIntStack Class

```java
// ResizeIntStack.java

public class ResizeIntStack {
    private int[] item;
    private int top;

    public ResizeIntStack() {
        item = new int[1];
        top = -1;
    }

    public boolean isEmpty() {
        return top == -1;
    }

    public boolean isFull() {
        return top == item.length-1;
    }

    public void clear() {
        item = new int[1];
        top = -1;
    }

    public void push(int x) {
        if (isFull())
            resize(2 * item.length);
        item[++top] = x;
    }

    private void resize(int size) {
        int[] temp = new int[size];
        for (int i = 0; i <= top; i++)
            temp[i] = item[i];
        item = temp;
    }
```

```
    public int pop() {
        if (isEmpty()) {
            System.out.println("Stack Underflow");
            System.exit(1);
        }
        int temp = item[top--];
        if (top == item.length/4)
            resize(item.length/2);
        return temp;
    }

    public int top() {
        if (isEmpty()) {
            System.out.println("Stack Underflow");
            System.exit(1);
        }
        return item[top];
    }
}
```

Visualizing the Resize Method

To help visualize the resizing algorithm, we create a new class, VisualResizeIntStack, which adds additional methods: pushResize() and popResize():

```java
public class VisualResizeIntStack {
    private int[] item;
    private int top;

    public VisualResizeIntStack() {
        item = new int[1];
        top = -1;
    }

    public boolean isEmpty() {
        return top == -1;
    }

    public boolean isFull() {
        return top == item.length-1;
    }

    public void clear() {
        item = new int[1];
        top = -1;
    }

    public void push(int x) {
        if (isFull())
            pushResize(2 * item.length);
        item[++top] = x;
    }

    private void pushResize(int size) {
        System.out.print("Count = " + (top+1) + "\tArray Size = "
                            + item.length + "  \t");
        int[] temp = new int[size];
        for (int i = 0; i <= top; i++)
            temp[i] = item[i];
        item = temp;
        System.out.println("Resizing...\tArray Size = "
                            + item.length + "\n");

    }
```

```java
    public int pop() {
        if (isEmpty()) {
            System.out.println("Stack Underflow");
            System.exit(1);
        }
        int temp = item[top--];
        if (top == item.length/4)
            popResize(item.length/2);
        return temp;
    }

    private void popResize(int size) {
        System.out.print("Count = " + top + "\tArray Size = "
                                     + item.length + "  \t");
        int[] temp = new int[size];
        for (int i = 0; i <= top; i++)
            temp[i] = item[i];
        item = temp;
        System.out.println("Resizing...\tArray Size = " + item.length
                                     + "\n");
    }

    public int top() {
        if (isEmpty()) {
            System.out.println("Stack Underflow");
            System.exit(1);
        }
        return item[top];
    }
}
```

Our client code will simply push 300 items on the stack and then pop the stack until empty.

```java
import java.io.*;

public class Test {
    public static void main(String[] args) {
        VisualResizeIntStack s = new VisualResizeIntStack();

        for (int i = 1; i <= 300; i++)
            s.push(i);
        while (!s.isEmpty())
            s.pop();
    }
}
```

The output clearly shows the dynamic resizing of the array that houses the stack:

```
Count = 1      Array Size = 1      Resizing...   Array Size = 2
Count = 2      Array Size = 2      Resizing...   Array Size = 4
Count = 4      Array Size = 4      Resizing...   Array Size = 8
Count = 8      Array Size = 8      Resizing...   Array Size = 16
Count = 16     Array Size = 16     Resizing...   Array Size = 32
Count = 32     Array Size = 32     Resizing...   Array Size = 64
Count = 64     Array Size = 64     Resizing...   Array Size = 128
Count = 128    Array Size = 128    Resizing...   Array Size = 256
Count = 256    Array Size = 256    Resizing...   Array Size = 512
Count = 128    Array Size = 512    Resizing...   Array Size = 256
Count = 64     Array Size = 256    Resizing...   Array Size = 128
Count = 32     Array Size = 128    Resizing...   Array Size = 64
Count = 16     Array Size = 64     Resizing...   Array Size = 32
Count = 8      Array Size = 32     Resizing...   Array Size = 16
Count = 4      Array Size = 16     Resizing...   Array Size = 8
Count = 2      Array Size = 8      Resizing...   Array Size = 4
Count = 1      Array Size = 4      Resizing...   Array Size = 2
Count = 0      Array Size = 2      Resizing...   Array Size = 1
```

Problem

Given a starting point in a maze, determine if there is a way out.

```
0  0  1  E  1  0  0  1  1  1
0  1  1  0  1  0  1  0  0  0
1  0  0  0  0  0  0  0  1  0
1  1  1  1  1  0  1  1  0  0
0  0  0  1  0  0  0  1  0  1
0  1  0  1  0  1  1  1  0  1
0  1  0  1  0  0  0  1  0  0
1  1  0  1  1  1  0  1  1  0
0  1  0  0  0  0  0  1  1  0
0  1  0  1  1  0  1  0  0  *
```

The maze is represented by a 10 x 10 array of 1's and 0's. There is one exit from the maze. The door to the exit contains an E. You may move vertically or horizontally in any direction that contains a 0; you may not move to a cell with a 1. If you move into the cell with the E, you have exited. If you are in a cell with 1's on all three sides, you must go back the way you came, *backtrack*, and try another path. You may not move diagonally.

Input

The input will be a 10 x 10 array of characters (1, 0, E, *). Each data line consists of one row of the maze.

Output

Print the maze with an '*' in the entry square, followed by the message "I AM FREE" if a way out exists from that point or "HELP, I AM TRAPPED" if a way out does not exist from that point.

Processing

Begin at the entry point and continue moving until you find a way out or you have no more moves to try. We must simulate the concept of backtracking, going back to the last crossing when blocked and turning another way. Two solutions will be presented.

Solution 1

If we put the last crossing on a stack, then when we pop the stack, we could get back to the last crossing. We will represent a crossing by putting the row and column number of each square we pass on the stack. When we pop the stack, we can then get back the last square we visited. From that point we could choose another direction.

Solution 2

We can put all possible moves from the square we are in on the stack. Then, when we have to backtrack, the square we pop off the stack would be the next one to try rather than the last crossing. For example:

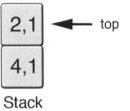

```
E  1  0  0  1
0  0  0  1  1
*  1  0  1  1
0  1  0  1  0
1  1  1  1  0
```

We start with the entry point `[3,1]` (note a lower array bound of 1). From here, there are two ways to go, `[4,1]` and `[2,1]`. We simply push both moves onto the stack.

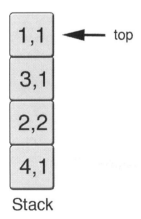

Stack

Next we pop the stack and move into square location `[2,1]`. We now decide all possible moves and push them on the stack once again. Then, we pop the stack to choose the next move. So the current position is `[2,1]`. This square does not contain an `E`, so we put the row and column number of each surrounding square that does not contain a `1` on the stack (i.e. all possible moves).

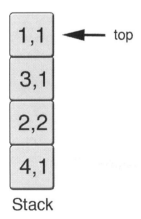

Stack

We now pop the stack and move into square position `[1,1]`. This location contains an `E` so `WE ARE FREE!!!`

Note

What would have happened if [1,1] had contained a 1 instead of an E? The position [1,1] would not have been pushed onto the stack.

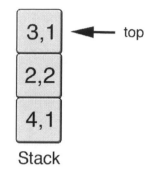

Stack

So instead of moving into [1,1], we would have moved into [3,1]. But this would then put us into an infinite loop. Square [3,1] was our starting square and we have been in a cycle from [3,1] to [2,1] to [3,1].

To avoid this problem, we will mark the squares we have visited with a period so we will not visit them again. Therefore, we will only put on the stack those squares that contain a 0 or E and not those squares that contain a 1 or period.

One Additional Problem to Consider

When we put [4,1] on the stack we knew by looking that there wasn't a square to its left. But how will the computer see this? We must therefore handle this as a special case. We're going to put a border of 1's around the whole maze. The borders of the maze will therefore be handled just like any other square.

```
1 1 1 1 1 1 1
1 E 1 0 0 1 1
1 0 0 0 1 1 1
1 * 1 0 1 1 1
1 0 1 0 1 0 1
1 1 1 1 1 0 1
1 1 1 1 1 1 1
```

To Summarize

At the beginning square we will examine the four adjacent squares and put the ones with a 0 or E in them on the stack. Mark the square we are in as having been visited by putting a period in the square. This will protect us against infinite loops. Get the next move from the stack (pop the stack). Make the square whose coordinates have been popped the current square. Repeat the process until you reach the exit point or try to backtrack and the stack is empty (no exit...we are surrounded by 1's and periods and the stack is empty).

Record Path Taken

This algorithm keeps track of possible moves by placing them in a stack. When we need to move, we take the top location in the stack, which represents the most recent alternative. If the stack is empty and we have not found the exit, there is NO WAY OUT. If we reach the square with the E, we have found a way out. BUT, the algorithm has not recorded that path.

Therefore, after a square has been marked as visited (contains a period), we will put its position in the stack. When we need to pop the stack to get the next move, we will test the new move to see if that position contains a period, a 0, or an E. If it contains a period, that position did not lead to a successful path. Just pop it off the stack and look at the next item on top of the stack to get another possible move.

If the exit point is reached, the path is represented in the stack along with the untried (and unneeded) alternative branch points. To list the path, we simply pop the stack and print each position whose value is a period.

```
// Square.java

public class Square {
    private int row;
    private int col;

    public Square(int r, int c) {
        row = r;
        col = c;
    }
```

```java
    public int getRow() {
        return row;
    }

    public int getCol() {
        return col;
    }

    public void setRow(int r) {
        row = r;
    }

    public void setCol(int c) {
        col = c;
    }
}
```

// **SquareStack.java**

```java
public class SquareStack {
    private Square[] item;
    private int top;

    public SquareStack() {
        item = new Square[1];
        top = -1;
    }

    public boolean isEmpty() {
        return top == -1;
    }

    public boolean isFull() {
        return top == item.length-1;
    }

    public void clear() {
        item = new Square[1];
        top = -1;
    }

    public void push(Square s) {
        if (isFull())
            resize(2 * item.length);
        item[++top] = s;
    }
```

```java
    private void resize(int size) {
        Square[] temp = new Square[size];
        for (int i = 0; i <= top; i++)
            temp[i] = item[i];
        item = temp;
    }

    public Square pop() {
        if (isEmpty()) {
            System.out.println("Stack Underflow");
            System.exit(1);
        }
        Square s = item[top--];
        if (top == item.length/4)
            resize(item.length/2);
        return s;
    }

    public Square top() {
        if (isEmpty()) {
            System.out.println("Stack Underflow");
            System.exit(1);
        }
        return(item[top]);
    }
}


// MazeDemo.java

import java.io.*;

public class MazeDemo {
    public static void main(String[] args) throws IOException {
        Maze m = new Maze();
        m.getMaze();
        m.processsmaze();
        m.outputPath();
    }
}
```

```java
// Maze.java

import java.io.*;
import java.util.*;

public class Maze {
    private Square move;
    private char[][] maze;
    private SquareStack s;

    public Maze() {
        s = new SquareStack();
        maze = new char[12][12];
    }

    public void getMaze() throws IOException {
        for (int row = 0; row < 12; ++row) {
            maze[row][0]  = '1';
            maze[row][11] = '1';
        }
        for (int col = 1; col < 11; ++col) {
            maze[0][col]  = '1';
            maze[11][col] = '1';
        }
        Scanner fileScan = new Scanner(new File("maze.txt"));
        for (int row = 1; row <= 10; ++row) {
            String line = fileScan.nextLine();
            String delims = "[ ]+";
            String[] tokens = line.split(delims);
            for (int col = 1; col <= 10; ++col)
                maze[row][col] = tokens[col-1].charAt(0);
        }
        fileScan.close();
    }
```

```java
// From the square MOVE, all adjacent squares containing
// a 0 or an E are put on the stack.

public void stackpossibles (Square move) {
    if ((maze[move.getRow()+1][move.getCol()] == '0') ||
        (maze[move.getRow()+1][move.getCol()] == 'E')) {
            Square newMove = new Square(move.getRow()+1,
                                            move.getCol());
            s.push(newMove);
    }
    if ((maze[move.getRow()-1][move.getCol()] == '0') ||
        (maze[move.getRow()-1][move.getCol()] == 'E')) {
            Square newMove = new Square(move.getRow()-1,
                                            move.getCol());
            s.push(newMove);
    }
    if ((maze[move.getRow()][move.getCol()+1] == '0') ||
        (maze[move.getRow()][move.getCol()+1] == 'E')) {
            Square newMove = new Square(move.getRow(),
                                            move.getCol()+1);
            s.push(newMove);
    }
    if ((maze[move.getRow()][move.getCol()-1] == '0') ||
        (maze[move.getRow()][move.getCol()-1] == 'E')) {
            Square newMove = new Square(move.getRow(),
                                            move.getCol()-1);
            s.push(newMove);
    }
}



// Maze is printed with surrounding 1's.

public void printmaze () {
    for (int row = 0; row < 12; ++row) {
        for (int col = 0; col < 12; ++col)
            System.out.print(" " + maze[row][col]);
        System.out.println();
    }
    System.out.println();
}
```

```java
// Outputs path taken through maze.

public void outputPath() {
    Square move;
    System.out.println("PATH TAKEN");
    while (!s.isEmpty()) {
        move = s.pop();
        if (maze[move.getRow()][move.getCol()] == '.')
            System.out.println(move.getRow() + "   " +
                                                move.getCol());
    }
}


// The maze is printed, and squares are visited until the
// square with the E is moved into or there are no more
// squares to try. The maze with the tried path is printed
// along with the outcome.

public void processmaze () {
    Square move = new Square(10, 10);
    boolean freed = maze[move.getRow()][move.getCol()] == 'E';
    boolean trapped = maze[move.getRow()][move.getCol()] == '1';
    maze[move.getRow()][move.getCol()] = '*';
    System.out.println("INITIAL MAZE");
    printmaze();
    while (!trapped && !freed) {
        maze[move.getRow()][move.getCol()] = '.';
        s.push(move);
        stackpossibles(move);
        trapped = s.isEmpty();
        while (!trapped &&
                    maze[move.getRow()][move.getCol()] == '.')) {
            move = s.pop();
            trapped = s.isEmpty();
        }
        freed = maze[move.getRow()][move.getCol()] == 'E';
    }
    if (freed) {
        maze[move.getRow()][move.getCol()] = '.';
        s.push(move);
    }
    System.out.println("FINAL MAZE");
    printmaze();
    if (freed)
        System.out.println("I AM FREE\n");
    else
        System.out.println("HELP, I AM TRAPPED\n");
}
}
```

```
// maze.txt

0  0  1  E  1  0  0  1  1  1
0  1  1  0  1  0  1  0  0  0
0  0  0  0  0  0  0  0  1  0
1  1  1  1  1  0  1  1  0  0
0  0  0  1  0  0  0  1  0  1
0  1  0  1  0  1  1  1  0  1
0  1  0  1  0  0  0  1  0  0
1  1  0  1  1  1  0  1  1  0
0  1  0  0  0  0  0  1  1  0
0  1  0  1  1  0  1  0  0  0
```

Maze Program Output

```
INITIAL MAZE

1  1  1  1  1  1  1  1  1  1  1  1
1  0  0  1  E  1  0  0  1  1  1  1
1  0  1  1  0  1  0  1  0  0  0  1
1  0  0  0  0  0  0  0  0  1  0  1
1  1  1  1  1  1  0  1  1  0  0  1
1  0  0  0  1  0  0  0  1  0  1  1
1  0  1  0  1  0  1  1  1  0  1  1
1  0  1  0  1  0  0  0  1  0  0  1
1  1  1  0  1  1  1  0  1  1  0  1
1  0  1  0  0  0  0  0  1  1  0  1
1  0  1  0  1  1  0  1  0  0  *  1
1  1  1  1  1  1  1  1  1  1  1  1


FINAL MAZE

1  1  1  1  1  1  1  1  1  1  1  1
1  .  .  1  .  1  0  0  1  1  1  1
1  .  1  1  .  1  0  1  .  .  .  1
1  .  .  .  .  .  .  .  .  1  .  1
1  1  1  1  1  1  0  1  1  .  .  1
1  0  0  0  1  0  0  0  1  .  1  1
1  0  1  0  1  0  1  1  1  .  1  1
1  0  1  0  1  0  0  0  1  .  .  1
1  1  1  0  1  1  1  0  1  1  .  1
1  0  1  0  0  0  0  0  1  1  .  1
1  0  1  0  1  1  0  1  .  .  .  1
1  1  1  1  1  1  1  1  1  1  1  1
```

```
I AM FREE

PATH TAKEN

1   4
2   4
3   4
3   5
3   6
3   7
3   8
2   8
2   9
2   10
3   10
4   10
4   9
5   9
6   9
7   9
7   10
8   10
9   10
10  10
```

```java
// StringStack.java

public class StringStack {
    private String[] item;
    private int top;

    public StringStack() {
        item = new String[1];
        top = -1;
    }

    public boolean isEmpty() {
        return top == -1;
    }

    public boolean isFull() {
        return top == item.length-1;
    }

    public void clear() {
        item = new String[1];
        top = -1;
    }

    public void push(String s) {
        if (isFull())
            resize(2 * item.length);
        item[++top] = s;
    }

    private void resize(int size) {
        String[] temp = new String[size];
        for (int i = 0; i <= top; i++)
            temp[i] = item[i];
        item = temp;
    }
```

```java
    public String pop() {
        if (isEmpty()) {
            System.out.println("Stack Underflow");
            System.exit(1);
        }
        String temp = item[top--];
        if (top == item.length/4)
            resize(item.length/2);
        return temp;
    }

    public String top() {
        if (isEmpty()) {
            System.out.println("Stack Underflow");
            System.exit(1);
        }
        return item[top];
    }
}
```

Stack of Objects

So far we have created classes for a stack of `ints`, `IntStack`, a stack of Squares, `SquareStack`, and a stack of Strings, `StringStack`. For each new object that we might want to manipulate with a stack, we would be forced to create a new stack class or modify an existing stack class with the appropriate code for the manipulation of that type of object, whether it be an `Automobile` object, an `Elephant` object, a `Student` object, etc. Anytime we modify code or create new code there is the chance of introducing errors. Also, creating multiple stack classes increases the amount of code that has to be maintained.

It would be more efficient if we could design a system around a single stack of indeterminate type on which the primitive routines could be defined. We could then create instances of such a stack as necessary, thus eliminating the need to create separate classes.

Java provides us with the tools to create and manipulate objects of indeterminate type. Note that all objects in Java are said to be derived from the superclass `Object`. An object of any type may be stored in an object of type `Object`. This allows us to implement a single stack class, `ObjectStack`, whose elements are of type `Object` but can hold objects of any type.

```
public class ObjectStack {
    private Object[] item;
    private int top;
```

As the `Object` class is at the top of Java's inheritance hierarchy, we would be able to insert an object of any type onto the stack:

```
public void push(Object o) {
    item[++top] = o;
}
```

We would also be able to remove an object of any type from the stack:

```
public Object pop() {
    return item[top--];
}
```

Let's take a closer look at how this works. Assume that we have a `Student` class and we want to manipulate `Student` objects on our `ObjectStack`. First we might instantiate a stack of objects:

```
ObjectStack s = new ObjectStack();
```

Then we might instantiate a `Student` object:

```
Student stud = new Student();
```

We can now push the `Student` object onto the `ObjectStack` as follows:

```
s.push(stud);
```

So far so good. Now let's pop the `Student` object from the `ObjectStack`:

```
stud = s.pop();
```

Oops. We're now presented with an incompatible types error! `stud` is of type `Student` and the object we're popping off the stack and assigning to `stud` is of type `Object`! What's going on?

When we push a `Student` object onto an `ObjectStack`, the `Student` object automatically gets cast up to an `Object`. When we pop the `ObjectStack`, an `Object` is then removed from the stack and returned. However, there is no automatic downcast from an `Object` to a `Student` object, which is what we're looking for. It's up to us to cast it back to the appropriate type:

```
stud = (Student) s.pop();
```

This casts the `Object` returned from the stack into a `Student` object that can now be assigned to `stud`.

Java provides the programmer with a series of wrapper classes (`Integer`, `Double`, `Character`, `Boolean`, etc.) defined in the `java.lang` package, that may be used to contain, or *wrap*, the primitive types. That is, an object of type `Integer` contains a single data element of type `int`, an object of type `Character` contains a single data element of type `char`, etc. The Java compiler automatically converts primitive types to their corresponding object wrapper classes (`int` and `Integer`, `char` and `Character`, etc.)

Our client code can push an `int` onto an `ObjectStack` as follows:

```
int x = 4;
s.push(x);
```

The `int x` is automatically wrapped into an `Integer` object and is then cast into an `Object` that is placed onto the `ObjectStack`.

Our code to pop the `ObjectStack` is as follows:

```
x = (Integer)s.pop();
```

Note that it is still necessary to cast the `Object` popped from the `ObjectStack` down into an `Integer` object. The `int` is then unwrapped from the `Integer` object and assigned to `x`. Note that it is always the programmer's responsibility "unwrap" the item extracted from the data structure prior to assigning it to a variable of primitive type.

Using an `Object` allows the programmer to define the features of a data structure without reference to a particular type, with the method using the data structure being responsible for properly interpreting the object placed on the data structure.

Note that utilizing an `ObjectStack` can expose us to subtle bugs in our programs that cannot be detected until runtime. The client code below will generate a run-time error:

```java
// BadCode.java

import java.io.*;
import java.util.Scanner;

public class BadCode {
    public static void main(String[] args) {
        ObjectStack s = new ObjectStack();

        String buf = new String("Hello, world.");
        s.push(buf);
        s.push(42);
        buf = (String) s.pop();
        System.out.println(buf);
    }
}
```

Why? When using an `ObjectStack`, we're forced to cast the popped object from the stack into an object of the appropriate type. However, when the programmer places different types of objects on the same `ObjectStack`, the client code must be sure to use the right cast, or a run-time error will occur.

In this example, a `String` object and then an `Integer` object is pushed, in that order, onto the `ObjectStack`. When the stack is popped, the Object popped from the stack is cast into a `String` rather than an `Integer`! Crash!

Note that this code cannot be type-checked at compile time. So when we use type casting with an implementation such as `ObjectStack` for different types of objects, we are assuming that clients will cast objects popped from the stack to the proper type.

ObjectStack Class

```java
// ObjectStack.java

public class ObjectStack {
    private Object[] item;
    private int top;

    public ObjectStack() {
        item = new Object[1];
        top = -1;
    }

    public boolean isEmpty() {
        return top == -1;
    }

    public boolean isFull() {
        return top == item.length-1;
    }

    public void clear() {
        item = new Object[1];
        top = -1;
    }
    public void push(Object o) {
        if (isFull())
            resize(2 * item.length);
        item[++top] = o;
    }

    private void resize(int size) {
        Object[] temp = new Object[size];
        for (int i = 0; i <= top; i++)
            temp[i] = item[i];
        item = temp;
    }
```

```
        public Object pop() {
            if (isEmpty()) {
                System.out.println("Stack Underflow");
                System.exit(1);
            }
            Object temp = item[top--];
            if (top == item.length/4)
                resize(item.length/2);
            return temp;
        }

        public Object top() {
            if (isEmpty()) {
                System.out.println("Stack Underflow");
                System.exit(1);
            }
            return item[top];
        }
    }
```

```java
// ObjectStackClient.java

public class Driver {
    public static void main(String[] args) {
        int x;
        char c;
        Object myObject;

        ObjectStack s = new ObjectStack();
        for (int i = 0; i < 10; i++)
            s.push(i);
        while (!s.isEmpty()) {
            x = (Integer) s.pop();
            System.out.print(x + " ");
        }
        System.out.println();
        for (int i = 65; i < 91; i++)
            s.push((char)i);
        while (!s.isEmpty()) {
            c = (Character) s.pop();
            System.out.print(c + " ");
        }
        System.out.println();


        // Identify different classes of objects using instanceof
        s.push(new Integer(2));
        s.push(new Integer(4));
        s.push(new Character('A'));
        s.push(new Character('B'));
        s.push(new Integer(6));
        s.push(new Character('C'));

        while (!s.isEmpty()) {
            myObject = s.pop();
            if (myObject instanceof Integer)
                System.out.println(((Integer) myObject).intValue());
            else if (myObject instanceof Character)
                System.out.println(((Character) myObject).charValue());
            else
                System.out.println("Neither.");
        }
    }
}
```

```
Output:

9 8 7 6 5 4 3 2 1 0
Z Y X W V U T S R Q P O N M L K J I H G F E D C B A
C
6
B
A
4
2
```

```java
// MazeDemo2.java

import java.io.*;

public class MazeDemo2 {
    public static void main(String[] args) throws IOException {
        Maze2 m = new Maze2();
        m.getMaze();
        m.processmaze();
        m.outputPath();
    }
}


// Maze2.java

import java.io.*;
import java.util.*;

public class Maze2 {
    private Square move;
    private char[][] maze;
    private ObjectStack s;

    public Maze2() {
        s = new ObjectStack();
        maze = new char[12][12];
    }
```

```java
// Read maze from file

public void getMaze() throws IOException {
    for (int row = 0; row < 12; ++row) {
        maze[row][0]  = '1';
        maze[row][11] = '1';
    }
    for (int col = 1; col < 11; ++col) {
        maze[0][col]  = '1';
        maze[11][col] = '1';
    }
    Scanner fileScan = new Scanner(new File("maze.txt"));
    for (int row = 1; row <= 10; ++row) {
        String line = fileScan.nextLine();
        String delims = "[ ]+";
        String[] tokens = line.split(delims);
        for (int col = 1; col <= 10; ++col)
            maze[row][col] = tokens[col-1].charAt(0);
        }
    fileScan.close();
}


// Maze is printed with surrounding 1's.

public void printmaze () {
    for (int row = 0; row < 12; ++row) {
        for (int col = 0; col < 12; ++col)
            System.out.print(" " + maze[row][col]);
        System.out.println();
    }
    System.out.println();
}


// Outputs path taken through maze.

public void outputPath() {
    Square move;
    System.out.println("PATH TAKEN");
    while (!s.isEmpty()) {
        move = (Square) s.pop();
        if (maze[move.getRow()][move.getCol()] == '.')
            System.out.println(move.getRow() + "   " +
                                               move.getCol());
    }
}
```

```
// From the square MOVE, all adjacent squares containing a 0
// or an E are put on the stack.

void stackpossibles (Square move) {
    if ((maze[move.getRow()+1][move.getCol()] == '0') ||
        (maze[move.getRow()+1][move.getCol()] == 'E')) {
            Square newMove = new Square(move.getRow()+1,
                                                move.getCol());
            s.push(newMove);
    }
    if ((maze[move.getRow()-1][move.getCol()] == '0') ||
        (maze[move.getRow()-1][move.getCol()] == 'E')) {
            Square newMove = new Square(move.getRow()-1,
                                                move.getCol());
            s.push(newMove);
    }
    if ((maze[move.getRow()][move.getCol()+1] == '0') ||
      (maze[move.getRow()][move.getCol()+1] == 'E')) {
            Square newMove = new Square(move.getRow(),
                                                move.getCol()+1);
            s.push(newMove);
    }
    if ((maze[move.getRow()][move.getCol()-1] == '0') ||
        (maze[move.getRow()][move.getCol()-1] == 'E')) {
            Square newMove = new Square(move.getRow(),
                                                move.getCol()-1);
            s.push(newMove);
    }
}
```

```
// The maze is printed, and squares are visited until the square
// with the E is moved into or there are no more squares to try.
// The maze with the tried path is printed along with
// the outcome.

public void processmaze () {
    Square move = new Square(10, 10);
    boolean freed = maze[move.getRow()][move.getCol()] == 'E';
    boolean trapped = maze[move.getRow()][move.getCol()] == '1';
    maze[move.getRow()][move.getCol()] = '*';
    System.out.println("INITIAL MAZE");
    printmaze();
    while (!trapped && !freed) {
        maze[move.getRow()][move.getCol()] = '.';
        s.push(move);
        stackpossibles(move);
        trapped = s.isEmpty();
        while (!trapped && (maze[move.getRow()][move.getCol()]
                                                == '.')) {

            move = (Square) s.pop();
            trapped = s.isEmpty();
        }
        freed = maze[move.getRow()][move.getCol()] == 'E';
    }
    if (freed) {
        maze[move.getRow()][move.getCol()] = '.';
        s.push(move);
    }
    System.out.println("FINAL MAZE");
    printmaze();
    if (freed)
        System.out.println("I AM FREE\n");
    else
        System.out.println("HELP, I AM TRAPPED\n");
    }
}
```

Evaluating Arithmetic Expressions with ObjectStack

Suppose we wanted to evaluate the following string of characters as an arithmetic expression:

```
( 5 + ( ( 4 * 2 ) * ( 2 + 3 ) ) )
```

Mathematically, we would first multiply 4 * 2 = 8, then add 2 + 3 = 5, then multiply those two results together, 8 * 5 = 40, and finally add 5 to that result, 5 + 40 = 45.

We can utilize two `ObjectStacks` to implement *Dijkstra's Two Stack Algorithm* as shown below:

1. Scan the expression from left to right. When an operand is encountered, push it onto the operand stack.

2. When an operator is encountered in the expression, push it onto the operator stack.

3. When a left parenthesis is encountered in the expression, ignore it.

4. When a right parenthesis is encountered in the expression, pop an operator off the operator stack. The two operands it must operate on must be the last two operands pushed onto the operand stack. We therefore pop the operand stack twice, perform the operation, and push the result back onto the operand stack so it will be available for use as an operand of the next operator popped off the operator stack.

5. When the entire infix expression has been scanned, the value left on the operand stack represents the value of the expression.

Shown below are the steps in the evaluation of the following expression:

```
( 5 + ( ( 4 * 2 ) * ( 2 + 3 ) ) )
```

Arithmetic Expression	Operand Stack	Operator Stack	Rule
(5 + ((4 * 2) * (2 + 3))) ^			3
(5 + ((4 * 2) * (2 + 3))) ^	5		1
(5 + ((4 * 2) * (2 + 3))) ^	5	+	2
(5 + ((4 * 2) * (2 + 3))) ^	5	+	3
(5 + ((4 * 2) * (2 + 3))) ^	5	+	3
(5 + ((4 * 2) * (2 + 3))) ^	5 4	+	1
(5 + ((4 * 2) * (2 + 3))) ^	5 4	+ *	2
(5 + ((4 * 2) * (2 + 3))) ^	5 4 2	+ *	1
(5 + ((4 * 2) * (2 + 3))) ^	5 8	+	4
(5 + ((4 * 2) * (2 + 3))) ^	5 8	+ *	2
(5 + ((4 * 2) * (2 + 3))) ^	5 8	+ *	3
(5 + ((4 * 2) * (2 + 3))) ^	5 8 2	+ *	1
(5 + ((4 * 2) * (2 + 3))) ^	5 8 2	+ * +	2
(5 + ((4 * 2) * (2 + 3))) ^	5 8 2 3	+ * +	1
(5 + ((4 * 2) * (2 + 3))) ^	5 8 5	+ *	4
(5 + ((4 * 2) * (2 + 3))) ^	5 40	+	4
(5 + ((4 * 2) * (2 + 3))) ^	45		4

Using our `ObjectStack` class, we present the code below to evaluate an arithmetic expression. Our code assumes that the arithmetic expression is fully parenthesized, with all characters separated by whitespace.

```java
// Evaluate.java

import java.io.*;
import java.util.Scanner;

public class Evaluate2 {
    public static void main(String[] args) throws IOException {
        ObjectStack operator = new ObjectStack();
        ObjectStack operand = new ObjectStack();
        Scanner fileScan = new Scanner(new File("expressions.txt"));

        while (fileScan.hasNext()) {
            String exp = fileScan.nextLine();
            System.out.println(exp);
            for (int i = 0; i < exp.length(); i++) {
                char ch = exp.charAt(i);
                if (ch >= '0' && ch <= '9')
                    operand.push(ch - 48);
                else if (ch == '+' || ch == '-' || ch == '*'
                                   || ch == '/' || ch == '^')
                    operator.push(ch);
                else if (ch == ')') {
                    int val2 = (Integer) operand.pop();
                    int val1 = (Integer) operand.pop();
                    char op =  (Character) operator.pop();
                    if (op == '+')
                        operand.push(val1 + val2);
                    else if (op == '-')
                        operand.push(val1 - val2);
                    else if (op == '*')
                        operand.push(val1 * val2);
                    else if (op == '/')
                        operand.push(val1 / val2);
                    else if (op == '^')
                        operand.push((int) Math.pow(val1, val2));
                }
            }
            System.out.println((Integer) operand.pop());
        }
        fileScan.close();
    }
}
```

Here are the arithmetic expressions in the `expressions.txt` text file:

```
( 3 + 2 )
( 1 + ( ( 2 + 3 ) * ( 4 * 5 ) ) )
( 1 - ( 2 * 8 ) )
( 8 + ( ( 4 * 2 ) * 6 ) )
( 3 ^ 4 )
```

The output to the above program is shown below:

```
( 3 + 2 )
5
( 1 + ( ( 2 + 3 ) * ( 4 * 5 ) ) )
101
( 1 - ( 2 * 8 ) )
-15
( 8 + ( ( 4 * 2 ) * 6 ) )
56
( 3 ^ 4 )
81
```

Final Note on ObjectStack Class

Note that in our `pop()` implementation of `ObjectStack`, the reference to the popped item remains in the array as the `top` pointer decrements.

```
public Object pop() {
    if (isEmpty()) {
        System.out.println("Stack Underflow");
        System.exit(1);
    }
    Object temp = item[top--];
    if (top == item.length/4)
        resize(item.length/2);
    return temp;
}
```

The object that was popped off the `ObjectStack` still exists within the array, but can no longer be accessed. To reclaim this memory, we can set the array location corresponding to the item popped from the stack to `null`.

```
public Object pop() {
    if (isEmpty()) {
        System.out.println("Stack Underflow");
        System.exit(1);
    }
    Object temp = item[top];
    item[top--] = null;
    if (top == item.length/4)
        resize(item.length/2);
    return temp;
}
```

ObjectStack Class – Final Version

```java
// ObjectStack.java

public class ObjectStack {
    private Object[] item;
    private int top;

    public ObjectStack() {
        item = new Object[1];
        top = -1;
    }

    public boolean isEmpty() {
        return top == -1;
    }

    public boolean isFull() {
        return top == item.length-1;
    }

    public void clear() {
        item = new Object[1];
        top = -1;
    }

    public void push(Object o) {
        if (isFull())
            resize(2 * item.length);
        item[++top] = o;
    }

    private void resize(int size) {
        Object[] temp = new Object[size];
        for (int i = 0; i <= top; i++)
            temp[i] = item[i];
        item = temp;
    }
```

```
public Object pop() {
    if (isEmpty()) {
        System.out.println("Stack Underflow.");
        System.exit(1);
    }
    Object temp = item[top];
    item[top--] = null;
    if (top == item.length/4)
        resize(item.length/2);
    return temp;
}

public Object top() {
    if (isEmpty()) {
        System.out.println("Stack Underflow.");
        System.exit(1);
    }
    return item[top];
}
}
```

Time Complexity for Stacks

	Average Case	Worst Case
Push:	O(1)	O(n)
Pop:	O(1)	O(n)
Top:	O(1)	O(1)

Prefix, Infix, and Postfix Notation

Consider the sum of a and b. We think of applying the operator "+" to the operands a and b and write the sum as $a+b$. However, we can also represent the sum of two numbers with the operator coming before the two operands, $+ab$, or with the operator coming after the two operands, $ab+$.

```
+ab    prefix notation

a+b    infix notation

ab+    postfix notation
```

Note that the prefixes **pre**, **in**, and **post** refer to the relative position of the operator with respect to the two operands.

Now suppose we wanted to convert an infix expression into prefix or postfix notation:

Rules to convert from infix to prefix notation:

1. Determine which operator has the highest precedence.

2. Convert that portion of the expression to prefix notation.

3. Treat that converted prefix sub-expression as one single operand (will be underlined).

4. Continue until the entire expression has been converted to prefix notation.

Let's convert a + b * c into prefix notation:

```
a + b * c

a + * b c

+ a * b c
```

Rules to convert from infix to postfix notation:

1. Determine which operator has the highest precedence.

2. Convert that portion of the expression to postfix notation.

3. Treat that converted postfix sub-expression as one single operand (will be underlined).

4. Continue until the entire expression has been converted to postfix notation.

Let's convert a + b * c into postfix notation:

```
a + b * c

a + b c *

a b c * +
```

Note that in the conversions above, operators with the highest precedence are converted first and that after a portion of the expression has been converted to prefix or postfix, it is to be treated as a single operand. Also note that the prefix and postfix results look different, although they are not the mirror image of each other.

In our next example we're going to use parentheses to override precedence in the original infix expression:

Infix to Prefix	Infix to Postfix
(a + b) * c	(a + b) * c
+ a b * c	a b + * c
* + a b c	a b + c *

Note that in these examples in which we use parentheses to show precedence of operators in the infix expression, we no longer need the parentheses to represent the expression in prefix or postfix notation. This is certainly an advantage of representing expressions in prefix or postfix notation (of course, at the cost of readability… at least to humans…).

Before proceeding, convert the two infix expressions below into prefix and postfix notation (note that the caret represents exponentiation):

```
(a + b) * (c – d)
a – b / (c * d ^ e)
```

…

…

I requested that you do not proceed until you have completed the examples above…

…

…

Here are the solutions:

infix to prefix

(a + b) * (c − d)

+ a b * − c d

* + a b − c d

infix to postfix

(a + b) * (c − d)

a b + * c d −

a b + c d − *

infix to prefix

a − b / (c * d ^ e)

a − b / (c * ^ d e)

a − b / * c ^ d e)

a − / b * c ^ d e)

− a / b * c ^ d e

infix to postfix

a − b / (c * d ^ e)

a − b / (c * d e ^)

a − b / c d e ^ *)

a − b c d e ^ * /)

a b c d e ^ * / −

Once again note that the prefix and postfix notations are different but that are not the mirror images of each other. Also note that parentheses are not needed in the prefix and postfix notations.

Evaluation of Postfix Expressions

Postfix notation (sometimes referred to as reverse Polish notation) makes for easy evaluation of expressions:

1 – The need for parentheses is eliminated.

2 – The priority of the operators is no longer relevant.

The order of the operators in the postfix expressions determines the actual order of operations in evaluating the expression and therefore parentheses are unnecessary. However, we do sacrifice the ability to note at a glance the operands associated with a particular operator.

In the example below, note how each operator follows its operands:

```
Infix expression: ( 5 - 3 ) * ( 4 + 6 )

Postfix expression: 5 3 - 4 6 + *
```

A postfix expression may be evaluated as follows:

1 - Parse the expression from left to right.

2 – When an operand is encountered, it gets pushed on the stack.

3 – When an operator is encountered, the two operands it must operate on must be the last two operands pushed onto the stack. We therefore pop the stack twice, perform the operation, and push the result back onto the stack so it will be available for us as an operand of the next operator.

4 – When you have parsed the entire string, the single value that remains on the stack is the result of the evaluation.

This evaluation process is much simpler than attempting a direct evaluation from an infix notation.

Algorithm to evaluate a postfix expression:

```
while there are more characters in the input string
     if the character is an operand
          push it onto the stack
     else the character must be an operator
          pop operand
          pop operand
          perform the operation
          push the result back onto the stack
result = pop(stack)
```

Example to evaluate postfix expression:

Infix expression: (5 - 3) * (4 + 6)

Postfix expression: 5 3 - 4 6 + *

Evaluate postfix expression: 5 3 - 4 6 + *

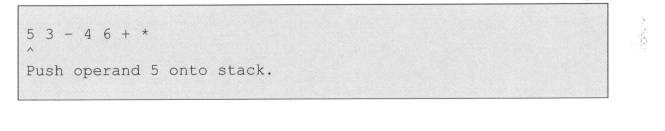

```
5 3 - 4 6 + *
^
Push operand 5 onto stack.
```

5 ← top of stack

Stack

```
5 3 - 4 6 + *
  ^
Push operand 3 onto stack.
```

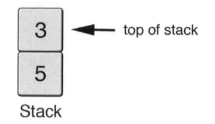

top of stack

Stack

```
5 3 - 4 6 + *
    ^
Operator encountered.

Pop the stack: op2 = 3
Pop the stack: op1 = 5
Perform the operation: op1 - op2 = 5 - 3 = 2
Push the result onto the stack.
```

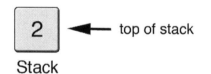

top of stack

Stack

```
5 3 - 4 6 + *
        ^
Push operand 4 onto stack.
```

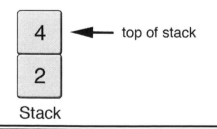

top of stack

Stack

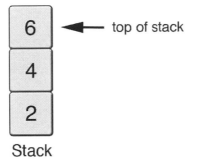

```
5 3 - 4 6 + *
        ^
Push operand 6 onto stack.
```

6 ← top of stack

4

2

Stack

```
5 3 - 4 6 + *
          ^
Operator encountered.

Pop the stack: op2 = 6
Pop the stack: op1 = 4
Perform the operation: op1 + op2 = 4 + 6 = 10
Push the result onto the stack.
```

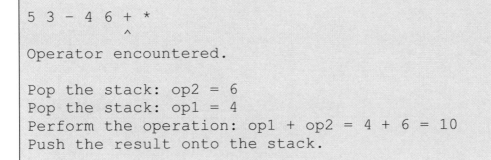

10 ← top of stack

2

Stack

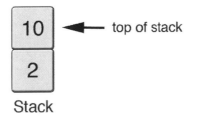

```
5 3 - 4 6 + *
        ^
Operator encountered.

Pop the stack: op2 = 10
Pop the stack: op1 = 2
Perform the operation: op1 * op2 = 10 * 2 = 20
Push the result onto the stack.
```

Stack

```
5 3 - 4 6 + *
          ^
There are no more characters in the input string.

Pop the stack: result = 20
```

Note: In the evaluation of any postfix expression, all division will be integer division.

Stack Algorithm to Convert Infix to Postfix

Compare infix and postfix expressions:

infix	postfix
3*4+9*5	34*95*+
3*(4+9)*5	349+*5*
3-4+5	34-5+
3-(4+5)	345+-

Note the following:

1. The operands appear in the same order in the infix and postfix expressions. Therefore, there is no need to change the order of the operands.

2. Each operator occurs further to the right in the postfix expression than in the infix expression, and the order of the operators may be changed.

Conversion of infix expression without parentheses:

Here are the translation rules to convert an infix expression, containing no parentheses, to postfix notation:

1. Scan the infix expression from left to right. When an operand is encountered, copy it immediately to the postfix expression.

2. When an operator is encountered in the infix expression, pop the operators from the stack and place them in the postfix expression until either the stack is empty or the operator on top of the stack has a lower priority than the operator encountered in the infix expression. Then push the operator encountered in the infix expression onto the stack.

3. When the entire infix expression has been scanned, pop operators from the stack and place them in the postfix expression until the stack is empty.

Example: 3*4+9*5

Infix	Stack	Postfix	Rule
3*4+9*5			
3*4+9*5 ^		3	1
3*4+9*5 ^	*	3	2
3*4+9*5 ^	*	34	1
3*4+9*5 ^		34*	2
3*4+9*5 ^	+	34*	2
3*4+9*5 ^	+	34*9	1
3*4+9*5 ^	+*	34*9	2
3*4+9*5 ^	+*	34*95	1
3*4+9*5 ^	+	34*95*	3
3*4+9*5 ^		34*95*+	3

Conversion of infix expression with parentheses:

A parenthesized sub-expression is treated as a single operand by the operators on either side of it in the infix expression. When a parenthesized sub-expression is encountered, the operators on the stack cannot be removed until the entire sub-expression has been translated. This is similar to a single operand being moved directly to the postfix expression without removing any operators from the stack.

The left parenthesis that precedes the sub-expression is pushed onto the stack and serves as a temporary bottom to the stack. The sub-expression is translated using the part of the stack above the left parenthesis. When the right parenthesis following the sub-expression is encountered, the left parenthesis is popped from the stack, exposing the operators beneath it.

We add the following three translation rules to convert an infix expression, containing parentheses, to postfix notation:

4. When a left parenthesis is encountered in the infix expression, push it onto the stack.

5. If a left parenthesis is encountered while unstacking operators according to rule 2, stop the unstacking and push the operator encountered in the infix expression onto the stack. Thus rule 2 treats a left parenthesis as if it were the bottom of the stack.

6. When a right parenthesis is encountered in the infix expression, pop the operators and place them in the postfix expression until a left parenthesis is encountered on the stack. Discard both left and right parenthesis.

Example: 2 * (3+4*5) *6

Infix	Stack	Postfix	Rule
2 * (3+4*5) *6			
2 * (3+4*5) *6 ^		2	1
2 * (3+4*5) *6 ^	*	2	2
2 * (3+4*5) *6 ^	* (	2	4
2 * (3+4*5) *6 ^	* (	23	1
2 * (3+4*5) *6 ^	* (+	23	5
2 * (3+4*5) *6 ^	* (+	234	1
2 * (3+4*5) *6 ^	* (+*	234	2
2 * (3+4*5) *6 ^	* (+*	2345	1
2 * (3+4*5) *6 ^	* (+	2345*	6
2 * (3+4*5) *6 ^	* (	2345*+	6
2 * (3+4*5) *6 ^	*	2345*+	6
2 * (3+4*5) *6 ^		2345*+*	2
2 * (3+4*5) *6 ^	*	2345*+*	2
2 * (3+4*5) *6 ^	*	2345*+*6	1
2 * (3+4*5) *6 ^		2345*+*6*	3

Note the following:
When the + is encountered in the infix expression, the * below the left parenthesis is not unstacked. The left parenthesis "protects" the * from being unstacked by any operator in the sub-expression. Only when the entire sub-expression has been translated and the left parenthesis has been removed can the * be unstacked.

In general, when a parenthesized sub-expression is encountered, translation of the main expression is interrupted while the sub-expression is translated, after which translation of the main expression resumes.

See if you can convert this infix expression into postfix notation.

((8 − 3 * (6 + 2) + 5 ^ 2) * 2)

1. Given an initially empty stack `s` that accepts integers, the following operations are performed:

```
s.push(10)
s.push(20)
s.pop()
s.push(30)
s.push(40)
s.push(50)
s.pop()
s.pop()
s.push(60)
s.pop()
s.pop()
s.push(70)
s.push(80)
s.pop()
```

a) Show the composition of the stack after these operations.

b) Display the correct order in which the integers are popped off the stack?

2. The string DATASTRUCTURES is subjected to the following sequence of stack operations, beginning with D and working left to right:

```
push - push - push - pop - pop - push - push - pop - push - push -
push - pop - push - push - push - pop - pop - pop - push - push - push
```

What output is produced from the pops of this initially empty stack?

3. Use the operations `push`, `pop`, `top`, and `isEmpty` to construct pseudocode operations that do each of the following:

a) Set `num` to the second element from the top of the stack, leaving the stack without its top two elements.

b) Set `num` to the second element from the top of the stack, leaving the stack unchanged.

---

c) Given an integer n, set `num` to the nth element from the top of the stack, leaving the stack without its top n elements.

d) Given an integer n, set `num` to the **nth** element from the top of the stack, leaving the stack unchanged.

e) Set `num` to the bottom element of the stack, leaving the stack empty.

f) Set `num` to the bottom element of the stack, leaving the stack unchanged.

g) Set `num` to the nth element from the bottom of the stack leaving the stack unchanged.

4. Consider a language that does not have arrays but does have stacks as a data type. That is, one can declare:

```
Stack s;
```

and the `push`, `pop`, `top` and `isEmpty` operations are defined. Describe, without using code or pseudo code, how the store and extract operations on a one-dimensional array can be implemented by using these stack primitive operations on two stacks. Note that the first item stored in the array is located at the bottom of the stack.

5. Given below is part of a class declaration and constructor for keeping two stacks within a single linear array. In this class, neither stack should overflow until all memory in the array is utilized and an entire stack should never be shifted to a different location within the array. For this class you should write the methods `push1()`, `push2()`, `pop1()`, `pop2()`, `clear1()`, `clear2()`, `isEmpty1()`, `isEmpty2()`, and `isFull()` to manipulate the two stacks. (Hint: The two stacks grow toward each other.) Don't worry about overflow or underflow and do not resize the array.

```
public class Stack {
    private int[] item;
    private int top1;
    private int top2;
    private int size;
```

```
public Stack(int max) {
    size = max;
    item = new int[size];
    top1 = -1;
    top2 = size;
}
```

6. Convert the formula we derived earlier for calculating the storage location of an element of a two-dimensional array stored in row-major order into postfix notation. You can use either conversion algorithm. Show all work.

```
location (list[i1, i2]) =

          base + [(i1 - L1) * (U2 - L2 + 1) + (i2 - L2)] * esize
```

7. Convert each infix expression below into postfix notation using the algorithmic technique just introduced of parsing the expression left to right. Additionally, evaluate the postfix expression. Note: In the evaluation of any postfix expression, all division will be integer division. Be sure to show all work.

```
1:   7 - 4 * 3 + 8

2:   6 * 3 + 5 * 4 + 2 * 6

3:   3 * 3 + 4 * 8 - 9 / 2 ^ 2

4:   9 - 4 * 3 - 5

5:   2 * ( 9 - 1 / 4 ) + 3

6:   ( 8 - 3 ) / ( 4 * 7 )

7:   2 * ( 6 * ( 3 + 4 ) ) - 8

8:   ( ( 4 * ( 3 + 8 ) + ( 5 - 2 ) / 2 ) - 3 ) ^ 2

9:   ( ( 4 - 2 * ( 7 - 1 ) + 2 ^ 2 ) * 6 )

10:  ( ( ( 2 ^ 3 ^ 4 ) ) )
```

❖ Computer Lab: Infix to Postfix Notation

One common way for a compiler for a high-level language to generate machine language instructions to evaluate arithmetic or Boolean expressions, involves a conversion of the expression from infix to postfix. Typically, the compiler does not require a fully parenthesized expression as input, but instead has a table of priorities which indicate the order in which operators will be applied within a pair of parentheses (the operator with highest priority is evaluated first).

For example, consider a compiler with the following set of priorities:

Operator	Priority
`^, ~, unary +, unary -`	6
`*, /`	5
`+, -`	4
`<, <=, =, <>, >, >=`	3
`and`	2
`or`	1

Then the expression:

```
A / B ^ C + D * E - A * C
```

will be evaluated as:

```
((A / (B ^ C)) + (D * E)) - (A * C)
```

and its postfix form would be:

```
A B C ^ / D E * + A C * -
```

For this lab, you are to design, implement, and test a Java program that reads infix expressions from a file, `infix.txt`, converts the infix expression to postfix notation, and evaluates the postfix expressions. We make the following simplifying assumptions:

• All operators and operands are one character long in the original infix expression.

• Allowable operators are +, -, *, / (integer division), ^ (exponentiation).

• All operators are left associative.

• There are no unary operators.

• Each expression is contained on its own line within the file.

• Parentheses can of course be used in normal fashion, and blanks should be allowed between symbols.

The infix expressions below should be read into your program from a file, `infix.txt`.

```
1:   8 + 4 * 2 - 6

2:   7 * 2 - 4 * 3 + 2 * 5

3:   2 * 3 * 4 - 8 + 9 / 3 / 3

4:   5 + 7 * 4 - 6

5:   4 * ( 3 + 2 * 4 ) - 7

6:   ( 5  + 7 ) / ( 9 - 5 )

7:   3 * ( 5 * ( 5 - 2 ) ) - 9

8:   ( ( 5 * ( 4 + 2 ) - ( 8 + 8 ) / 2 ) - 9 ) ^ 3

9:   ( ( 5 + 5 * ( 6 - 2 ) + 4 ^ 2 ) * 8 )

10:  ( ( ( 3 ^ 4 ) ) )
```

Be sure that your program outputs the original infix expression, its postfix equivalent, as well as the evaluation of the postfix expression. All output should be sent to a file called `csis.txt`. This output file will be submitted along with your source code for the lab.

The only stack class that should be used in this lab is the `ObjectStack` class that we developed. You should use at least the following classes and interface in the lab:

```
Driver                  InfixToPostfix
ObjectStack             EvalPostfix
ObjectStackInterface
```

The only user-defined static function in the lab should be `main()`. No floats, doubles, or scientific notation should be used.

For extra credit, your program should also be able to handle these ill-formed expressions below, indicating that such an expression is erroneous, identifying the type of error, and going on to process the next infix expression.

```
1 + * 2            adjacent operators
1 2 * 3 ^ 4        adjacent operands
( 1 + 2            missing parenthesis
( 1 + 2 ) * 3 )    extra parenthesis
```

★ Stack Lab Note 1: Scanner Class

You can use Java's `Scanner` class to open a file for input.

Required declarations:

```
import java.io.*;
import java.util.Scanner;

public static void main(String[] args) throws IOException {
```

To open a file for input and create a `Scanner` object:

```
Scanner fileScan = new Scanner(new File("infix.txt"));
```

To read a line from the file using the Scanner object:

```
while (fileScan.hasNext()) {
    String buf = fileScan.nextLine();
```

To close the `Scanner` object:

```
fileScan.close();
```

★ Stack Lab Note 2: Operator Precedence

The conversion from infix to postfix will require the comparison of operator priorities. Here's a method that will take an operator as input and return its priority:

```
private int priority(char op) {
    switch (op) {
        case '^': return 3;
        case '*':
        case '/': return 2;
        case '+':
        case '-': return 1;
        default : return 0;
    }
}
```

★ Stack Lab Note 3: Program Documentation

I've provided a document on the use of Javadoc that can be found in this link on Canvas:

```
Files | Java Review | Javadoc Program Documentation
```

In particular, note the following guidelines:

• Every class must have a Javadoc class comment.

• Every method must have a Javadoc method comment.

• Every method parameter must have an `@param` tag.

• Every method with a return statement must have an `@return` tag.

• Generate the HTML Javadoc documentation for your project and be sure to submit the folder that contains the Javadoc documentation in the zip archive when submitting the lab.

★ Stack Lab Note 4: Interfaces
Each data structure in your project must implement an interface for that data structure. The interface files must be included in the zip archive for your code.

★ Stack Lab Note 5: Class Diagram
Shown below is the class diagram for my solution to the stack lab.

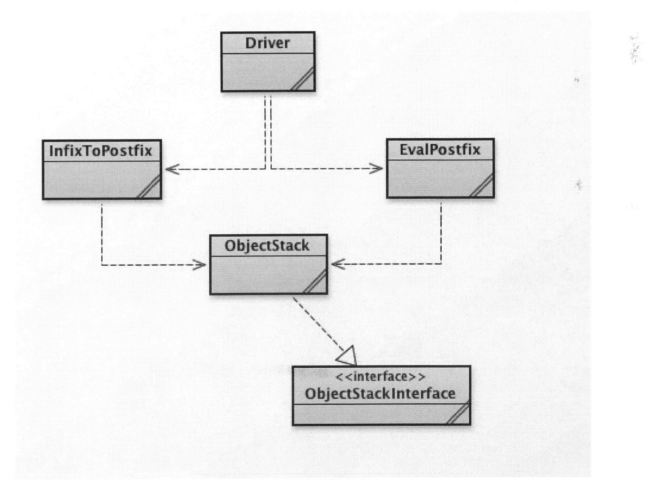

Sudoku is a puzzle where you fill in numbers 1-9 on a 9x9 board such that no number is duplicated in any row, column, or 3x3 sub-grid. For more information about the puzzle, see Wikipedia: `http://en.wikipedia.org/wiki/Sudoku`

For this lab, you are to design, implement, and test a Java program which solves a Sudoku puzzle. The input will consist of 9 lines of 9 characters each. Each character is a numeral (1-9) or a space, representing a blank square. The output must similarly consist of 9 lines of 9 characters each. Each character must be a numeral (1-9), and the whole output must be a solution to the input puzzle. For example:

```
Sample input
53 7  6 195
98  6 863 4 83 1 726 6 28
419 5 8 79

Sample output
534678912 672195348 198342567 859761423 426853791
713924856 961537284 287419635 345286179
```

You will need to devise a `SudokuBoard` class to support the methods below as well as any other methods you deem appropriate:

```
void place(r,c,n)      place numeral n at position (r,c)

void print()           outputs the Sudoku board

int get(r,c)           return the numeral at position (r,c)

void remove(r,c)       remove the numeral at position (r,c)

bool canPlace(r,c,n)   true iff the board would allow placing n at (r,c)

bool solved()          true iff there are no blank spots on the board
```

The simplest underlying implementation for storage would be an array of 9 strings, one for each row. The basic algorithm uses a stack. The following is a sketch of the ideas. It is up to you to flesh this out into an algorithm, and implement that algorithm.

Repeatedly, determine the most constrained square on the board, i.e., the one that will accept the fewest numerals, if there is one. Place the smallest acceptable numeral on the square. Push its position r and c onto the stack. But if there isn't any square, backtrack by popping c and r, and continuing with the next acceptable numeral. Stop when the board is solved.

Chapter 5. Recursion

Introduction to Recursion
Implementation of Recursion
Recursive Arithmetic
Recursive Examples – Part 1
Recursion with Arrays
Multiplying Rabbits
Recursive Examples – Part 2
Towers of Hanoi
Advantages and Disadvantages of Recursion
❖ Written Homework: Recursion
❖ Computer Lab: The Game of Nim Lab
❖ Computer Lab: Recursive Base Conversion

Introduction to Recursion

Recursive Definitions

A recursive definition is one in which the object being defined is used as part of the definition. For example, the word *descendant* may be defined as follows:

> "A descendant of a person is an offspring or a descendant of an offspring of a person."

In this definition, all the descendants of the person are simply and precisely accounted for. A non-recursive definition of descendant that attempts to take all possibilities into account is the following:

> "A descendant of a person is a son or daughter, or a grandson or granddaughter, or a great-grandson or great-granddaughter of the person, etc."

In this case, the definition is longer than the recursive definition and avoids infinite lengths through the use of "etc.". Dictionaries often try to avoid recursion in their definitions. If we were to look up the word descendant in a dictionary, we would find the following definition:

> "one who has a specific person among one's ancestors"

However, an *ancestor* is defined as:

> "one from whom a person is descended"

Thus the recursion is still present, though indirectly. If we were to look up the word recursion in a dictionary, we might find:

> Recursive, adj., see recursive.

Implementation of Recursion

One important application of stacks is in the implementation of recursive functions in programming languages. A recursive function is a function that calls itself! But if a function calls itself over and over, how will the function ever terminate? Won't we be stuck in an endless loop? Why would we ever need such a function?

In order for a recursive function to terminate properly, we must follow two rules:

Each recursive function must always call itself to solve a simplified version of the original problem (recurrence relation).

Repeated simplification must lead to a trivial version of the problem that can be solved without any further recursive calls (base case).

So recursion is a process in which the result of each repetition is dependent upon the result of the next repetition. We'll see that recursion simplifies program structure at the cost of function calls.

Factorial Example - Iterative

Given a positive integer n, $n!$ is defined as the product of all integers between 1 and n:

```
5! = 5 * 4 * 3 * 2 * 1 = 120

3! = 3 * 2 * 1 = 6

0! is defined as equal to 1
```

We can write our factorial definition as follows:

```
if n = 0 then n! = 1

if n > 0 then n! = n * (n-1) * (n-2) * (n-3) * ... * 1
```

The method below demonstrates an iterative method that evaluates $n!$.

```
public static int fact(int n) {
    int prod  = 1;

    for (int i = 1; i <= n; ++i)
        prod *= i;
    return prod;
}
```

Factorial Example - Recursive

We can refine the definition without the previous use of ... if we recognize that:

```
5!   = 5 * 4 * 3 * 2 * 1

     = 5 * 4!
```

In fact, for any $n > 0$:

```
n! = n * (n-1)!
```

i.e., multiplying n by the product of all integers from 1 to $n-1$ yields the product of all integers from 1 to n. Therefore our new recursive factorial definition becomes:

```
if n = 0    then n! = 1

if n > 0    then n! = n * (n-1)!
```

Note that the second expression uses factorial within its definition of factorial when $n > 0$. Thus, we have a recursive statement (recurrence relation). The first expression does not use factorial in its definition of factorial, when $n = 0$, and is therefore referred to as the base case.

This recursive definition might seem to be circular since it defines the factorial function in terms of itself. But this is not true. The definition is not circular. Here's why:

Note that 0! is defined directly as 1. Since 0! has been defined, defining 1! as 1 * 0! is not circular at all. Also, once 1! has been defined, defining 2! as 2 * 1! is straightforward. Note how this recursive factorial definition follows the two rules we set up for recursion to work correctly:

• Each recursive function must always call itself to solve a simplified version of the original problem.

• Each time there is a recursive factorial call, it is to a simpler case of itself. Repeated simplification must lead to a trivial version of the problem that can be solved without any further recursive calls. Eventually we reach the most simplified case where the factorial of 0 is defined as 1 and does not require a recursive call to calculate the value.

So we can say:

```
5! = 5 * 4!
      4! = 4 * 3!
           3! = 3 * 2!
                2! = 2 * 1!
                     1! = 1 * 0!
                          0! = 1
```

Note that each case is reduced to a simpler case until we reach the case of 0! = 1. We no longer need to make a recursive call to calculate a partial solution to our problem because 0! is not defined recursively. It is the limiting case (rule 2) for our recursive definition. This process of leaving off the solution to partial solutions until reaching the limiting case is called the recursive descent.

At this point the recursion can terminate and we can now work our way back up returning solutions to each of the problems we were not able to complete. This process of getting values and completing each of the partial problems is called the recursive ascent.

```
5! = 5 * 4!                                        120
      4! = 4 * 3!                                   24
           3! = 3 * 2!                               6
                2! = 2 * 1!                        2
  Recursive               1! = 1 * 0!          1   Recursive
  Descent                      0! = 1          1   Ascent
```

Stack of Execution States

In programming, recursion refers to the writing of a function that calls or invokes itself. Programming languages that allow recursive programs use an internal stack to save the current execution state, or activation record, (all the local variables, the return address, etc.) before the function calls itself. Then, as the function returns or exits, the previous execution state is retrieved from the stack and execution of the program continues. If a function calls itself 5 times, there will be 5 different execution states on the stack. One by one the program would exit each of the execution levels before it terminated completely.

We're going to examine the execution of the recursive factorial function along with the stack of execution states. Here is our initial code for the recursive factorial function:

```
public static void main(String[] args) {
    System.out.println(fact(4));
}

public static int fact(int n) {
    int x, y;

    if (n == 0)
        return 1;
    x = n-1;
    y = fact(x);
    return n * y;
}
```

Look closely at the `fact()` method. Note that `x = n-1` and `y` is the factorial of `x` (i.e. `n-1`). Therefore we are returning `n * y` which is really `n * (n-1)!` which is our definition for factorial.

Although variables `x` and `y` are unnecessary, they have been added to allow us to visualize the stack and the recursive descent and recursive ascent more clearly. We'll shortly rewrite the `fact()` method without the use of `x` and `y`.

Remember that a recursive method call is just like any other recursive call. When the call is made, the local variables must be placed on the stack along with the return address. Each time a method (or a recursive method) returns, it returns to the point immediately following the point from which it was called. This return point is the return address that is popped off the stack.

To help in the visualization of the factorial method, we're going to use symbols (+, #) to represent return addresses in our code:

```
public static void main(String[] args) {
+    System.out.println(fact(4));
}

public static int fact(int n) {
    int x, y;

    if (n == 0)
        return 1;
    x = n-1;
#   y = fact(x);
    return n * y;
}
```

We'll see that in main(), when fact(4) is called, the return address, + will be placed on the stack. In function fact(), when fact(x) is called, the return address # will be placed on the stack. So we're going to examine the execution of the factorial recursive function along with the stack of execution states:

Stack View 1

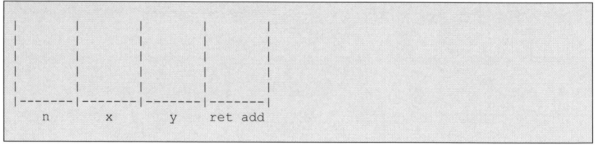

We begin the program and execute the System.out.println statement in main(). At that point we must make a call to the fact() method, so the return address + must be placed on the stack:

Stack View 2

```
|        |        |        |        |
|        |        |        |        |
|        |        |        |        |
|        |        |        |        |
|        |        |        |   +    |
|--------|--------|--------|--------|
    n        x        y      ret add
```

As we call the method, the actual parameter 4 must be passed to the formal parameter n. The test n == 0 is evaluated as false so we execute the statement x = n - 1 and make the recursive call, y = fact(x). But first the local variables must be saved on the stack along with the return address:

Stack View 3

```
|        |        |        |        |
|        |        |        |        |
|        |        |        |        |
|        |        |        |        |
|   4    |   3    |        |   +    |
|--------|--------|--------|--------|
    n        x        y      ret add
```

As we call the method again, the actual parameter 3 (x = 3) must be passed to the formal parameter n. The test n == 0 is evaluated as false so we execute the statement x = n - 1 and make the next recursive call y = fact(x). But first the local variables must be saved on the stack along with the return address:

Stack View 4

```
|        |        |        |        |
|        |        |        |        |
|        |        |        |        |
|   3    |   2    |        |   #    |
|   4    |   3    |        |   +    |
|--------|--------|--------|--------|
    n        x        y      ret add
```

As we call the method again, the actual parameter 2 (x = 2) must be passed to the formal parameter n. The test n == 0 is evaluated as false so we execute the statement x = n - 1 and make the next recursive call y = fact(x). But first the local variables must be saved on the stack along with the return address:

Stack View 5

```
|       |       |       |       |       |
|       |       |       |       |       |
|   2   |   1   |       |       |   #   |
|   3   |   2   |       |       |   #   |
|   4   |   3   |       |       |   +   |
|-------|-------|-------|-------|
    n       x       y     ret add
```

As we call the method again, the actual parameter 1 (x = 1) must be passed to the formal parameter n. The test n == 0 is evaluated as false so we execute the statement x = n - 1 and make the next recursive call y = fact(x). But first the local variables must be saved on the stack along with the return address:

Stack View 6

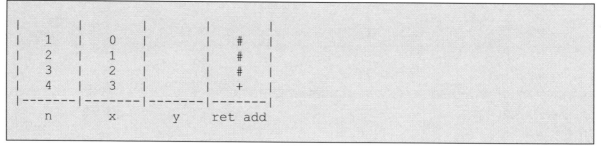

```
|       |       |       |       |       |
|   1   |   0   |       |       |   #   |
|   2   |   1   |       |       |   #   |
|   3   |   2   |       |       |   #   |
|   4   |   3   |       |       |   +   |
|-------|-------|-------|-------|
    n       x       y     ret add
```

As we call the method again, the actual parameter 0 (x = 0) must be passed to the formal parameter n. The test n == 0 is now evaluated as true so the method ends and returns the value 1 (i.e., 0! = 1).

We've now completed the recursive descent and are about to make the recursive ascent. When we leave the method, we must pop the stack to get the return address and to allow the local variables on top of the stack to be used again with new invocation of the method. The new return address is # so the function return value of 1 is assigned to y. n now has the value 2 and x has the value 1.

Stack View 7

```
|       |       |       |       |
|       |       |       |       |
|   2   |   1   |   1   |   #   |
|   3   |   2   |       |   #   |
|   4   |   3   |       |   +   |
|-------|-------|-------|-------|
    n       x       y    ret add
```

The next statement is to return n * y or 1 * 2 or 2 as a method return value. So the return address is popped again from the stack and we return 2 to y:

Stack View 8

```
|       |       |       |       |
|       |       |       |       |
|       |       |       |       |
|   3   |   2   |   2   |   #   |
|   4   |   3   |       |   +   |
|-------|-------|-------|-------|
    n       x       y    ret add
```

Once again, the next statement is to return n * y or 3 * 2 or 6 as a method return value. So the return address is popped again from the stack and we return 6 to y:

Stack View 9

```
|       |       |       |       |
|       |       |       |       |
|       |       |       |       |
|       |       |       |       |
|   4   |   3   |   6   |   +   |
|-------|-------|-------|-------|
    n       x       y    ret add
```

Finally, the next statement is to return n * y or 4 * 6 or 24 as a method return value. But this time the return address, +, is popped off the stack:

Stack View 10

```
|        |        |        |        |        |
|        |        |        |        |        |
|        |        |        |        |        |
|        |        |        |        |        |
|        |        |        |        |        |
|--------|--------|--------|--------|        |
    n        x        y     ret add
```

The value `24` is now returned to the `System.out.println()` statement in `main()` where it is then output. When we reach the closing brace in `main()` and thus leave the `main()` method, the compiler attempts to pop the stack to get the next return address. However, the stack is now empty so the compiler returns control back to the operating system.

Here's the recursive algorithm to compute `n!` a bit more succinctly:

```java
// fact1.java - factorial method 1

public static int fact(int n) {
    if (n == 0)
        return 1;
    return n * fact(n - 1);
}
```

This program's implementation of the `fact()` method that evaluates factorial is much simpler to write than its counterpart's iterative implementation found above. Notice that the first `if` statement corresponds to the termination statement in the recursive definition. The second statement in the function return `n * fact(n - 1);` corresponds to the recursive statement in the original definition.

In all recursive functions, the exit conditions for the function must lead in execution before all other recursive statements. If this were not true the function would never terminate. (Technically, the function would cause the program-execution stack to overflow: a condition called a stack-overflow.)

Here is a simplified version of the preceding factorial function:

```
// fact2.java - factorial method 2

public static int fact(int n) {
    return n == 0 ? 1 : n * fact(n - 1);
}
```

Recursive Arithmetic

From the 1950's to the 1970's, the first computers often only came equipped with hardware to perform addition and subtraction, but not much multiplication and division. To multiply or divide it was necessary to write your own programs. So let's see if we can develop a recursive algorithm to multiply two numbers.

Let's take a look at the product of two integers, a * b, where a and b are positive integers. a * b may be iteratively defined as a added to itself b times. However, a recursive definition may look like this:

```
if b = 1, then a * b = a

if b > 1, then a * b = a + a * (b - 1)
```

For example, we can use our recursive multiplication definition to evaluate 6 * 3:

```
6 * 3 = 6 + 6 * 2
      = 6 + 6 + 6 * 1
      = 6 + 6 + 6
      = 18
```

We can write a recursive function to calculate the multiplication of two numbers by closely following the recursive definition. The general idea is to add a to the product of a and b-1:

```java
// mult.java

public static int mult(int a, int b) {
    if (b == 1)
        return a;
    return a + mult(a, b-1);
}
```

1. See if you can determine the output of the following program. Assume the input stream is: HELLO.:

```java
import java.io.*;

public class Driver {
    public static void main(String[] args) throws IOException {
        System.out.println("Enter string delimited by period: ");
        foo();
    }

    public static void foo() throws IOException {
        char c = (char) System.in.read();
        if (c != '.')
            foo();
        System.out.print(c);
    }
}
```

Don't go any further until you have determined the output of the program above...

:
:

I mean it. Don't continue until you have calculated the output...

:
:

The output appears on the next page.

:
:

OK. Here's the output:

```
.OLLEH
```

2. Method to sum integers from 1 to num:

```
// sum1.java

public static int sum(int num) {
    if (num = 1)
        return 1;
    return num + sum(num-1);
}
```

3a. Non-recursive method to output the reverse of the integers in a number. So 123 get output as 321:

```
// reverse1.java

public static void reverse(int num) {
    do {
        System.out.println(num % 10);
        num = num / 10;
    }
    while num != 0;
}
```

3b. Recursive method to output the reverse of the integers in a number:

```
// reverse2.java

public static void reverse(int num) {
    System.out.print(num % 10);
    if (num / 10 != 0)
        reverse(num / 10);
}
```

4. Recursive method to compute the greatest common divisor (GCD) of two integers:

Euclid devised a clever algorithm for computing the greatest common divisor (GCD) of two integers. According to Euclid's algorithm:

```
GCD(m, n)   = GCD(n, m), if n > m              (1)
            = m, if n = 0                      (2)
            = GCD(n, m % n), otherwise (if n > 0)   (3)
```

- Step (1) - Interchanges the order of the arguments if $n > m$.

- Step (2) - If the 2nd argument is zero, the GCD is equal to the first argument.

- Step (3) - The GCD is recursively defined in terms of itself.

Note that the process must terminate since $m \% n$ will decrease to a value of 0 in a finite number of steps.

For example:

```
GCD(26, 4)   = GCD(4, 26 % 4)
             = GCD(4, 2)
             = GCD(2, 4 % 2)
             = GCD(2, 0)
             = 2
```

The method invokes itself until the second parameter has a value of 0. When this happens, the method value is the value of the first parameter.

Here's the recursive method to compute the GCD(m, n). Note how this directly follows the recursive definition of the GCD shown above:

```java
// gcd.java

public static int gcd(int m, int n) {
    if (n > m)
        return gcd(n, m);
    else if (n == 0)
        return m;
    else return gcd(n, gcd(m % n));
}
```

Recursion with Arrays

Example 1 – Sum Array Elements

Let's develop a recursive algorithm to sum up the elements of an array.

If the array has only one element, the sum is the single element:

$$\text{sum}(a_1, a_2, ..., a_n) = a_1, \qquad \text{for } n = 1$$

If the array has more than one element, the sum is the last element plus the sum of the first $n-1$ elements:

$$\text{sum}(a_1, a_2, ..., a_n) = a_n + \text{sum}(a_1, a_2, ..., a_{n-1}), \qquad \text{for } n > 1$$

Here's a recursive method to sum up the elements of an array based on the above algorithm:

```
// sum2.java

public static int sum2(int[] num, int n) {
    if (n == 1)
        return num[0];
    return num[n-1] + sum2(num, n-1);
}
```

This method can also be written as:

```
// sum3.java

public static int sum3(int[] num, int n) {
    return n == 1 ? num[0] : num[n-1] + sum(num, n-1);
}
```

Example 2 - Print Elements of an Array:
Although this is a simple algorithm to write iteratively, I present a recursive algorithm to output the elements of an array. Can you see the limiting case?

```
// print.java

public static void print(int[] num, int n) {
    if (n == 1)
        System.out.println(num[0]);
    else    {
        print(num, n-1);
        System.out.println(num[n-1]);
    }
}
```

Example 3 - Print Elements of Array Backwards:
This method will recursively output the contents of the array backwards. Again, this is a simple task to perform iteratively.

```
// bprint.java

public static void bprint(int[] num, int n) {
    if (n == 1)
        System.out.println(num[0]);
    else {
        System.out.println(num[n-1]);
        bprint(num, n-1);
    }
}
```

Note that this last recursive example is somewhat different that the other examples in that all the work is done before the recursive ascent begins. The recursive call in this example is the last statement before the closing brace of the method. Therefore, the return address that is placed onto the stack before the recursive method `bprint` is called each time is the closing brace of the `if` statement. As a result, nothing of importance is placed upon the stack during the recursive descent. This situation is referred to as *tail-end recursion* and would be more properly coded using iteration.

Example 4 - Find Largest Element in Array

The solution to finding the largest of n integers is to find the largest of the first $n-1$ integers and then compare that result to the last number:

```java
// largest.java

public static int largest(int[] num, int n) {
    if (n == 1)
        return num[0];
    int temp = largest(num, n-1);
    return num[n-1] > temp ? num[n-1] : temp;
}
```

Multiplying Rabbits

Rabbits are very prolific breeders. If rabbits did not die, their population would quickly get out of hand. Let's make the following assumptions:

1. Rabbits never die.

2. A rabbit reaches sexual maturity exactly two months after birth (that is, at the beginning of its third month of life).

3. Rabbits are always born in male-female pairs. At the beginning of every month, each sexually mature male-female pair gives birth to exactly one male-female pair.

Assume we started with a single newborn male-female pair. How many pairs would there be in month 6, counting the births that took place at the beginning of month 6?

month 1:	1 pair, the original
month 2:	1 pair still, since it is not sexually mature
month 3:	2 pairs; the original pair has reached sexually maturity and has given birth to a second pair
month 4:	3 pairs; the original pair has given birth again, but the pair born at the beginning of month 3 is not yet sexually mature
month 5:	5 pairs; all rabbits alive in month 3 (2 such pairs) are now sexually mature. Add their offspring to those pair alive in month 4 (3 pairs) to yield 5 pairs
month 6:	8 pairs; 3 pairs sexually mature plus 5 pairs alive in the previous month

In order to construct a recursive solution for computing `rabbit(n)`, the number of pairs in month n, we must determine how `rabbit(n-1)` can be used to compute `rabbit(n)`. If it were the case that all pairs of rabbits who were alive in month n-1 gave birth to a pair at the start of month n, we would have:

```
rabbit(n) = 2 * rabbit(n-1)
```

But this is not correct since not all the rabbits who were alive in month n-1 are sexually mature at the start of month n. Only those who were alive in month n-2 are ready to reproduce at the start of month n.

Therefore:

```
rabbit(n) = rabbit(n-1) + rabbit(n-2)
```

What should be the simplified or special case?

```
rabbit(2) = rabbit(1) + rabbit(0)
```

But we might need to specify the number of pairs alive in month 0, and it seems artificial to say its equal to 0. A better alternative is to treat `rabbit(2)` itself as a special case with the value equal to 1. Therefore the recursive definition has two simplified cases, `rabbit(2)` and `rabbit(1)`.

Therefore:

```
rabbit(n) = 1 if n <= 2
          = rabbit(n-1) + rabbit(n-2) if n > 2
```

Note, the series of numbers `rabbit(1)`, `rabbit(2)`, `rabbit(3)` ... is known as the Fibonacci series 1, 1, 2, 3, 5, 8, ... Each element in this series is the sum of the two preceding elements.

Therefore:

```
rabbit(6) = rabbit(5) + rabbit(4)
          = rabbit(4) + rabbit(3) + rabbit(3) + rabbit(2)
          = rabbit(3) + rabbit(2) + rabbit(2) + rabbit(1)
                                        + rabbit(2) + rabbit(1) + 1
          = rabbit(2) + rabbit(1) + 1 + 1 + 1 + 1 + 1 + 1
          = 1 + 1 + 6
          = 8
```

Here is the recursive function to calculate a Fibonacci number:

```
// fib.java

public static int fib(int n) {
    if (n <= 2)
        return 1;
    return fib(n-1) + fib(n-2);
}
```

Recursive Examples – Part 2

1. Recursive Method to Reverse a String

Suppose we want to reverse the contents of a `StringBuilder`. In the method below, `buf` is the `StringBuilder` to be reversed, `m` contains the index of the first element of the `StringBuilder` which is initially `0`, and `max` contains the index of the last element of the `StringBuilder`, which is equal to the length of the `StringBuilder` - 1:

```java
// reverse3.java

public static void reverse (StringBuilder buf, int m, int n) {
    swap(buf[m], buf[n]);
    if ((n - m) >= 2)
        reverse(buf, m + 1, n - 1);
}
```

This method reverses the `StringBuilder` `buf` from the outside in. Note that if we were to place the `swap()` method call after the `if` statement, the `StringBuilder` in `buf` would be reversed from the inside out.

2. Recursive Method to Display a String in Reverse Order

In the method below, `buf` is the `String` to be displayed in reverse order, `m` contains the index of the first element of the String which is initially `0`, and `max` contains the index of the last element of the `String`, which is equal to the length of the `String` -1:

```java
// reverseDisplay.java

public static void reverseDisplay(char[] buf, int m, int n) {
    if(m < n)
        reverseDisplay(buf, m + 1, n);
    System.out.println(buf[m]);
}
```

Note that when the `System.out.println()` statement is below the `if` statement, the `String` in `buf` is displayed in reverse order. If the `System.out.println()` statement was above the `if` statement, the `String` would be displayed in forward order.

Recursive Algorithm to Search a Dictionary

Our strategy in searching a dictionary is called divide and conquer. We divide the problem into two halves and attempt to solve (conquer) the appropriate half. The base case is when there is only one page in the Dictionary.

```
search(Dictionary, Word)
if (Dictionary is one page in size)
     scan the page for Word
else
    open Dictionary to point near the middle
    determine which half of Dictionary contains Word
    if (Word is in first half of Dictionary)
        search (first half of Dictionary, Word)
    else
        search (second half of Dictionary, Word)
```

This recursive algorithm to search a dictionary is the heart of the recursive binary search algorithm shown below.

Iterative Binary Search

Binary search is an algorithm to search a sorted array. It involves picking the midpoint of a range in a sorted array, and determining which side of the midpoint a desired value should lie in. This happens in a loop, which stops when the desired value is found or the range becomes zero and the value is known not to be present. Each time the loop is executed, the midpoint is found between first and last. Then the same process is performed on a smaller range in the array.

```
// binarySearch.java

public static int binarySearch(int[] num, int max, int id) {
    private int mid;

    int i = 0;
    int j = max-1;
    while (i <= j) {
        mid = (i + j) / 2;
        if (num[mid] > id)
            j = mid - 1;
        else if (num[mid] < id)
            i = mid + 1;
        else return mid;
    }
    return -1;
}
```

Recursive Binary Search

Binary search is often written using recursion, instead of iteration as shown above. The key idea is that the algorithm decides to search the right or left half of the array, which is a simpler version of the original problem. In the recursive binary search method below, note how the parameters to the recursive calls are adjusted to specify either the right or left half of the array. What kind of recursion do we see here?

```
// recursiveBinarySearch

public static int recursiveBinarySearch(int[] num, int i, int j,
                                                        int id) {
    private int mid;

    if (i > j)
        return -1;
    mid = (i + j) / 2;
    if (num[mid] > id)
        return recursiveBinarySearch(num, i, mid-1, id);
    else if (num[mid] < id)
        return recursiveBinarySearch(num, mid+1, j, id);
    else return mid;
}
```

Towers of Hanoi

In the beginning of creation, God presented a problem to the priests at the Temple of Brahma. The problem was this. Three diamond rods were placed on a brass plate. On one of the diamond rods, God placed 64 golden discs, each one smaller than the one underneath. The priests had to move all of the discs from the initial diamond rod to a second diamond rod obeying the following two rules:

Rule 1: Only one disc could be moved at a time.

Rule 2: A larger disc could not be placed on a smaller disc.

The time that it takes the priests to move all of the discs to solve the problem will be the time of creation!

Let's consider the problem of five discs instead of 64.

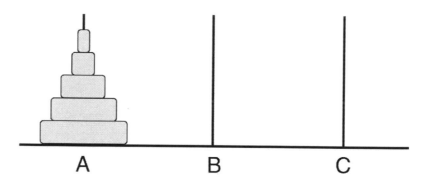

Suppose the problem is to move the stack of five discs from rod A to rod C:

• Part of the solution will be to move the bottom disc from rod A to rod C, as a single move.

• Before we can do that, we need to move the four discs on top of it out of the way (to rod B)

• After we have moved the large disc from rod A to rod C, we then need to move the four discs on rod B back on top of the large disc on rod C to complete the solution.

We have the following three step solution moving n discs from rod A to rod C. Keep in mind that only one disc can be moved at a time and a larger disc cannot be placed on top of a smaller disc.

1. Move top $n-1$ discs from rod A to rod B (i.e., move the top four discs to rod B):

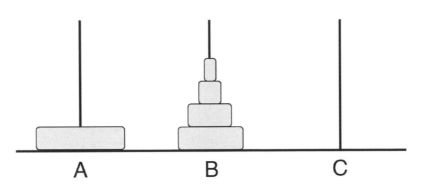

2. Move disc n from rod A to rod C (i.e., move the remaining disc on rod A to rod C):

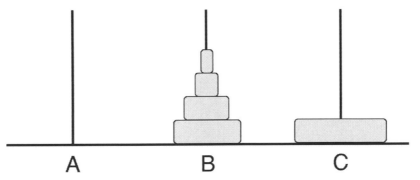

3. Move $n-1$ discs from rod B to rod C (i.e., move the discs on rod B to rod C):

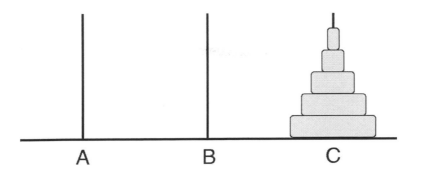

Notice that part of solving the five disc problem, is to solve the four disc problem (with a different destination rod). Here is where recursion comes in. In steps 1 and 3 the function will call itself recursively to solve the simpler problem of moving n-1 discs:

• The first step is the implementation of the solution using rods A and C in place of rods A and B and n-1 discs in place of n.

• The third step is the implementation of the solution using rods A and B in place of rods A and C and n-1 discs in place of n.

• For the second step, we just need to output instructions for moving the disc in question.

The trivial case, the one that can be solved without further recursive calls, is the problem of moving zero discs, which can be solved without taking any action. We must come up with a recursive method move() to print out step-by-step instructions for moving the discs.

Here's our recursive algorithm to move 3 discs:

```
// tower.java

public static void main(String[] args) {
    move(3, 'A', 'C', 'B');
}

public static void move(int num, char source, char dest, char aux) {
    if (num > 0) {
        move(num-1, source, aux, dest);
        System.out.println("Move disc " + num + " from rod " +
                            source + " to rod " + dest);
        move(num-1, aux, dest, source);
    }
}
```

Note that in the call to the `move()` function:

```
A is the source rod
C is the destination rod
B is the auxiliary rod
```

Here's the output produced by the program:

```
Move disc 1 from rod A to rod C.
Move disc 2 from rod A to rod B.
Move disc 1 from rod C to rod B.
Move disc 3 from rod A to rod C.
Move disc 1 from rod B to rod A.
Move disc 2 from rod B to rod C.
Move disc 1 from rod A to rod C.
```

Note that the total number of moves is equal to 2^n-1 or 2^3-1 or 7.

Calculate the Time of Creation
In the original Tower of Hanoi problem, the world will end when all 64 discs have been moved from rod A to rod C. We can calculate the time of creation as follows:

- Total moves = $2^{64} - 1 = 1.84 \times 10^{19}$

- There are 3.15×10^7 seconds/year

- If the priests make 1 move/second, it will take 5.84×10^{11} years (584 billion years) to complete the moves (assuming there are no mistakes)

- The age of the universe is ~13.8 billion years, 1.38×10^{10} years

- So the world will endure about 42 times as long as it already has.

A Crab Canon for Douglas Hofstadter

The blog below was posted by Julie Galef on June 16, 2011 and is reprinted with permission of the author.

Since it first came out in 1979, Douglas Hofstadter's Pulitzer Prize-winning book "Gödel, Escher, Bach: An Eternal Golden Braid" has widened the eyes of multiple generations of nerdy kids, and I was certainly no exception. The book draws all sorts of parallels between music, art, math, and computer science, ultimately shaping them into a bold thesis about how consciousness arises from self-reference and recursion. It's also a very playful book, full of puzzles, puns, and imagined dialogues between Achilles and a tortoise which weave in and out of the main chapters, illustrating the concepts therein.

One of those dialogues, titled "Crab Canon," seems puzzling when you begin reading it – sprinkled with seeming non-sequiturs, the word choice a bit awkward and off-kilter. Then shortly after the halfway point, when you start to see recent lines repeated, in reverse order, you realize: the whole dialogue is a line-level palindrome. The first line is the same as the last, the second line is the same as the second-to-last, and so on. But because Hofstadter chooses his sentences carefully, they often have different meanings when they reoccur in the reverse order. So, for example, the following bit of dialogue in the first half…

Tortoise: Tell me, what's it like to be your age? Is it true that one has no worries at all?
Achilles: To be precise, one has no frets.
Tortoise: Oh, well, it's all the same to me.
Achilles: Fiddle. It makes a big difference, you know.
Tortoise: Say, don't you play the guitar?

… becomes this bit of dialogue in the second half:

Achilles: Say, don't you play the guitar?
Tortoise: Fiddle. It makes a big difference, you know.
Achilles: Oh, well, it's all the same to me.
Tortoise: To be precise, one has no frets.
Achilles: Tell me, what's it like to be your age? Is it true that one has no worries at all?

Hofstadter does "cheat" a bit, by allowing himself to vary punctuation (for example, "He often plays, the fool" reoccurs later in a new context as "He often plays the fool"). Nevertheless, it's an impressive execution of a clever conceit.

Thumbing through Gödel, Escher, Bach again recently, I came across the Crab Canon and was struck with the desire to attempt a similar feat myself: a line-level palindrome that tells a linear story, that is, a story in which a series of non-repeating events occur.

It's maddeningly difficult trying to come up with lines that make sense, that in fact make a *different* sense, in both directions. And because all of the lines interlock -- each relying simultaneously on the line preceding it, the line following it, and its mirror-image line -- changing any one line in the poem tends to set off a ripple effect of necessary changes to all the other lines as well.

I eventually figured out a few crucial tricks, like relying on ambiguous pronouns ("they," "their") and using images that carry a different meaning depending on what's already happened. Below is the final result – my own canon, in homage to the book that dazzled my teenaged self years ago:

SEASIDE CANON, for Douglas Hofstadter

by Julia Galef

The ocean was still.
In an empty sky, two gulls turned lazy arcs, and
their keening cries echoed
off the cliff and disappeared into the sea.
When the child, scrambling up the rocks, slipped
out of her parents' reach,
they called to her. She was already
so high, but those distant peaks beyond --
they called to her. She was already
out of her parents' reach
when the child, scrambling up the rocks, slipped
off the cliff and disappeared into the sea.
Their keening cries echoed
in an empty sky. Two gulls turned lazy arcs, and
the ocean was still.

Advantages and Disadvantages of Recursion

Advantages
• Because it is usually shorter and its logic more explicit, a recursive solution may be easier to understand.

• When applied to certain problems, a recursive solution may execute faster due to a reduction in the number of operations that must be performed.

• A recursive solution may be much easier to devise than the equivalent iterative solution, thus facilitating problem solution.

Disadvantages
• Recursive solutions most often execute more slowly than iterative solutions due to the fact that program "states" must be saved and restored.

• Understanding the actions generated by a recursive solution may be difficult and time consuming. Thus, debugging recursive solutions can be difficult.

• Because a function repeatedly calls itself (and, thus, a function is repeatedly re-entered), a great deal of main memory may be needed to create and link allocation records, and to store new instances of local variables declared within the function, and copies of parameters passed into the function at each level of recursion.

1. The method below was presented in the course documents:

```
import java.io.*;

public class Driver {
    public static void main(String[] args) throws
                                java.io.IOException {
        System.out.println("Enter string: ");
        foo();
    }

    public static void foo() throws java.io.IOException {
        char c = (char) System.in.read();
        if (c != '.')
            foo();
        System.out.print(c);
    }
}
```

Its purpose is to reverse the characters in an input stream. For example, if the input to the method is:

```
HELLO.
```

then the output produced by the method is:

```
.OLLEH
```

See if you can modify the method so the period does not appear in the output stream. Note that I do not want you to give as the solution:

```
if (c != '.')
    System.out.print(c);
```

2. Consider an algorithm for the integer division of two integers:

```
26 / 8 = 1 + 18 / 8
       = 1 + 1 + 10 / 8
       = 1 + 1 + 1 + 2 / 8
       = 3
```

Using this algorithm, write a recursive definition (base case and recurrence relation) for integer division. Then write a recursive method for division that accepts two integers and returns their integer quotient.

3. Write a recursive method to perform integer exponentiation given that:

```
xⁿ = 1 if n = 0

xⁿ = x * xⁿ⁻¹ if n > 0
```

4. Given the code below, what is the value of `foo (52)`? Show the recursive descent and recursive ascent.

```
public int foo (int n) {
    if (n == 1)
        return 0;
    else
        return 1 + foo(n/2);
}
```

5. If an array contains n elements, what are the maximum number of recursive calls made by the binary search algorithm?

6. A palindrome is a string that reads the same forwards and backwards. Consider some examples:

- Able was I ere I saw Elba.
- Was it a rat I saw?
- Madam! I'm Adam.
- Live not on evil, madam, live not on evil.
- Red rum, sir, is murder!
- A man a plan a canal Panama.
- Otto

Design a recursive method with the following signature:

```
public boolean palindrome(String phrase, int left, int right);
```

that will determine whether or not a given String, `phrase`, is a palindrome. Note that `left` and `right` contain the index of the first and last String character, respectively. You may assume that all spaces and punctuation have been removed from the String and that the String contains all lower case characters.

Here's our recursive definition for a palindrome:

If the outer two characters match, then the String is a palindrome if the remaining String is a palindrome.

❖ Computer Lab: The Game of Nim

The game of Nim is played as follows:

Some number of sticks are placed in a pile. Two players alternate in removing either one or two sticks from the pile. The player to remove the last stick loses.

If the pile consists or two or three sticks, the player who goes first can win by removing either one or two sticks respectively, thus forcing their opponent to pick up the last stick. Thus two and three are called winning positions. A losing position is one in which the player who goes second can win no matter what the first player does.

Write a Java program that contains a simple recursive method:

```
public void nim(int n);
```

that simulates a good Nim player. A good Nim player is one who always wins, if he has a winning strategy. A winning strategy is one in which the player can win at `nim(n)`, where n is the number of sticks, if the player can come up with a strategy in which they can defeat their opponent at `nim(n-1)`. This suggests that we can write a recursive procedure to determine if a player has a winning strategy and what their next move should be.

See if you can write this simple recursive method to determine if n is a winning or losing position. Also write a driver program that will present to the user a session of this game to determine if n is a winning or losing position. Have n range from 1 to 20. This doesn't have to be a long recursive program. It is more in the spirit of the Towers of Hanoi problem (i.e., short and somewhat tricky.)

❖ Computer Lab: Recursive Base Conversion

Given an integer, `num`, whose binary representation is `length` digits long, write a recursive function:

```
string binPrint(int num, int length);
```

that returns a string containing the binary representation of `num`, including leading zeros.

For example:

```
binPrint(14, 5);
```

would return

```
01110
```

Use the following observations to create the recursive function:

if `length == 0`, then you do nothing. If `length > 0`, then you want to first create a string containing the results of calling `binPrint(num/2, length-1)`, and then concatenate either a `'0'` or `'1'` depending on the last digit in `num`.

For example, to do `binPrint(14,5)`, you first recursively call `binPrint(7,4)`, which returns `"0111"`, and then you append, in this case, a `'0'`, giving `"01110"`.

Chapter 6. Queues

Introduction to Queues
Queue Primitive Operations
Queue Representation in Java
Circular Queue Representation
IntQueue Class
ObjectQueue Class
❖ Written Homework: Queues
❖ Computer Lab: Multilevel Feedback Queue Simulation
❖ Computer Lab: Deques
❖ Computer Lab: Printer Queues
❖ Computer Lab: Priority Queues

Introduction to Queues

A queue is an ordered set of items from which items may be deleted at one end (called the front of the queue) and into which items may be inserted at the other end (called the rear or the queue).

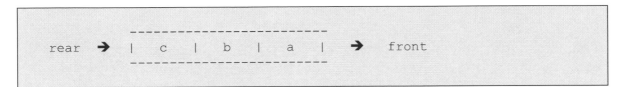

Note that a queue is defined as a data structure that holds a series of items to be processed on a First In First Out (FIFO) basis (though some queues can be sorted in priority). The first element inserted into the queue is the first element to be removed. The main difference between a stack and a queue is that a stack is only accessed from one end, while a queue is accessed from both ends.

Everybody has experience with queues as they are commonplace. Queues occur at gas stations, fast food counters, shopping centers, anyplace where many people (customers) line up for few resources (salespeople, cashiers, gas pumps, etc.) The customers are dealt with in the order that they arrived. New additions are made to the rear of the queue, as new customers enter the line. Items are removed from the front of the queue, as customers get serviced.

Note that the removal order for a queue is the opposite of that for a stack. In a queue, the item that is removed is the item that has been present in the queue for the longest period of time while in a stack the item that is removed is the item that has been present in the stack for the shortest period of time.

Queues are very common in the functioning of computers. The purpose of a queue is to provide some form of buffering. For example, when you send a printing job to a printer, it is inserted into the rear of the printer queue. Each job is then printed in the order in which it was sent to the printer.

The following consists of a queue that has three integers:

```
             ------------------------------
rear  →   |    30    |    20    |    10    |    →    front
             ------------------------------
```

The operations of adding two new items: 40 and 50, to the queue occurs in the rear:

```
             ------------------------------------------
rear  →   |   50   |   40   |   30   |   20   |   10   |    →    front
             ------------------------------------------
```

The operations of removing two items from the queue would yield the queue:

```
             ----------------------------
rear  →   |   50   |   40   |   30   |    →    front
             ----------------------------
```

Queue Primitive Operations

- `q.insert(x)` - inserts item x into the rear of queue q. Overflow occurs if you attempt to insert an element into a full queue.

- `q.remove()` - deletes the item at the front of queue q and returns its value. Underflow occurs if you attempt to remove an element from an empty queue.

- `q.query()` - returns the front element of queue q without deleting the element from the queue. Note that it is also illegal to query an empty queue. This condition is also called underflow.

- `q.isEmpty()` - determines whether or not queue q contains any elements. This primitive operation returns `true` if there are currently no elements in the queue or `false` if the queue contains at least one element.

- `q.isFull()` - determines whether or not queue q has reached it maximum capacity for holding elements. This primitive operation returns `true` if the queue is at full capacity or `false` if the queue can still contain more elements.

- `q.clear()` - removes all elements from queue q.

Queue Representation in Java

We shall again use an array for storing the items in the queue. The queue is allowed to grow and shrink within the bounds of the array. This time, however, it will be necessary to declare two variables, `front` and `rear`, to hold the positions within the array of the first and last elements of the queue.

front – points to the next element in the queue to be removed

rear – points to the last element inserted into the queue

We start with `front` pointing to 0 and `rear` pointing to –1 because nothing has yet been added to the queue. We can use the fact that `rear < front` to indicate an empty queue.

Inserting an item into the queue would first require incrementing the `rear` pointer and then performing a store operation on the array at the location at which `rear` is pointing:

```
   |-----|
4  |     |
   |-----|
3  |     |
   |-----|
2  |     |
   |-----|
1  |     |
   |-----|
0  |  2  | ← front  ← rear
   |-----|
```

Note that `rear == front` indicates that there is one element in the queue.

Inserting another item into the queue would also require first incrementing the `rear` pointer and then performing the store operation on the array at that location:

```
   |-----|
4  |     |
   |-----|
3  |     |
   |-----|
2  |     |
   |-----|
1  |  4  | ← rear
   |-----|
0  |  2  | ← front
   |-----|
```

Note that `rear > front` would indicate that there is more than one element in the queue.

Deleting an element from the queue would first require an array extract operation at the location in the array where the `front` pointer is pointing (we always delete the element at the front of the queue). We must then update the `front` pointer:

```
    |-----|
 4  |     |
    |-----|
 3  |     |
    |-----|
 2  |     |
    |-----|
 1  |  4  |  ← rear   ← front
    |-----|
 0  |     |
    |-----|
```

Once again, `rear == front` and we have one element in our queue.

We can summarize as follows:

```
rear < front: queue empty
rear = front: queue contains one element
rear > front: queue contains more than one element
```

Queue Declarations

Our Queue class might look like this:

```
public class Queue {
     private int[] item;
     private int front;
     private int rear;
}
```

Again, our `Queue insert` operation requires our first updating the `rear` pointer and then performing the store operation:

```
public void insert(int x) {
     item[++rear] = x;
}
```

To `remove` an element from the queue, we first do an extract operation at the location in the queue that the `front` pointer is pointing. Then we must update the `front` pointer:

```
public int remove() {
      int temp = item[front];
      ++front;
      return temp;
}
```

Queue Example

Let's look at the dynamic nature of a queue according to our **insert** and **remove** methods defined above. We will use an array of five elements to hold the `Queue`:

We begin with an empty `Queue`:

Insert an item into the queue:

```
      |-----|
   4  |     |
      |-----|
   3  |     |
      |-----|
   2  |     |
      |-----|
   1  |     |
      |-----|
   0  |  2  |  ← front   ← rear
      |-----|
```

Insert an item into the queue:

```
      |-----|
   4  |     |
      |-----|
   3  |     |
      |-----|
   2  |     |
      |-----|
   1  |  4  |  ← rear
      |-----|
   0  |  2  |  ← front
      |-----|
```

Insert an item into the queue:

```
      |-----|
   4  |     |
      |-----|
   3  |     |
      |-----|
   2  |  6  |  ← rear
      |-----|
   1  |  4  |
      |-----|
   0  |  2  |  ← front
      |-----|
```

Remove an item from the queue:

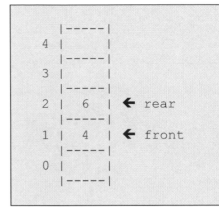

```
      |-----|
  4 | |     |
      |-----|
  3 | |     |
      |-----|
  2 | |  6  |  ← rear
      |-----|
  1 | |  4  |  ← front
      |-----|
  0 | |     |
      |-----|
```

Remove an item from the queue:

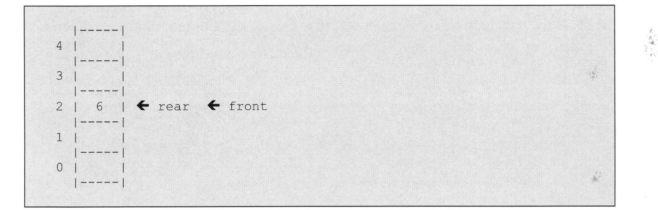

```
      |-----|
  4 | |     |
      |-----|
  3 | |     |
      |-----|
  2 | |  6  |  ← rear    ← front
      |-----|
  1 | |     |
      |-----|
  0 | |     |
      |-----|
```

Insert an item into the queue:

```
      |-----|
  4 | |     |
      |-----|
  3 | |  7  |  ← rear
      |-----|
  2 | |  6  |  ← front
      |-----|
  1 | |     |
      |-----|
  0 | |     |
      |-----|
```

Insert an item into the queue:

```
    |-----|
4 |  8  | ← rear
    |-----|
3 |  7  |
    |-----|
2 |  6  | ← front
    |-----|
1 |     |
    |-----|
0 |     |
    |-----|
```

Note that although our array can hold five elements, and we only have three elements in our Queue, we are not able to insert any more elements into the queue. We've reached the "top" of the array and our queue is considered full! Let's see what happens if we remove these remaining elements from the queue:

Remove an item from the queue:

```
    |-----|
4 |  8  | ← rear
    |-----|
3 |  7  | ← front
    |-----|
2 |     |
    |-----|
1 |     |
    |-----|
0 |     |
    |-----|
```

Remove an item from the queue:

```
    |------|
 4  |  8   |  ← rear    ← front
    |------|
 3  |      |
    |------|
 2  |      |
    |------|
 1  |      |
    |------|
 0  |      |
    |------|
```

Remove an item from the queue:

```
                ← front
    |------|
 4  |      |  ← rear
    |------|
 3  |      |
    |------|
 2  |      |
    |------|
 1  |      |
    |------|
 0  |      |
    |------|
```

Note that we now have a situation in which we have a full queue (we've reached the "top" of the array) and in which `rear < front`, which indicates an empty queue! We've reached the absurd situation where the queue is empty, yet no new elements can be inserted. Our queue is both full and empty at the same time!

Therefore our array representation as outlined is unacceptable!

Circular Queue Representation

We somehow need to avoid the possibility of running out of room in the queue while there are still "free" array locations we can use to store data in the queue.

Solution 1

Any time an item is removed from the queue (i.e., pulled from the bottom of the array), all the elements of the array can move down one slot and the `front` and `rear` pointers can be adjusted accordingly.

Here's an example. We start with a queue containing three elements:

Now we remove an element from the queue:

We now move the remaining elements of the queue down one position and adjust the `front` and `rear` pointers:

We now have all of the queue elements residing at the bottom of the array and have the remaining space in the array available to hold additional queue elements.

Unfortunately, the problem with this technique is that there are too many data movements involved. Imagine a queue containing 5,000 data elements, each data element containing 10,000 bytes of information. Just think of the number of data movements that would be required each time a `remove` operation was performed on the queue! It's too inefficient a process!

Solution 2
Rather than move all the data items down one position each time a remove operation is performed, just wait until an element is inserted into the top location in the array and then move all the elements back down to the bottom of the array.

Here's an example. We start with a queue containing two items:

We insert an item into the queue:

```
    |-----|
 4  |  8  | ← rear
    |-----|
 3  |  7  |
    |-----|
 2  |  6  | ← front
    |-----|
 1  |     |
    |-----|
 0  |     |
    |-----|
```

We've just inserted an item into the top element of the array, so it's now time to move all the elements of the queue down to the "bottom" of the array and adjust the `front` and `rear` pointers accordingly:

```
    |-----|
 4  |     |
    |-----|
 3  |     |
    |-----|
 2  |  8  | ← rear
    |-----|
 1  |  7  |
    |-----|
 0  |  6  | ← front
    |-----|
```

While this is a better solution then previous one, there are still too many data movements involved. We must look further for a solution that involves no additional data movements.

Solution 3: Circular Queue Representation

Our final solution is to redefine the data structure used to store the queue. Rather than use a linear array with a beginning and an end, let's use a finite structure with no beginning and no end, i.e., a circle, or rather, a circular array structure to hold the elements of the queue:

Think of the array that holds the queue as a circular object rather than as a linear object. Imagine the first element of the array as immediately following the last element. Therefore, even if the last element of the array is occupied, a new value can be inserted behind it in the first element of the array as long as that first element is empty.

So let's assume the queue contains three items in positions 2, 3, and 4 of a five-element array:

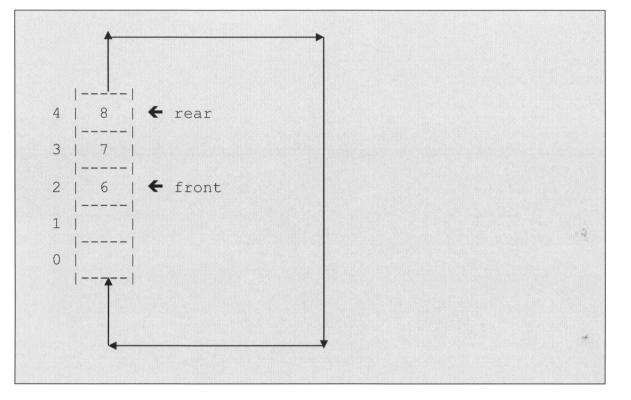

Although the array is not full, the last element of the array is occupied. If an attempt is now made to insert a new item into the queue, it can be placed into position 0 of the array:

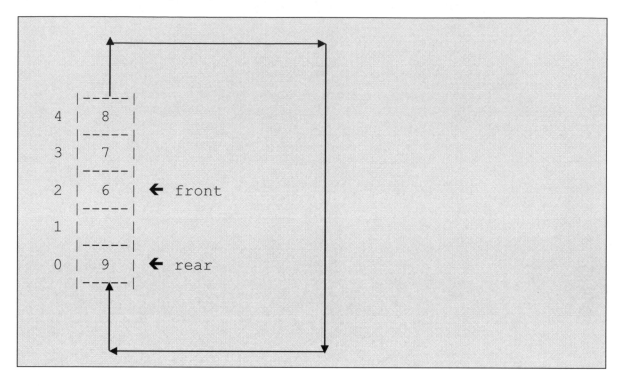

Note the order of items inserted into the queue is: 6, 7, 8, and 9. Now let's remove an item from the queue:

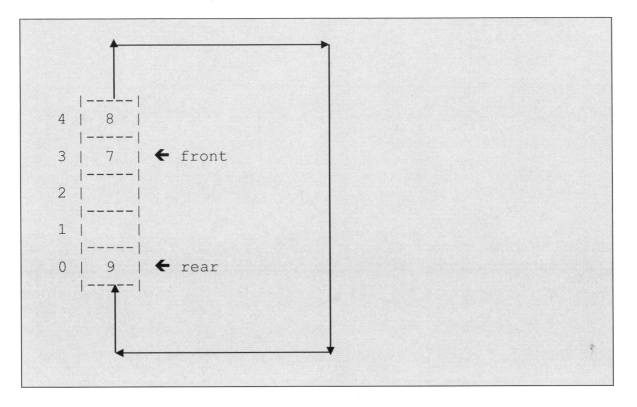

Remove another item from the queue:

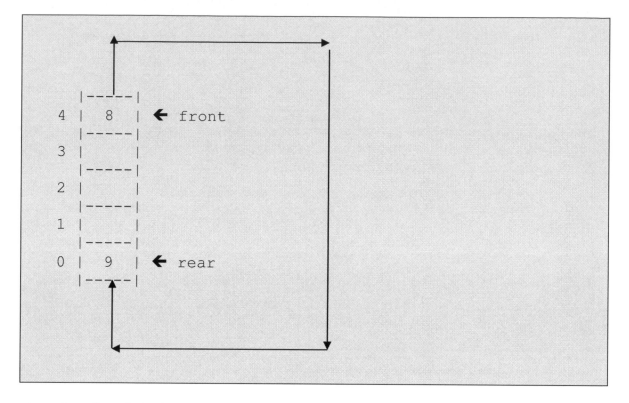

Insert an item into the queue:

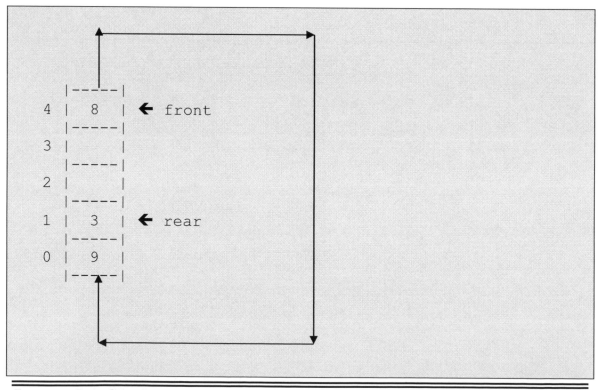

Note that `rear < front` in the above queue. However, in our previous implementation, `rear < front` implied an empty queue. But that is plainly not the case here. It is difficult under this circular queue representation, using the relative positions of `front` and `rear`, to determine when the queue is empty!

Therefore, rather than use the relative values of `front` and `rear` to determine whether or not a queue is empty or full, we're simply going to add a counter, `count`, that will be incremented when we insert an element into the queue and will be decremented when we remove an element from a queue. If `count == 0`, the queue is empty and if `count == item.length`, the queue is full.

Remember that `front` will point to the next item to be removed and `rear` will point to the last item inserted. We therefore start out with an empty queue where `front == 0` and `rear == -1`. When we want to insert an item into the queue, we first update the `rear` pointer and then perform the insertion. When we want to remove an item from the queue, we first extract the item from the array and then we update the `front` pointer.

For example, we start off with an empty queue. `count == 0`.

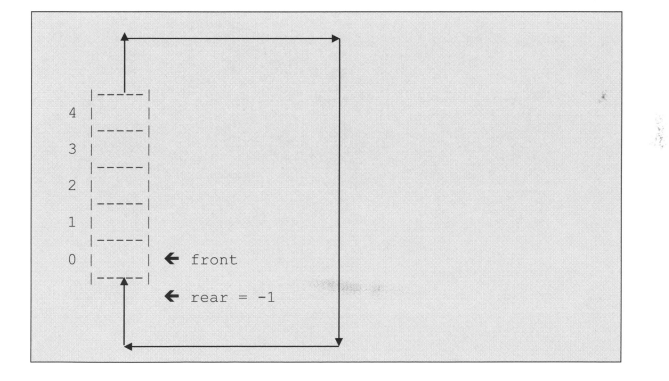

We now insert an item into the queue. Note that `front` now points to the next item to be removed and `rear` points to the last item inserted. `count == 1`.

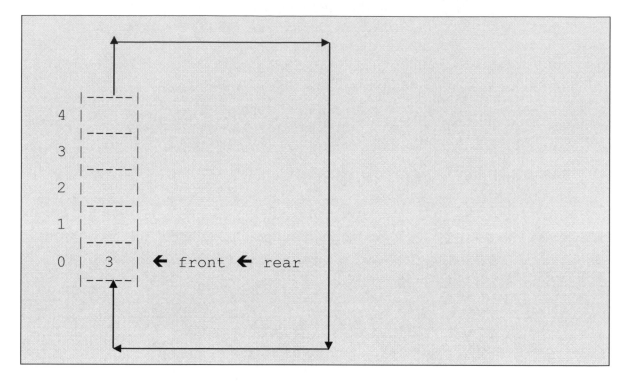

Insert an item into the queue. `count == 2`.

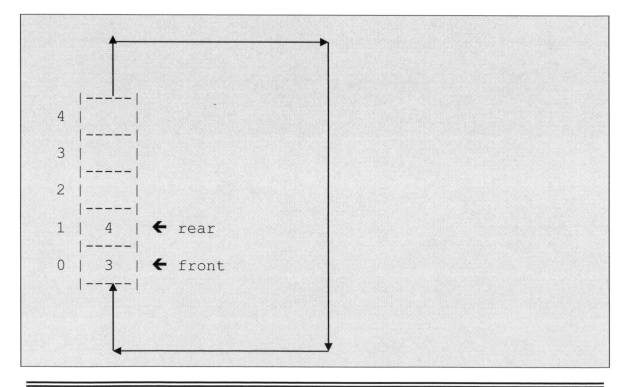

Insert an item into the queue. `count == 3`.

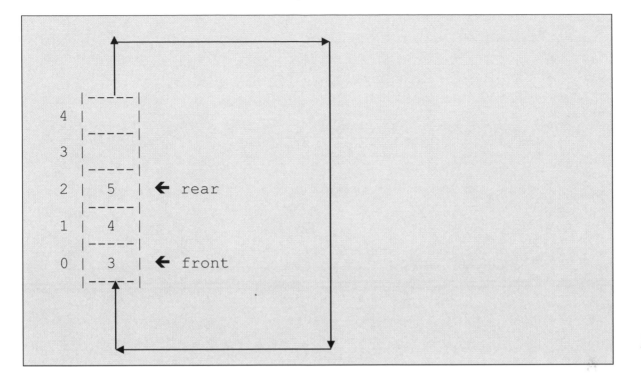

Remove an item from the queue. `count == 2`.

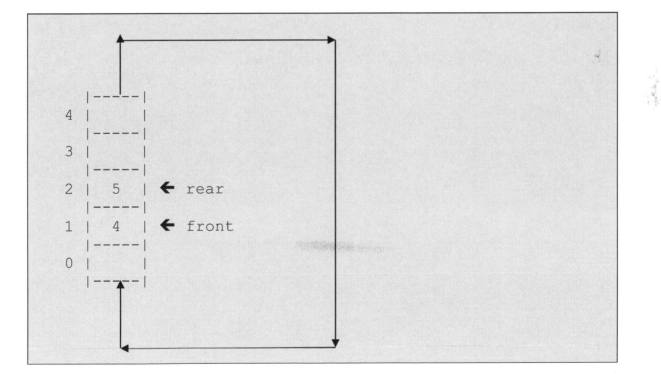

Remove an item from the queue. `count == 1`.

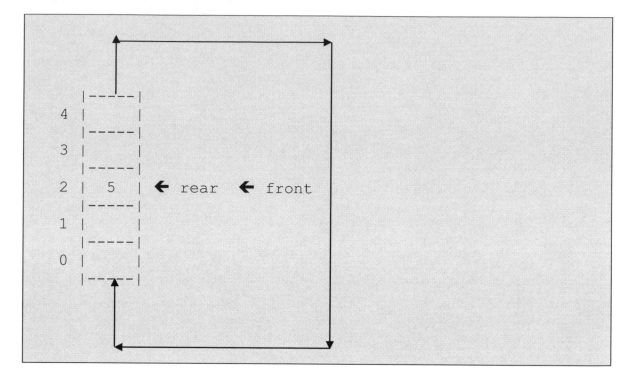

Remove an item from the queue. `count == 0`. Therefore the queue is empty.

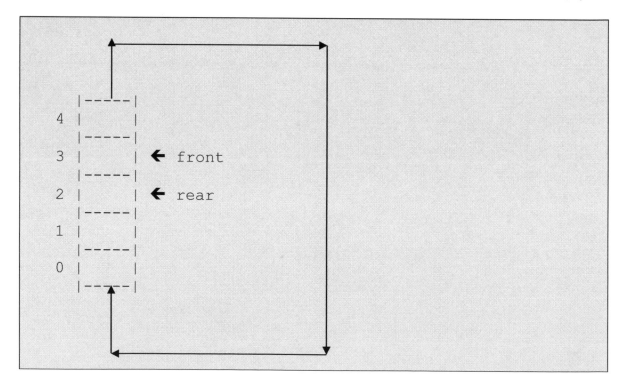

```
// IntQueue.java

public class IntQueue {
    private int[] item;
    private int front;
    private int rear;
    private int count;

    public IntQueue() {
        item = new int[1];
        front = 0;
        rear  = -1;
        count = 0;
    }

    public boolean isEmpty() {
        return count == 0;
    }

    public boolean isFull() {
        return count == item.length;
    }

    public void clear() {
        item = new int[1];
        front = 0;
        rear  = -1;
        count = 0;
    }

    public void insert(int x) {
        if (isFull())
            resize(2 * item.length);
        rear = (rear+1) % item.length;
        item[rear] = x;
        ++count;
    }
```

```
public int remove() {
    if (isEmpty()) {
        System.out.println("Queue Underflow");
        System.exit(1);
    }
    int temp = item[front];
    front = (front+1) % item.length;
    --count;
    if (count == item.length/4 && item.length != 1)
        resize(item.length/2);
    return temp;
}

public int query() {
    if (isEmpty()) {
        System.out.println("Queue Underflow");
        System.exit(1);
    }
    return item[front];
}

private void resize(int size) {
    int[] temp = new int[size];
    for (int i = 0; i < count; ++i) {
        temp[i] = item[front];
        front = (front+1) % item.length;
    }
    front = 0;
    rear = count-1;
    item = temp;
}
}
```

A Note About the `remove()` Method

In the `ObjectStack` class, the `pop()` method checks the size of the array and if the array is ¼ full, we resize the array to ½ full.

```
if (top == item.length/4)
    resize(item.length/2);
```

Note that the `remove()` method of the `IntQueue` class performs an extra check before resizing the array:

```
if (count == item.length/4 && item.length != 1)
    resize(item.length/2);
```

This extra check, `item.length != 1`, prevents us from resizing the array when the array contains a single element. This test of a *boundary condition* ensures that we do not attempt to resize the array to size 0. For example, suppose we start with an empty queue:

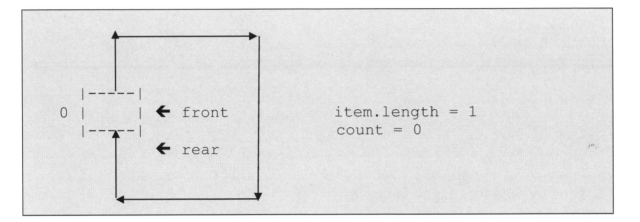

Let's insert a single item into the queue:

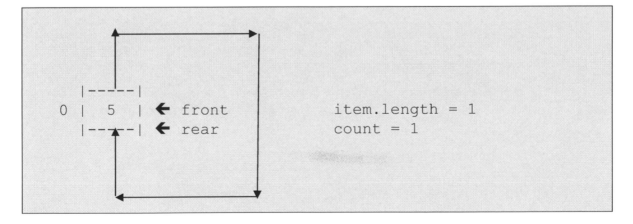

Now let's see what happens if we attempt to remove an item from the queue *without* the test in the `remove()` method for `item.length != 1`:

```
if (count == item.length/4)
    resize(item.length/2);
```

Executing the statements in the `remove()` method just before the if-statement we get the following:

```
item.length = 1
count = 0;
item.length/4 = 0
item.length/2 = 0
```

As `count` and `item.length/4` are both equal to 0, the `resize()` method will be called. However, the new size of the array sent to the `resize()` method will be `item.length/2 = 0`. So it is necessary to trap this boundary condition in the `remove()` method to prevent a resize of the array when the array is of size 1. Thus the need for the additional test:

```
if (count == item.length/4 && item.length != 1)
    resize(item.length/2);
```

```java
// ObjectQueue.java

public class ObjectQueue {
    private Object[] item;
    private int front;
    private int rear;
    private int count;

    public ObjectQueue() {
        item = new Object[1];
        front = 0;
        rear  = -1;
        count = 0;
    }

    public boolean isEmpty() {
        return count == 0;
    }

    public boolean isFull() {
        return count == item.length;
    }

    public void clear() {
        item = new Object[1];
        front = 0;
        rear  = -1;
        count = 0;
    }

    public void insert(Object o) {
        if (isFull())
            resize(2 * item.length);
        rear = (rear+1) % item.length;
        item[rear] = o;
        ++count;
    }
```

```java
    public Object remove() {
        if (isEmpty()) {
            System.out.println("Queue Underflow");
            System.exit(1);
        }
        Object temp = item[front];
        item[front] = null;
        front = (front+1) % item.length;
        --count;
        if (count == item.length/4 && item.length != 1)
            resize(item.length/2);
        return temp;
    }

    public Object query() {
        if (isEmpty()) {
            System.out.println("Queue Underflow");
            System.exit(1);
        }
        return item[front];
    }

    private void resize(int size) {
        Object[] temp = new Object[size];
        for (int i = 0; i < count; ++i) {
            temp[i] = item[front];
            front = (front+1) % item.length;
        }
        front = 0;
        rear = count-1;
        item = temp;
    }
}
```

Time Complexity for Queues

	Average Case	Worst Case
Insert:	O(1)	O(n)
Remove:	O(1)	O(n)
Query:	O(1)	O(1)

1. Describe how you might use a stack and a queue to determine whether or not a string was a palindrome?

2. If an array is not considered circular, the text suggests that each remove operation must shift down every remaining element of a queue. An alternative method is to postpone shifting until rear equals the last index of the array. When that situation occurs and an attempt is made to insert an element into the queue, the entire queue is shifted down so that the first element of the queue is in the first position of the array. What are the advantages of this method over performing a shift at each remove operation? What are the disadvantages?

3. What does the following code fragment do to the queue q?

```
ObjectStack s = new ObjectStack();
while (!q.isEmpty())
    s.push(q.remove());
while (!s.isEmpty())
    q.insert(s.pop());
```

4. Describe how you might implement a queue using two stacks. Hint: If you push elements onto a stack and then pop them all, they appear in reverse order. If you repeat this process, they're now back in order.

5. Perform a hand simulation of the Multi-Level Feedback Queue Simulation Lab to ensure that you understand the algorithm. Your output should agree with the partial output provided in the lab document.

❖ Computer Lab: Multi-Level Feedback Queue Simulation

In a time-sharing computer system, many users share the computer simultaneously. Such a system typically has a single CPU (the processor) and one main memory. Several user programs are placed in main storage at once (usually in a waiting queue(s)) and the processor is switched rapidly between the jobs according to some job scheduling policy.

Jobs (processes) are usually given a limited amount of CPU time called a time slice or quantum. If a process does not complete before its CPU time expires, the CPU is preempted and given to the next waiting process. Eventually each process will acquire the CPU for a long enough period of time sufficient to complete its required job.

In this lab you will write a Java program that will simulate an operating system's job scheduling policy to determine which process will be assigned the CPU when it becomes available. We will utilize a system of queues to simulate a sophisticated job scheduling mechanism, the multi-level feedback queue (MFQ).

A new process enters the queuing network at the rear of the top queue. It moves through that queue FIFO until it moves to the front of the queue and gets the CPU. If the job completes or relinquishes the CPU to wait for I/O completion or completion of some other event, the job leaves the queuing network. If the quantum expires before the process voluntarily relinquishes the CPU, the process is removed from the CPU and placed at the rear of the next lower-level queue (preemption). The process is next serviced when it reaches the front of that queue if the first queue is empty. As long as the process continues using the full quantum provided at each level, it continues to move to the rear of the next lower queue. Usually there is some bottom-level queue through that the process circulates round robin until it completes.

Multi-Level Feedback Queue

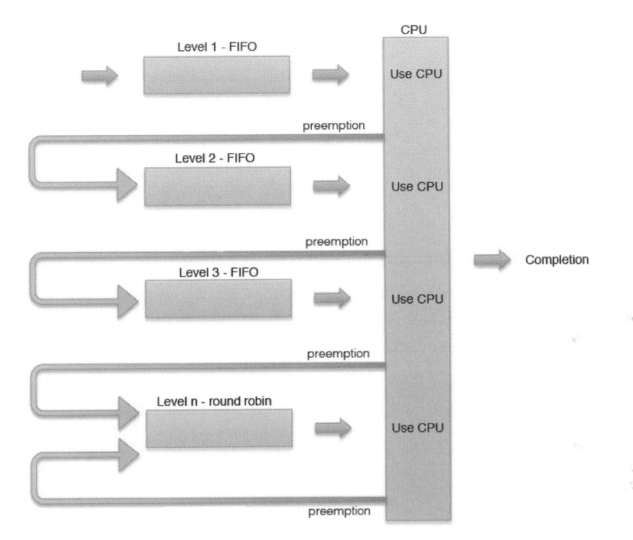

In the multi-level feedback scheme, the quantum given to processes as they move to each lower level queue becomes larger. Thus, the longer a process has been in the queuing network, the larger quantum it is assigned each time it gets the CPU. But it may not get the CPU very often because processes in the higher queues are given higher priority. A process in a given queue cannot run unless all higher-level queues are empty. A process can also be preempted by a new process entering the queuing system.

In this way, new processes enter the network with very high priority and get fast service if they are either interactive or I/O bound. Processes that are CPU bound consume their full quantum, unless preempted, and then are placed at the rear of the next lower-priority queue. The longer a process uses the CPU, the lower its priority becomes, until it reaches the lowest-priority queue in the network where it circulates round robin until completion. If the time quantum given to each process from queue level $i = 2^i$ time units, and a job does not complete within its time quantum, it gets moved down to the next lower queue, giving it twice as much CPU time.

Process from Queue i	Quantum Given to Process: $i = 2^i$
1	2
2	4
3	8
4	16

The input to this simulation will consist of job requests, each composed of three elements:

- Arrival time - Time job is initially submitted to the system
- Process identifier (pid) - Identifies each process as it travels through the system
- CPU time - CPU time required by the process to complete its job

The output, displayed in a tabular format, should include a table entry each time a job enters the system indicating the:

- Event
- System time
- Process identifier (pid)
- CPU time needed

When a process completes and leaves the system, an appropriate table entry should be output to indicate the:

- Event
- System time
- Process identifier (pid)
- Total time in the system
- Identity of the lowest-level queue in which the process resided
- Response time

Be sure that your program sends all output to a file called `csis.txt`. This output file will be submitted along with your source code for the lab.

When the simulation is complete, you should also output the following:

- Total number of jobs

- Total time of all jobs in system: sum of the time each job is in the system

- Average response time: where response time is defined as the interval from the time a process enters the system (enters queue 1) to the time of first response, or the time it first given to the CPU

- Average turnaround time for the jobs: where turnaround time is defined as the interval from the time a process enters the system (enters queue 1) to the time of its completion

- Average waiting time: where waiting time is the amount of time that a process is kept waiting in a queue(s)

- Average throughput for the system as a whole: the number of jobs divided by the sum of total time of all jobs in the system

Be sure all your data is properly labeled and all average values are displayed to two decimal places.

For extra credit, present a visual display of the simulation.

Here is the data set, `mfq5.txt`, which your program should run on:

Arrival Time	Process ID	CPU Time
2	101	3
6	102	2
11	103	5
12	104	12
17	105	1
23	106	9
31	107	2
68	108	2
68	109	6
68	110	1
70	111	5
75	112	1
76	113	12
79	114	11
92	115	8
92	116	2
92	117	1
94	118	3
96	119	15
98	120	7

To check your code, here are the first couple of lines of output and the last couple of lines of output that your program should generate:

Event	System Time	PID	CPU Time Needed	Total Time In System	Lowest Level Queue	Response Time
Arrival	2	101	3			
Departure	5	101		3	2	0
:						
:						
:						
Departure	141	109		73	4	1
Departure	142	119		46	4	0

★ Queue Lab Note 1: Classes

The only queue class that should be used in this lab is the `ObjectQueue` class that we developed. You should also add the `ObjectQueueInterface` to your project. Additionally, you should utilize at least the following classes in the lab:

```
Driver, Mfq, Job, Cpu, Clock
```

The `Job` class might include these class variables:

`pid`: Identifies each process as it travels through the system

`arrivalTime`: Time job entered the system

`cpuTimeRequired`: Total CPU time needed by job when job enters the system

`cpuTimeRemaining`: Time remaining for completion of job

`currentQueue`: Location of the current queue of the job

The `Cpu` class might include these class variables:

`job`: Holds current Job on the CPU

`cpuQuantumClock`: keeps track of time quanta remaining for current job on CPU

`busyFlag`: determines whether or not there is a job on the CPU

★ Queue Lab Note 2: Input Queue

Along with the four queues that you will be using for this lab, I would also recommend creating an input queue. Before the lab simulation begins, read each line of input from `mfq.txt`, insert the data into a newly created `Job` object, and then insert the `Job` object into the input queue. Once the simulation begins, you can query the `Job` object at the front of the input queue to determine whether or not it's time for the `Job` object to enter the simulation, i.e., is the system time equal to the arrival time of the `Job` object at the front of the queue?

★ Queue Lab Note 3: Driver Class

Here's my driver for the lab. Feel free to use it, but it's not required.

```java
import java.io.*;

public class Driver {
    public static void main(String[] args) throws IOException{
        PrintWriter pw = new PrintWriter(new FileWriter("csis.txt"));
        Mfq mfq = new Mfq(pw);
        mfq.getJobs();
        mfq.outputHeader();
        mfq.runSimulation();
        mfq.outStats();
        pw.close();
    }
}
```

★ Queue Lab Note 4: For Testing Purposes:

Read a line of Job data from the input file, instantiate a new Job object, populate the Job object with the data just read, and insert the Job object into the Input Queue. Repeat for all jobs in the input file.

Once all of the jobs have been removed from the input file and inserted into the Input Queue, I would recommend removing the Job at the front of the Input Queue and output the information contained in the Job object. Repeat until the Input Queue is empty. Your output should reflect the input file.

Once you have this working, you know your `ObjectQueue` primitives are fine and you can move forward with the simulation.

★ Queue Lab Note 5: Flowchart

Presented below is a flowchart to help you think about the simulation lab.

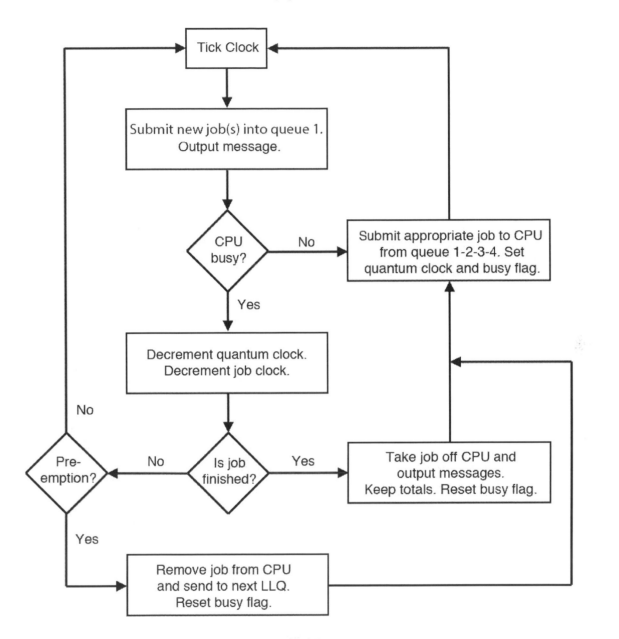

Note that preemption can occur if a job has the CPU and its time quantum has expired or if a job is sitting in queue 1.

★ Queue Lab Note 6: Debugging

In the `ObjectQueue` class, the `System.out.println()` error messages aren't very helpful since they only pertain to the very last method call (`insert()`, `remove()`, `query()`). The code below can be added to these methods and will use Java's exception system to show the path of which methods were executed along with a class name and a line number where the program crashed.

```
if (isEmpty()) {
    new Exception("Remove Runtime Error:
                            Queue Underflow").printStackTrace();
    System.exit(1);
}
```

For example, when `ObjectQueue.remove()` executes `System.exit(1)`, it will first print a message like this:

```
java.lang.Exception: Remove Runtime Error: Queue Underflow
    at feedBackQ.ObjectQueue.remove(ObjectQueue.java:59)
    at feedBackQ.SystemManager.runSimulation(SystemManager.java:38)
    at feedBackQ.Launcher.main(Launcher.java:15)
```

This slightly cryptic output is a snapshot of the method stack along with class names and line numbers. The top line is the exception itself, the second line is the method and exact line the program crashed at, the third line is the method that called the method that crashed, etc.

★ Queue Lab Note 7: String Class Split Method to Parse Strings

When reading in data from a file on a line-by-line basis, we often have the need to parse (i.e., divide up) the string to extract the individual pieces of information.

The queue lab requires that you read data from the `mfq.txt` input file that contains three integers per line. You will need to read each line of data as a string and parse the string to grab each of the three integers on the line.

We use the `Scanner` class to read each line from the input file.

You could then use the `StringTokenizer` class to parse each line read from the input file. However, the `StringTokenizer` class is losing favor to the `split()` method found in the `String` class.

I've provided a document on the use of the `split()` method that can be found in this link on Canvas:

```
Files | Java Review
```

Here's how you would parse the string:

```
"All you     need     is         love.":
```

```
String phrase = "All you     need     is         love.";
String delims = "[ ]+";
String[] tokens = phrase.split(delims);
```

The `split()` method returns an array containing the tokens. To see what the tokens are, just loop through the array:

```
for (int i = 0; i < tokens.length; i++)
   System.out.println(tokens[i]);
```

Note that the tokens returned are strings and, for this lab, you will have to convert the string tokens into integers using the `parseInt()` method from Java's `Integer` class.

Note that if a string begins with one (or more) delimiters, then the first token that the `split()` method returns will be the empty string (`""`). Now, depending upon which version of the data file you downloaded, there might be space(s) before the arrival time for the first three lines of data:

No Extra Spaces			Extra Spaces		
2	101	3	2	101	3
7	102	1	7	102	1
9	103	7	9	103	7
12	104	5	12	104	5

In either case, your program can take this into account by using code similar to this:

```
int i = tokens[0].equals("") ? 1 : 0;
```

You can then use `i` appropriately as an index into the `tokens` array

```
tokens[i]
tokens[i+1]
tokens[i+2]
etc.
```

★ Queue Lab Note 8: Program Documentation

I've provided a document on the use of Javadoc that can be found in this link on Canvas:

```
Files | Java Review | Javadoc Program Documentation
```

In particular, note the following guidelines:

• Every class must have a Javadoc class comment.

• Every method must have a Javadoc method comment.

• Every method parameter must have an `@param` tag.

• Every method with a return statement must have an `@return` tag.

• Generate the HTML Javadoc documentation for your project and be sure to submit the folder that contains the Javadoc documentation in the zip archive when submitting the lab.

★ Queue Lab Note 9: Interfaces
Each data structure in your project must implement an interface for that data structure. The interface files must be included in the zip archive for your code.

★ Queue Lab Note 10: Class Diagram
Shown below is the class diagram for my solution to the queue lab.

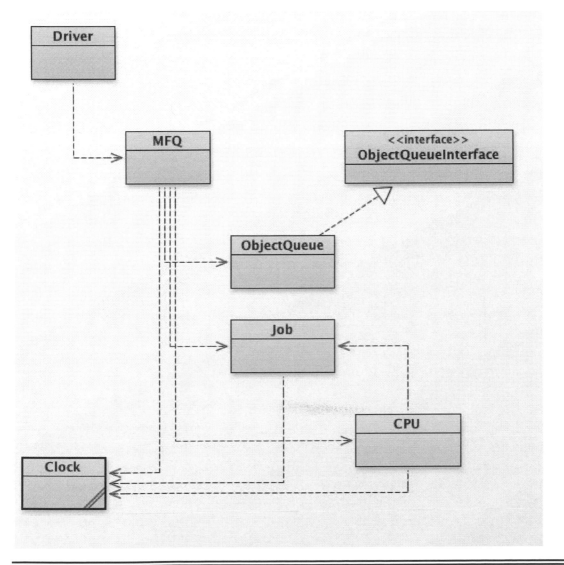

❖ Computer Lab: Deques

A deque (double ended queue) is an ordered set of items from which items may be deleted at either end and into which items may be inserted at either end. In order to fully implement a `Deque` class, we would need to implement the following primitive operations:

- `clear()`
removes all items from deque

- `isEmpty()`
determines whether or not the deque contains any items

- `isFull()`
determines whether or not the deque can contain any more items

- `insertTop()`
inserts item into top of deque

- `insertBottom()`
inserts item into bottom of deque

- `removeTop()`
removes element from top of deque

- `removeBottom()`
removes item from bottom of deque

- `queryTop()`
returns top element from deque without modifying the deque

- `queryBottom()`
returns bottom element from deque without modifying the deque

The following assignment will necessitate the implementation of the above mentioned deque:

The Laurel Parking Garage contains a single lane that can hold up to 10 cars. Cars arrive at the south end of the garage and pull as far up to the north end of the garage as possible. When it is time for a car to leave the parking garage, they exit from the north end.

If a customer arrives to pick up a car that is not the northernmost, all cars to the north of his car are moved out and stacked up, his car is driven out, and the other cars are unstacked and restored in the same order that they were in originally. Whenever a car leaves, all cars to the south are moved forward so that at all times all the empty spaces are in the south part of the garage. If there is no room for a car upon its arrival, the car gets queued until a free space becomes available.

Write a Java program that reads a group of input lines from the file, `carfile.txt`. This file contains either an `'a'` for arrival or a `'d'` for departure, as well as a three digit license plate number. Cars are assumed to arrive and depart in the order specified by the input file. When a car departs, a message should be printed indicating the license plate number and the number of times the car was moved within the garage (including the departure itself but not the arrival). Note that no cars will leave the waiting queue before being brought into the garage.

All program output should be saved in a file called `csis.txt`

The contents of `carfile.dat` are shown below:

```
a    101
a    102
a    103
a    104
d    102
a    105
a    106
d    101
d    104
a    107
a    108
a    109
a    110
d    110
d    106
a    111
d    103
d    109
a    112
a    113
a    114
a    115
a    116
```

```
a    117
d    114
a    118
a    119
a    120
a    121
d    111
a    122
a    123
a    124
d    108
d    105
a    125
d    113
a    126
d    117
d    112
d    116
a    127
d    119
a    128
d    120
d    107
d    125
d    121
d    115
a    129
d    123
d    127
d    122
d    128
a    130
d    129
d    118
d    126
d    130
d    124
```

❖ Computer Lab: Printer Queues

One useful application of queues is in simulation. A simulation program is one which attempts to model a real-world situation to learn something about the situation. Each object and action in the real situation has its counterpart in the program. If the simulation is accurate, that is, if the program successfully mirrors the real world, then the result of the program should mirror the result of the actual actions being simulated. Thus it is possible to understand what occurs in the real world situation without observing its occurrence.

This lab will require you to solve the following problem: There have been complaints from students in the computer lab that their print jobs from the network printer seem to take a long time to print. Should the CSIS department purchase another printer?

Your assignment is to write a simulation program that models a printer queue. The input to this simulation will consist of print job requests, each composed of three elements:

- Arrival Time: time print job is initially submitted to the printer queue

- Print Job Identifer (`pjid`): identifies each print job as it travels through the simulation

- Number Pages: the number of pages to be printed

If nothing is currently being printed, the print job submitted is immediately sent to the printer and printed. If there is a job currently being printed, then the new print job is entered at the rear of the queue. When a print job finishes, the queue is checked and if it is not empty then the first job in the queue is removed from the queue and it is printed. You can assume that the printer prints at a speed of four pages per minute.

The output, displayed in a tabular format, should include a table entry each time a print job enters the printer queue indicating the current time, the print job identifier, and the number of pages required to be printed. When a print job completes and leaves the printer, an appropriate table entry should indicate the current time, the print job identifier, and the total time in the simulation.

After all the print jobs have been processed, your program should output the following results:

- the number of print jobs completed

- the average waiting time in the queue (service time)

- total time of all print jobs in system

- average response time - where response time is defined as the interval from the time a print job enters the simulation to the time it gets the printer

- average turnaround time for the print jobs - where turnaround time is defined as the interval from the time a print job enters the simulation to the time of its completion

- average waiting time in the print queue - where waiting time is the amount of time that a print job is kept waiting in a queue

- maximum waiting time in the print queue - where waiting time is the amount of time that a print job is kept waiting in a queue

- average throughput for the system as a whole - the number of print jobs divided by the sum of total time of all print jobs in the system

Be sure all your data is properly labeled and all average values are displayed to two decimal places. All program output should be saved in a file called `csis.txt`.

On a separate sheet of paper answer the following questions:

- How would each of the results above be affected if two printers were used?

- How would each of the results above be affected if the number of print jobs were doubled?

- How would each of the results above be affected if the printer printed at 5 pages per minute?

❖ Computer Labs: Priority Queues

Write a Java program to simulate the behavior of a simple computer system capable of executing only one job at a time. When the system is free to start executing a new job, it chooses, from among those jobs waiting to run, the job with the highest priority.

The input consists of 0 or more job requests, each composed of four elements:

- Job Name: 3 digit code

- Priority Class: 1, 2, 3, or 4

- Time of Submission: integer representing seconds

- Seconds of CPU Time Required: integer

The jobs are ordered in the input file by increasing time of submission. Jobs with a lower priority class number have a higher priority, and vice versa. Jobs within a class are processed first-come first-served.

The output should include a message each time a job is submitted to a queue and each time a job begins or ends execution announcing the current time and job name. When the simulation is complete, output the average waiting time per job (where waiting time lasts from the time of submission to the moment execution begins).

Note that all program output should be saved in a file called csis.txt.

Job Name	Priority Class	Time of Submission	CPU Time Required
101	3	2	5
102	2	3	4
103	4	3	5
104	1	5	2
105	2	6	1
106	3	8	2
107	3	14	3
108	4	14	2
109	4	35	4
110	2	37	3
111	4	38	3
112	1	38	6
113	2	38	4
114	3	39	1
115	2	41	2
116	1	50	2

Chapter 7. Linear and Non-Linear Linked Lists

Introduction to Linear Linked Lists

Sequential Storage of Arrays

One of the big advantages of arrays is that you can allocate memory for a large number of variables without writing a lot of code. It's also simple to initialize or change their values "all at once" with a while or for loop. Additionally, we can have direct access to any array element with the use of the correct index into the array.

However, the big disadvantage of using an array is that the size of an array is fixed and you may not always know exactly how many items you will need to store. You may be reading in data from a file, and you won't necessarily know how big to make your array to hold the data.

Another problem with arrays is that rearranging elements in the array can be time consuming. Suppose you have 1,000 elements in an array and you decide that you want the $1,000^{th}$ element to be the second element and the second to be the third and the third to be the fourth and so on. You'll have to shift all the elements down one place. This is not very efficient.

The drawbacks of sequential storage also become apparent when we use the array to represent stacks and queues:

• A fixed amount of storage remains allocated to the stack or queue, even when the data structure is actually using a smaller amount of storage, or perhaps no storage at all.

• No more than the fixed amount of storage may be allocated to the array that houses the stack or queue. If the stack or queue grows too much, the overflow condition will occur.

Linked Lists

In a sequential representation, the items of an array are implicitly ordered by the sequential order of storage. For example, if `num[i]` represents an element of an array, `num[i+1]` represents the next element of the array.

Now suppose that the items of a data structure were explicitly ordered. This would mean that every element of the data structure would have to contain within itself the address in memory of the next element of the data structure.

Note that in this new representation we can no longer use the fact that items are related by their location or address as in an array. Individual items in this data structure must have explicit pointers to the location of the other data items within the data structure. This gives rise to a new type of data structure called the *linear linked list*.

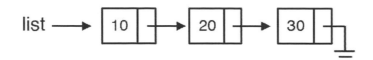

A linear linked list consists of a collection of *nodes* (items), each of which contains two fields:

• information field (info) – holds the actual data element on the list

• next address field (next) – contains the address in memory (pointer) to the next node in the list

Note that linear linked lists are typically drawn with boxes representing nodes, and pointers are drawn as arrows that connect one node to another. Thus, the arrows represent the links between the nodes, and each node contains data for one element.

The entire linked list is accessed via an external pointer, list, which points to (contains the address of) the first node in the list. Note that the external pointer is not included within a node but its value is accessed directly by referencing a pointer variable.

The next address field of the last node in the list contains a special pointer value, null, which is not a valid address but is used to signify the end of a list. The null pointer is represented by the symbol:

A list with no nodes is called the empty list or null list and is represented below. In this case the external pointer list has the null value:

list ⌐

Data elements of a linear linked list are contained in the `info` field of the list and must be of the same data type (`int, char, struct,` etc). As each node contains within itself (within its `next` field) a pointer to the next node in the list, we are able to traverse the list and access the nodes of the list in order (that is, from first to last).

The linked list is a dynamic structure and can change size as the program executes. Nodes can be inserted and deleted at any position of a list (beginning, between nodes, at the end). Only the first node, accessed by the `list` pointer, is known. From there links between nodes can be used to move from one node to another node. Theoretically, there is no upper limit on the length of a list, but practically, a computer's memory size is the limit.

Here's an example of a new node being inserted into the middle of the list without causing the other elements to change their locations in memory. Notice that this can be done with just the manipulation of two pointers and requires no data movements:

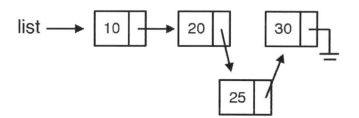

Working with linear linked lists can be fun because they are easy to draw, yet give a useful way to organize data. In certain places lists can be tricky, but a good drawing can go a long way toward clarifying such a situation. Actually, I cannot emphasize this enough. It's a good idea to draw pictures when you're trying to build and understand linked list code. Generally, all you need to do is to draw a box for each node and an arrow going from each node to the next to represent the 'next' pointer.

Linked Lists vs. Arrays

Notice that the above list gives numbers in numeric order. You might wonder how this compares with storing an ordered list of numbers in an array. The key difference is that an array gives random access in that you can directly access any data item by its index number. This allows one to use binary search instead of the slower sequential search, for example. A linked list gives only sequential access to the data, so that only sequential search is available. For example, to read the millionth element of a linked list, you must read the 999,999 elements that precede it!

However, there are other comparisons that could be made between the two. Although the array method allows the faster search to be used, if we want to insert a new item after the one found, we are in trouble! There is probably no room in the array to insert a new item at this point. Instead, all items to the right of this location have to be slid over to the next array location. This is a slow process but does make room to insert the new item. As we will see more clearly when we code linked lists, it is fairly easy to insert a new item into an ordered linked list. In fact, it is just a matter of changing a couple of pointers (as shown above).

Deletion of an item from an ordered list is also a simple matter of changing a pointer, whereas in an ordered array, all of the data to the right has to be shifted left to fill in the hole left upon deletion. Thus, once again, the linked list is faster and more flexible. In general, a linked list is probably the better method if you are going to dynamically insert and delete items a lot. (A linked list is one example of a *dynamic data structure*. This means that it can easily grow, contract, and change as needed. An array is a *static data structure*.)

Another comparison could be made based on the amount of space that the two methods use. With the array scheme, you would need to set the size of the array in advance, overestimating the amount of space needed. However, the linked list method also wastes space, in that it needs room in each node for a pointer. In general it is not possible to say which method wastes more space.

Writing linked list code is a bit more complicated than using arrays, but for many applications such as:

- Information retrieval
- Programming language development
- Simulation
- Storage management techniques

using a linked list instead of an array can be much more efficient.

Primitive Operations on Linear Linked Lists

The primitive linear linked list operations are shown below:

```
p.getNode()
```

Returns a newly created node and sets the contents of a reference variable named `p` to the newly created node.

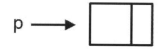

```
p.freeNode()
```

Returns the node that `p` references to the source of unused nodes and makes the node available for reuse.

```
p.getInfo()
```

Returns the data in the information portion of a node that `p` references.

> `x = p.getInfo()` assigns the contents of the `info` field of the node referenced by `p` to `x`.

```
p.setInfo(x)
```

Assigns a new value to the info portion of a node referenced by `p`.

> `p.setInfo(x)` assigns the contents of `x` to the `info` field of the node referenced by `p`.

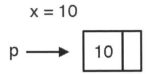

$$x = 10$$

```
p.getNext()
```

Returns the reference in the `next` field of a node that `p` references.

> `q = p.getNext()` assigns to `q` the contents of the `next` field of the node referenced to by `p`.

Given the following linear linked list:

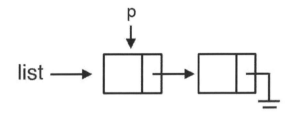

then `q = p.getNext()` results in the following:

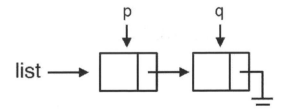

```
p.setNext(q)
```

Assigns the contents of reference variable q to the next field of the node referenced by p.

Given the following linear linked list:

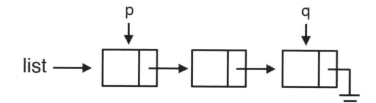

then p.setNext(q) results in the following:

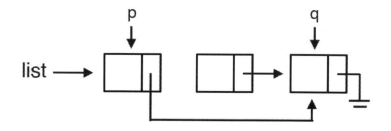

Three List Algorithms

Algorithm 1: Given a linear linked list of integers, create an algorithm that will add a node with the data value of 10 to the front of the list:

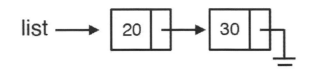

```
p.getnode()
```

p is a reference to a newly created node:

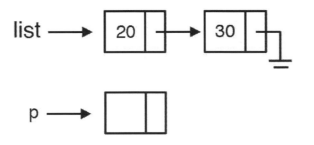

```
p.setInfo(x)
```

Inserts an integer x into the info portion of the node that is referenced by p:

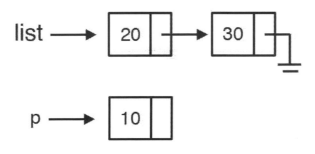

```
p.setNext(list)
```

We now want the node referenced by p to reference the node that list references (since list references the first node in the list). So we must set the next field of the node that p references, to the node that list references:

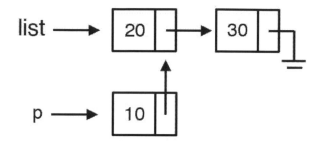

```
list = p
```

Finally, since list is the external reference to the first node in the linear linked list, its value must be modified to reference the new first node of the list. This changes the value of list to the value of p:

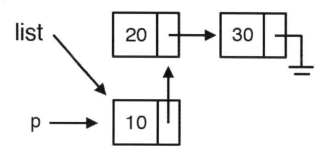

Note at this point the reference p is not needed and can be simply disregarded:

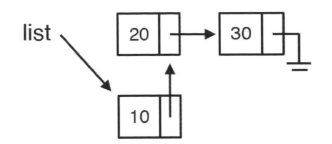

Put together, we have an algorithm for adding an integer to the front of a linear linked list:

```
p.getNode()
p.setInfo(x)
p.setNext(list)
list = p
```

Let's test this algorithm to see if it works for an initially empty list:

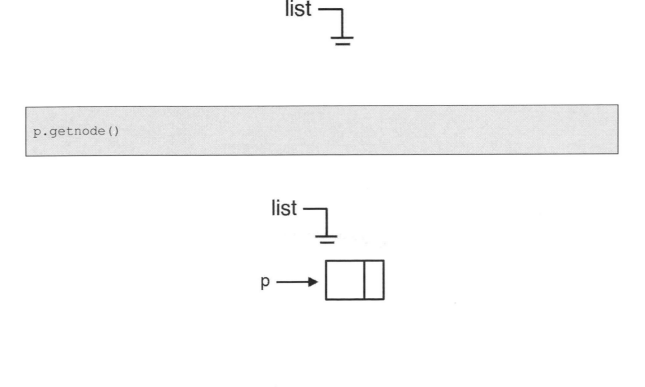

```
p.getnode()
```

```
p.setInfo(x)
```

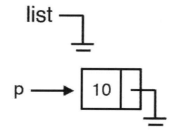

```
p.setNext(list)
```

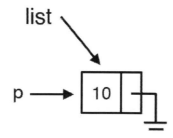

```
list = p
```

Again, reference p is not needed and can be simply disregarded:

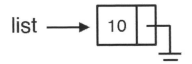

Algorithm 2: Remove the first node of a non-empty list and store the value of its `info` field in a variable x.

```
p = list
```

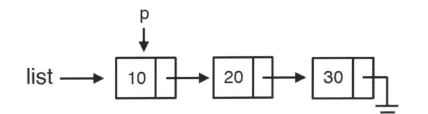

```
list = p.getNext()
```

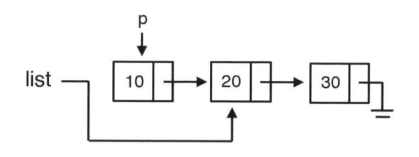

```
x = p.getInfo()
```

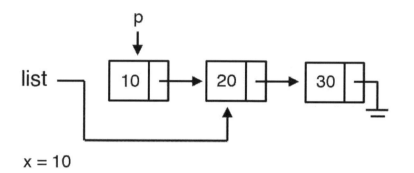

x = 10

```
p.freeNode()
```

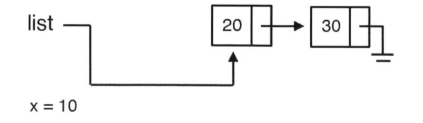

x = 10

Put together, we have an algorithm for deleting any integer from the front of a linear linked list:

```
p = list
list = p.getNext()
x = p.getInfo()
p.freeNode()
```

Let's test this algorithm to see if it works for a list with a single node:

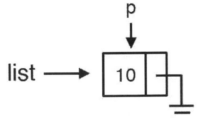

```
p = list
```

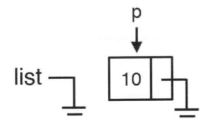

```
list = p.getNext()
```

```
x = p.getInfo()
```

x = 10

```
p.freeNode()
```

x = 10

We can summarize these two new algorithms as follows:

Add a node to the front of a linear linked list:

```
p.getNode()
p.setInfo(x)
p.setNext(list)
list = p
```

Remove the first node of a linear linked list:

```
p = list
list = p.getNext()
x = p.getInfo()
p.freeNode()
```

Look closely at our two algorithms. Can you figure out exactly what it is that we have defined?

.
.
.
.
.
.
.
.
.
.
.
.
.
.
.
.
.
.

If we are using a linear linked list to represent a stack, then our two algorithms above have implemented the `push` and `pop` operations on stacks!

Time Complexity for Stacks Implemented as Linear Linked Lists

	Average Case	Worst Case
Push:	O(1)	O(1)
Pop:	O(1)	O(1)
Top:	O(1)	O(1)

Algorithm 3: Given a linear linked list of integers, create an algorithm that will traverse, or visit, each node in the list and output the data in each of the `info` fields.

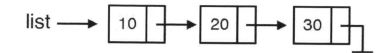

```
p = list
while (p != null)
    output(p.getInfo())
    p = p.getNext()
```

Can you see the importance of ensuring that there is a `null` value in the `next` field of the last node in the linear linked list?

Linked Implementation of Queues

As seen previously, a stack can be represented using linear linked lists. In the implementation of this representation, each node contains a data field for the information and a reference to the next node on the list. The top element on the stack is the item at the front of the list. When the list is `null`, the stack is empty.

Implementing stacks as linked lists provides a solution to the problem of dynamically growing stacks, as a linked list is a dynamic data structure. The stack can grow or shrink as the program demands it to. However, if a small and/or fixed amount of data is being dealt with, it is often simpler to implement the stack as an array.

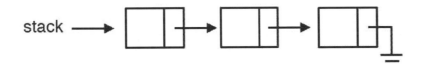

The second way of designing queues is also to use linear linked lists. The main difference between linked lists and arrays is that of flexibility. An array, once declared, is of a fixed size and cannot change. Conversely, a linked list is of a variable size. When a new item is added it is simply linked to the end of the queue.

Thus the problem with an array implementation of queues is that it wastes memory if the queue varies in size during its existence. This is because the size of the array will have to be the size of the largest amount of data ever in the queue. Remember we cannot extend or reduce the size of the array, so it must account for the largest number initially. This is wasteful especially in instances where the size of data is usually small, but occasionally becomes very large.

A linked list implementation of a queue is performed by linking together elements to form a chain. Two references are needed to mark the front and back of the queue. Without these references it would be very easy to lose track of where the queue begins and ends.

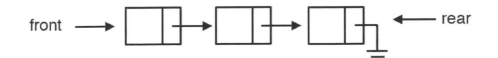

Remember that items are deleted from the front of a queue and items are inserted into the rear of a queue.

The list reference, `front`, points to the first element of the linear linked list and represents the front of the queue. Another pointer, `rear`, points to the last element in the linked list and represents the rear of the queue:

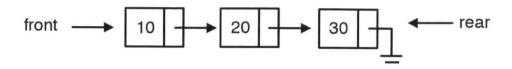

Here is an algorithm to remove an element from the front of the queue:

```
p = front
if (p != null)
    x = p.getInfo()
    front = p.getNext()
    if front == null
        rear = null
    p.freeNode()
```

Let's work through the algorithm step-by-step:

```
p = front
```

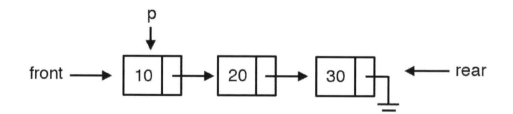

```
if (p != null)
    x = p.getInfo()
```

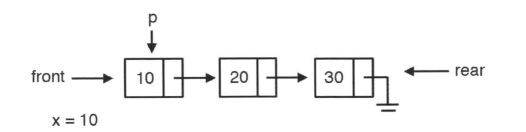

```
front = p.getNext()
```

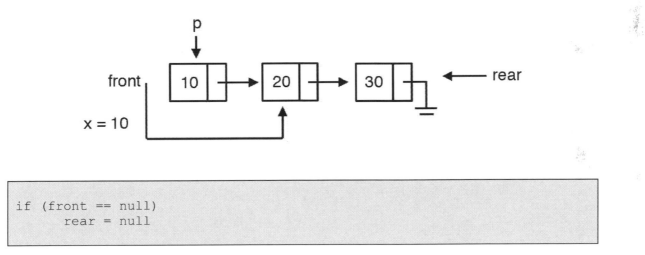

```
if (front == null)
    rear = null
```

This statement becomes valid if we are attempting to delete an item from a queue that only contains one item.

```
p.freeNode()
```

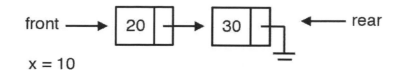

x = 10

It is left as an exercise to work through this algorithm to delete an element from the front of a queue that contains only one element:

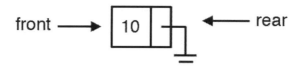

After working through the exercise, can you determine how an empty queue is represented?

Presented below is an algorithm to insert an element into the rear of the queue:

```
p.getNode()
p.setInfo(x)
p.setNext(null)
if (front == null)
    front = p
else
    rear.setNext(p)
rear = p
```

Let's begin with a queue initially containing two items and work through the algorithm step-by-step:

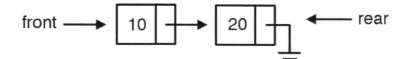

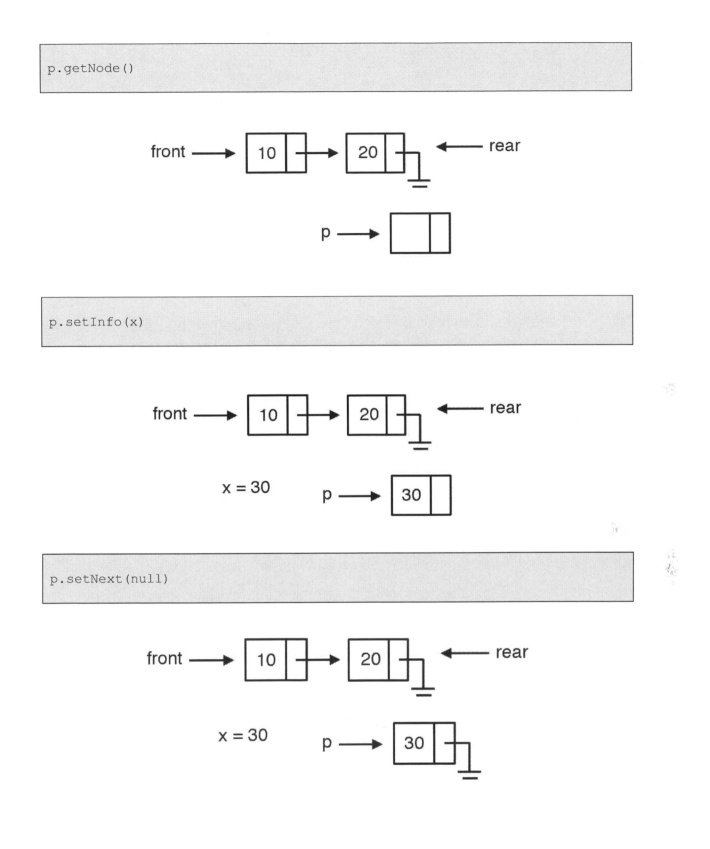

```
if (front == null)
    front = p
else
    rear.setNext(p)
```

Note we execute the `else` clause here. If we were working with an empty queue, the `if` clause would have been executed.

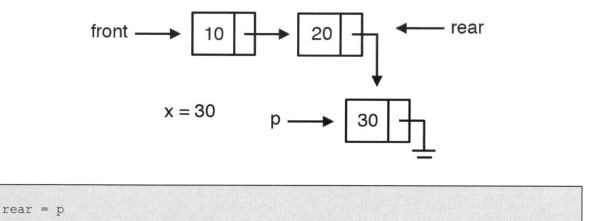

```
rear = p
```

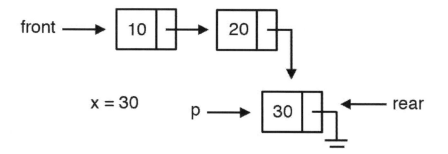

It is left as an exercise to insert an item into an initially empty queue:

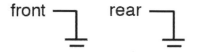

Time Complexity for Queues Implemented using Linear Linked Lists

	Average Case	Worst Case
Insert:	O(1)	O(1)
Remove:	O(1)	O(1)
Query:	O(1)	O(1)

Linked List as a Data Structure

Linear linked lists are not just used for representations of stacks and queues. They are data structures in their own right, because they have properties the other data structures do not. For example, we've previously discussed that it is easy to insert and delete elements from the middle of a list without any data movements. The amount of work required is independent of the size of the list. All that is necessary is to:

- allocate a new node

- insert the information into the node

- adjust two references

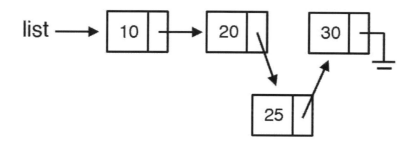

Algorithm 1

Given a pointer `p` to a node in a linear linked list, write an algorithm, `insertAfter`, which will insert a node <u>after</u> the node referenced by `p`:

```
q.getNode()
q.setInfo(x)
q.setNext(p.getNext())
p.setNext(q)
```

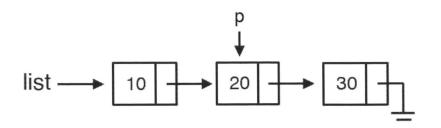

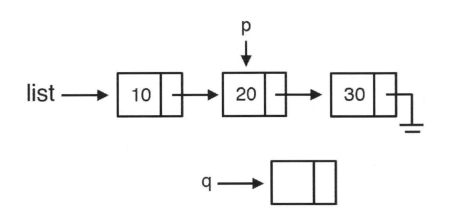

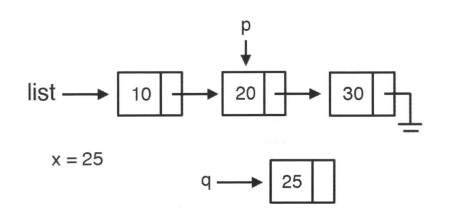

x = 25

```
q.setNext(p.getNext())
```

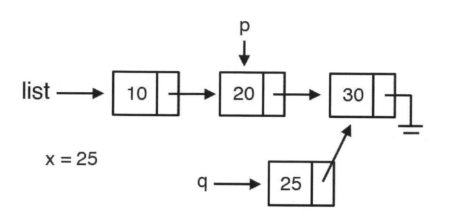

```
p.setNext(q)
```

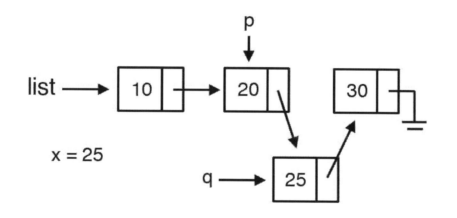

Note that an item can only be inserted after a given node, not before the node. This is because there is no way to proceed from a given node to its predecessor in a list without traversing the list from the beginning.

Algorithm 2
Given a pointer p to a node in a linear linked list, write an algorithm, `deleteAfter`, which will delete a node <u>after</u> the node referenced by p:

```
q = p.getNext()
x = q.getInfo()
p.setNext(q.getNext())
q.freeNode()
```

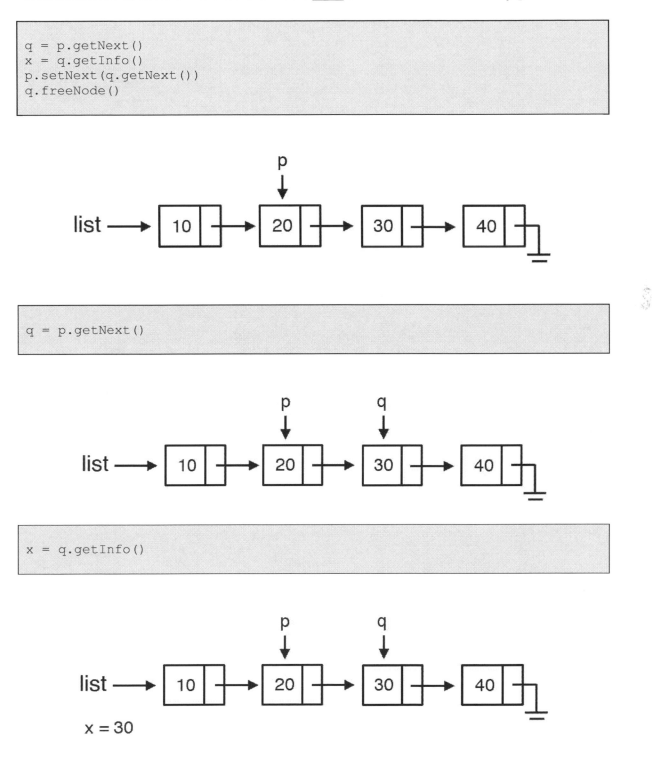

```
q = p.getNext()
```

```
x = q.getInfo()
```

x = 30

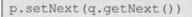

```
p.setNext(q.getNext())
```

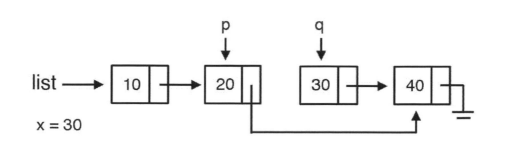

```
q.freeNode()
```

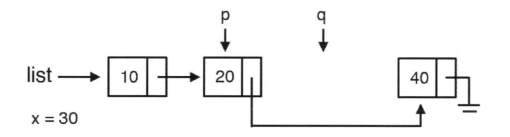

Again, we cannot just be given a reference to the node we want to delete. This is because the `next` field of the node's predecessor must be changed to reference the node's successor and there is no direct way of reaching the predecessor of a given node.

Two Examples of List Operations

Example 1

Suppose we wanted to delete all occurrences of the number 4 from a linear linked list. We would have to traverse the list for nodes with 4 in the `info` field and delete that node. But to delete a node, its predecessor must be known. Therefore we must use two references, p and q, to traverse the list. p will be considered the lead reference and q will be considered the lag reference, i.e., p will traverse the list and q will always reference the predecessor of p. Note the practice of using two references, one following the other, is very common when working with lists.

Two algorithms will be used:

`deleteFront()` will be used to delete the node from the front of the list.

`deleteAfter()` will be used to delete a node from the middle of the list.

```
p = list
q = null
while p != null
     if p.getInfo() == 4
          p = p.getNext()
          if q == null
               x = deleteFront()
          else
               x = deleteAfter(q)
     else
          q = p
          p = p.getNext()
```

It is left as an exercise to work through the algorithm. Be sure to draw pictures as you work through the algorithm line by line.

Example 2

Assume a linear linked list is ordered so that the smaller items precede the larger ones (i.e., the list is sorted). We want to insert an item **x** into this list in its proper place. Two algorithms are used:

insertFront() will be used to insert a node at the front of the list.

insertAfter() will be used to insert a node into the middle of the list.

```
p = list
q = null
while p != null and x > p.getInfo()
    q = p
    P = p.getNext()
if q = = null
    list.insertFront(x)
else
    q.insertAfter(x)
```

Again, it is left as an exercise to work through the algorithm. Be sure to draw pictures as you work through the algorithm line by line.

Java Implementation of Linear Linked Lists

ListNode Class
We first declare a `ListNode` class and define the class instance variables and constructors as follows:

```
public class ListNode {
    private int info;
    private ListNode next;

    public ListNode() {
        info = 0;
        next = null;
    }

    public ListNode(int i) {
        info = i;
        next = null;
    }

    public ListNode (int i, ListNode p) {
        info = i;
        next = p;
    }
```

Note that we declare the `ListNode` class to contain a reference to a `ListNode` object. It's a reference to the next node in the list.

We access the `info` field of the node as:

```
    public void setInfo(int i) {
        info = i;
    }

    public int getInfo() {
        return info;
    }
```

We access the `next` field of the node as:

```
public void setNext(ListNode p) {
    next = p;
}

public ListNode getNext() {
    return next;
}
}
```

List Class

We can now implement the pseudocode algorithms as `List` class methods. First, we declare a `List` class and make the class instance variable and constructor declarations as follows:

```
public class List {
    private ListNode list;

    public List() {
        list = null;
    }
```

Next we can write algorithms to return the first and last items in the list.

```
// Returns the first item in a list

public int getFirst() {
    if (list == null) {
        System.out.println("Runtime Error: getFirst()");
        System.exit(1);
    }
    return list.getInfo();
}
```

```
// Returns the last item in a list

public int getLast() {
    if (list == null) {
        System.out.println("Runtime Error: getLast()");
        System.exit(1);
     }
    ListNode p = list;
    while (p.getNext() != null)
        p = p.getNext();
    return p.getInfo();
}
```

Next we implement algorithms to add and remove nodes from the front and rear of the linear linked list:

```
// Adds an item to the front of a list

public void addFirst(int i) {
    ListNode p = new ListNode(i, list);
    list = p;
}


// Adds an item to the front of a list

public void addFirst(ListNode p) {
    if (p == null) {
        System.out.println("Runtime Error: addFirst()");
        System.exit(1);
    }
    p.setNext(list);
    list = p;
}
```

```java
// Adds an item to the end of the list

public void addLast(int i) {
    ListNode p = new ListNode(i);
    if (list == null)
        list = p;
    else {
        ListNode q = list;
        while (q.getNext() != null)
            q = q.getNext();
        q.setNext(p);
    }
}


// Adds an item to the end of the list

public void addLast(ListNode p) {
    if (p == null) {
        System.out.println("Runtime Error: addLast");
        System.exit(1);
    }
    p.setNext(null);
    if (list == null)
        list = p;
    else {
        ListNode q = list;
        while (q.getNext() != null)
            q = q.getNext();
        q.setNext(p);
    }
}
```

Note that we presented two methods to insert a new node at the front of the list and we presented two methods to insert a new node at the rear of the list. Can you see why?

```java
// Removes the first item from the list

public int removeFirst() {
    if (list == null) {
        System.out.println("Runtime Error: removeFirst()");
        System.exit(1);
    }
    ListNode p = list;
    list = p.getNext();
    return p.getInfo();
}


 // Removes the last item from the list

public int removeLast() {
    if (list == null) {
        System.out.println("Runtime Error: removeLast()");
        System.exit(1);
    }
    ListNode p = list;
    ListNode q = null;
    while (p.getNext() != null) {
        q = p;
        p = p.getNext();
    }
    if (q == null)
        list = null;
    else
        q.setNext(null);
    return p.getInfo();
}
```

The next few methods implement the `insertAfter` and `deleteAfter` algorithms:

```
// Inserts a node after the node referenced by p

public void insertAfter(ListNode p, int i) {
    if (list == null || p == null) {
        System.out.println("Runtime Error: insertAfter()");
        System.exit(1);
    }
    ListNode q = new ListNode(i, p.getNext());
    p.setNext(q);
}

// Alternate code using one line to do the insertion

public void insertAfter(ListNode p, int i) {
    if (list == null || p == null) {
        System.out.println("Runtime Error: insertAfter()");
        System.exit(1);
    }
    p.setNext(new ListNode(i, p.getNext()));
}

// Inserts a node after the node referenced by p

public void insertAfter(ListNode p, ListNode q) {
    if (list == null || p == null || q == null) {
        System.out.println("Runtime Error: insertAfter()");
        System.exit(1);
    }
    q.setNext(p.getNext());
    p.setNext(q);
}


// Deletes the node after the node referenced by p

 public int deleteAfter(ListNode p) {
    if (list == null || p == null || p.getNext() == null) {
        System.out.println("Runtime Error: deleteAfter()");
        System.exit(1);
    }
    ListNode q = p.getNext();
    p.setNext(q.getNext());
    return q.getInfo();
}
```

Next we implement an algorithm to traverse a linear linked list and output the data in the info fields.

```
// Traverse a linear linked list and output the data in info fields

public void traverse() {
    ListNode p = list;
    while (p != null) {
        System.out.println(p.getInfo());
        p = p.getNext();
    }
}
```

Here are methods to insert an element into an ordered (sorted) list and to remove an element from a list:

```
// Inserts an item into its correct location in an ordered list

public void insert(int i) {
    ListNode p = list;
    ListNode q = null;
    while (p != null && p.getInfo() < i) {
        q = p;
        p = p.getNext();
    }
    if (q == null)
        addFirst(i);
    else
        insertAfter(q, i);
}


// Inserts an item into its correct location in an ordered list

public void insert(ListNode r) {
    ListNode p = list;
    ListNode q = null;
    while (p != null && p.getInfo() < r.getInfo()) {
        q = p;
        p = p.getNext();
    }
    if (q == null)
        addFirst(r);
    else
        insertAfter(q, r);
}
```

```
// Removes the first occurrence of an item in a list

public int remove(int i) {
    ListNode p = list;
    ListNode q = null;
    while (p != null && p.getInfo() != i) {
        q = p;
        p = p.getNext();
    }
    if (p == null)
        return -1;
    else return q == null ? removeFirst() : deleteAfter(q);
}
```

This method determines whether or not an item is found within a list:

```
// Returns true if the item is found in the list

public boolean contains(int i) {
    ListNode p = list;
    while (p != null && p.getInfo() != i)
        p = p.getNext();
    return p != null;
}
```

Additional useful methods for manipulating a linear linked list are presented:

```
// Determines whether or not a list is empty

public boolean isEmpty() {
    return list == null;
}


// Removes all elements from the list

public void clear() {
    list = null;
}
```

```java
    // Returns the number of elements in the list

public int size() {
    int count = 0;
    ListNode p = list;
    while (p != null) {
        ++count;
        p = p.getNext();
    }
    return count;
}



    // Returns sum of the integers in the list

public int sumElements() {
    int sum = 0;
    ListNode p = list;

    while (p != null) {
        sum += p.getInfo();
        p = p.getNext();
    }
    return sum;
}


// Returns the first reference to the node with the requested value;
// otherwise, returns null

public ListNode select(int i) {
    ListNode p = list;
    while (p != null)
        if (p.getInfo() == i)
            return p;
        else
            p = p.getNext();
    return null;
}
```

```java
// Makes a copy of a list
// q set to null to satisfy the compiler

public List copyList() {
    ListNode p;
    ListNode q = null;

    List newList = new List();
    ListNode r = list;
    while (r != null) {
        p = new ListNode(r.getInfo(), null);
        if (newList.isEmpty())
            newList.addLast(p);
        else
            q.setNext(p);
        q = p;
        r = r.getNext();
    }
    return newList;
}


// Reverses a list

public void reverse() {
    ListNode p = list;
    ListNode q = null;
    ListNode r;

    while (p != null) {
        r = q;
        q = p;
        p = p.getNext();
        q.setNext(r);
    }
    list = q;
}
```

Finally, here are a couple of methods to return the first and last nodes in a list:

```
// Returns the first node in the list

  public ListNode getFirstNode() {
      return list;
  }


// Returns the last node in the list

  public ListNode getLastNode() {
      if (list == null)
          return null;
      ListNode p = list;
      while (p.getNext() != null)
          p = p.getNext();
      return p;
  }
```

List Classes

```java
// ListNode.java

public class ListNode {
    private int info;
    private ListNode next;

    // Default constructor
    public ListNode() {
        info = 0;
        next = null;
    }

    // One-arg constructor
    public ListNode (int i) {
        info = i;
        next = null;
    }

    // Two-arg constructor
    public ListNode (int i, ListNode p) {
        info = i;
        next = p;
    }

    // Sets info field
    public void setInfo(int i) {
        info = i;
    }

    // Returns item in info field
    public int getInfo() {
        return info;
    }

    // Sets next field
    public void setNext(ListNode p) {
        next = p;
    }

    // Returns a reference to the last node in the list
    public ListNode getNext() {
        return next;
    }
}
```

```java
// List.java

public class List {
    private ListNode list;


    // Constructs an empty list
    public List() {
        list = null;
    }


    // Returns the first node in the list
    public ListNode getFirstNode() {
        return list;
    }


    // Returns the last node in the list
    public ListNode getLastNode() {
        if (list == null)
            return null;
        ListNode p = list;
        while (p.getNext() != null)
            p = p.getNext();
        return p;
    }


    // Returns the first item in a list
    public int getFirst() {
        if (list == null) {
            System.out.println("Runtime Error: getFirst()");
            System.exit(1);
        }
        return list.getInfo();
    }


    // Returns the last item in a list
    public int getLast() {
        if (list == null) {
            System.out.println("Runtime Error: getLast()");
            System.exit(1);
        }
        ListNode p = list;
        while (p.getNext() != null)
            p = p.getNext();
        return p.getInfo();
    }
```

```java
// Adds an item to the front of a list
public void addFirst(int i) {
    ListNode p = new ListNode(i, list);
    list = p;
}


// Adds an item to the front of a list
public void addFirst(ListNode p) {
    if (p == null) {
        System.out.println("Runtime Error: addFirst()");
        System.exit(1);
    }
    p.setNext(list);
    list = p;
}


// Adds an item to the end of the list
public void addLast(int i) {
    ListNode p = new ListNode(i);
    if (list == null)
        list = p;
    else {
        ListNode q = list;
        while (q.getNext() != null)
            q = q.getNext();
        q.setNext(p);
    }
}


// Adds an item to the end of the list
public void addLast(ListNode p) {
    if (p == null) {
        System.out.println("Runtime Error: addLast()");
        System.exit(1);
    }
    p.setNext(null);
    if (list == null)
        list = p;
    else {
        ListNode q = list;
        while (q.getNext() != null)
            q = q.getNext();
        q.setNext(p);
    }
}
```

```java
// Removes the first item from the list
public int removeFirst() {
    if (list == null) {
        System.out.println("Runtime Error: removeFirst()");
        System.exit(1);
    }
    ListNode p = list;
    list = p.getNext();
    return p.getInfo();
}


// Removes the last item from the list
public int removeLast() {
    if (list == null) {
        System.out.println("Runtime Error: removeLast()");
        System.exit(1);
    }
    ListNode p = list;
    ListNode q = null;
    while (p.getNext() != null) {
        q = p;
        p = p.getNext();
    }
    if (q == null)
        list = null;
    else
        q.setNext(null);
    return p.getInfo();
}


// Inserts a node after the node referenced by p
public void insertAfter(ListNode p, int i) {
    if (list == null || p == null) {
        System.out.println("Runtime Error: insertAfter()");
        System.exit(1);
    }
    ListNode q = new ListNode(i, p.getNext());
    p.setNext(q);
}


// Inserts a node after the node referenced by p
public void insertAfter(ListNode p, ListNode q) {
    if (list == null || p == null || q == null) {
        System.out.println("Runtime Error: insertAfter()");
        System.exit(1);
    }
    q.setNext(p.getNext());
    p.setNext(q);
}
```

```java
// Deletes the node after the node referenced by p
public int deleteAfter(ListNode p) {
    if (list == null || p == null || p.getNext() == null) {
        System.out.println("Runtime Error: deleteAfter()");
        System.exit(1);
    }
    ListNode q = p.getNext();
    p.setNext(q.getNext());
    return q.getInfo();
}


// Traverses a list and outputs data from the info fields
public void traverse() {
    ListNode p = list;
    while (p != null) {
        System.out.println(p.getInfo());
        p = p.getNext();
    }
}


// Inserts an item into its correct location within an ordered list
public void insert(int i) {
    ListNode p = list;
    ListNode q = null;
    while (p != null && p.getInfo() < i) {
        q = p;
        p = p.getNext();
    }
    if (q == null)
        addFirst(i);
    else
        insertAfter(q, i);
}


// Inserts an item into its correct location in an ordered list
public void insert(ListNode r) {
    ListNode p = list;
    ListNode q = null;
    while (p != null && p.getInfo() < r.getInfo()) {
        q = p;
        p = p.getNext();
    }
    if (q == null)
        addFirst(r);
    else
        insertAfter(q, r);
}
```

```java
// Removes the first occurrence of an item in a list
public int remove(int i) {
    ListNode p = list;
    ListNode q = null;
    while (p != null && p.getInfo() != i) {
        q = p;
        p = p.getNext();
    }
    if (p == null)
        return -1;
    else return q == null ? removeFirst() : deleteAfter(q);
}


// Returns true if the item is found in the list
public boolean contains(int i) {
    ListNode p = list;
    while (p != null && p.getInfo() != i)
        p = p.getNext();
    return p != null;
}


// Determines whether or not a list is empty
public boolean isEmpty() {
    return list == null;
}


// Removes all elements from a list
public void clear() {
    list = null;
}


// Returns the number of elements in the list
public int size() {
    int count = 0;
    ListNode p = list;
    while (p != null) {
        ++count;
        p = p.getNext();
    }
    return count;
}
```

```java
// Returns sum of the integers in the list
public int sumElements() {
    int sum = 0;
    ListNode p = list;

    while (p != null) {
        sum += p.getInfo();
        p = p.getNext();
    }
    return sum;
}


// Returns a reference to the node with the requested value
// Returns null otherwise
public ListNode select(int i) {
    ListNode p = list;
    while (p != null)
        if (p.getInfo() == i)
            return p;
        else
            p = p.getNext();
    return null;
}


// Makes a copy of a list
public List copyList() {
    ListNode p;
    ListNode q = null;  // to satisfy compiler
    ListNode r = list;

    List newList = new List();
    while (r != null) {
        p = new ListNode(r.getInfo(), null);
        if (newList.isEmpty())
            newList.addLast(p);
        else
            q.setNext(p);
        q = p;
        r = r.getNext();
    }
    return newList;
}
```

```
// Reverses a list
public void reverse() {
    ListNode p = list;
    ListNode q = null;
    ListNode r;

    while (p != null) {
        r = q;
        q = p;
        p = p.getNext();
        q.setNext(r);
    }
    list = q;
}
}
```

```java
// TestList.java

public class TestList {
    public static void main() {
        List list = new List();

        System.out.println(list.isEmpty());

        for (int i = 1; i <= 5; i++)
            list.addLast(i);
        list.traverse();
        System.out.println();

        list.addFirst(100);
        list.addLast(200);
        list.traverse();
        System.out.println();

        list.removeFirst();
        list.removeLast();
        list.traverse();
        System.out.println();

        System.out.println(list.size());
        System.out.println();

        list.addLast(500);
        list.addLast(25);
        list.traverse();
        System.out.println();

        list.remove(3);
        list.traverse();
        System.out.println();

        System.out.println(list.sumElements());
        System.out.println();

        List newList = list.copyList();
        list.traverse();
        System.out.println();
        newList.traverse();
        System.out.println();

        ListNode p = list.select(5);
        list.deleteAfter(p);
        list.traverse();
        System.out.println();
```

```
        ListNode r = list.select(5);
        list.insertAfter(r, 100);
        list.traverse();
        System.out.println();
    }
}
```

Here's the output produced by the above example:

```
true
1
2
3
4
5

100
1
2
3
4
5
200

1
2
3
4
5

5

1
2
3
4
5
500
25
```

```
1
2
4
5
500
25

537

1
2
4
5
500
25

1
2
4
5
500
25

1
2
4
5
25

1
2
4
5
100
25
```

ListLast Classes Tracking Last Node in List

Presented below are the `ListLast` classes that also keeps track of the last node in the list. This code will be more efficient in programs that require access to the last nodes in very long lists.

```
// ListNode.java
public class ListNode {
    private int info;
    private ListNode next;

    // Default ctor
    public ListNode() {
        info = 0;
        next = null;
    }

    // One-arg ctor
    public ListNode (int i) {
        info = i;
        next = null;
    }

    // Two-arg ctor
    public ListNode (int i, ListNode p) {
        info = i;
        next = p;
    }

    // Sets info field
    public void setInfo(int i) {
        info = i;
    }

    // Returns item in info field
    public int getInfo() {
        return info;
    }

    // Sets next field
    public void setNext(ListNode p) {
        next = p;
    }

    // Returns item in info field
    public ListNode getNext() {
        return next;
    }
}
```

```java
// ListLast.java

public class ListLast {
    private ListNode list;
    private ListNode last;


    // Constructs an empty list
    public ListLast() {
        list = null;
        last = null;
    }


    // Returns the first node in the list
    public ListNode getFirstNode() {
        return list;
    }

    // Returns the last node in the list
    public ListNode getLastNode() {
        return last;
    }


    // Returns the first item in the list
    public int getFirst() {
        if (list == null) {
            System.out.println("Runtime Error: getFirst()");
            System.exit(1);
        }
        return list.getInfo();
    }


    // Returns the last item in the list
    public int getLast() {
        if (list == null) {
            System.out.println("Runtime Error: getLast()");
            System.exit(1);
        }
        return last.getInfo();
    }


    // Adds an item to the front of a list
    public void addFirst(int i) {
        ListNode p = new ListNode(i, list);
        if (list == null)
            last = p;
        list = p;
    }
```

```java
// Adds a node to the front of the list
public void addFirst(ListNode p) {
    if (p == null) {
        System.out.println("Runtime Error: addFirst()");
        System.exit(1);
    }
    p.setNext(list);
    if (list == null)
        last = p;
    list = p;
}


// Adds an item to the end of the list
public void addLast(int i) {
    ListNode p = new ListNode(i);
    if (list == null)
        list = p;
    else
        last.setNext(p);
    last = p;
}


// Adds a node to the end of the list
public void addLast(ListNode p) {
    if (p == null) {
        System.out.println("Runtime Error: addLast()");
        System.exit(1);
    }
    p.setNext(null);
    if (list == null)
        list = p;
    else
        last.setNext(p);
    last = p;
}


// Removes the first item from the list
public int removeFirst() {
    if (list == null) {
        System.out.println("Runtime Error: removeFirst()");
        System.exit(1);
    }
    ListNode p = list;
    list = p.getNext();
    if (list == null)
        last = null;
    return p.getInfo();
}
```

```java
// Removes the last item from the list
public int removeLast() {
    if (list == null) {
        System.out.println("Runtime Error: removeLast()");
        System.exit(1);
    }
    ListNode p = list;
    ListNode q = null;
    while (p.getNext() != null) {
        q = p;
        p = p.getNext();
    }
    if (q == null) {
        list = null;
        last = null;
    }
    else {
        q.setNext(null);
        last = q;
    }
    return p.getInfo();
}


// Inserts a node after the node referenced by p
public void insertAfter(ListNode p, int i) {
    if (list == null || p == null) {
        System.out.println("Runtime Error: insertAfter()");
        System.exit(1);
    }
    ListNode q = new ListNode(i, p.getNext());
    p.setNext(q);
    if (q.getNext() == null)
        last = q;
}


// Inserts a node after the node referenced by p
public void insertAfter(ListNode p, ListNode q) {
    if (list == null || p == null || q == null) {
        System.out.println("Runtime Error: insertAfter()");
        System.exit(1);
    }
    q.setNext(p.getNext());
    p.setNext(q);
    if (last.getNext() != null)
        last = q;
}
```

```
// Deletes the node after the node referenced by p
public int deleteAfter(ListNode p) {
    if (list == null || p == null || p.getNext() == null) {
        System.out.println("Runtime Error: deleteAfter()");
        System.exit(1);
    }
    ListNode q = p.getNext();
    p.setNext(q.getNext());
    if (p.getNext() == null)
        last = p;
    return q.getInfo();
}


// Traverses a list and outputs data from the info fields
public void traverse() {
    ListNode p = list;
    while (p != null) {
        System.out.println(p.getInfo());
        p = p.getNext();
    }
}


// Inserts an item into its correct location within an ordered list
public void insert(int i) {
    ListNode p = list;
    ListNode q = null;
    while (p != null && i > p.getInfo()) {
        q = p;
        p = p.getNext();
    }
    if (q == null)
        addFirst(i);
    else
        insertAfter(q, i);
}


// Inserts an item into its correct location within an ordered list
public void insert(ListNode r) {
    ListNode p = list;
    ListNode q = null;
    while (p != null && r.getInfo() > p.getInfo()) {
        q = p;
        p = p.getNext();
    }
    if (q == null)
        addFirst(r);
    else
        insertAfter(q, r);
}
```

```java
// Removes the first occurrence of an item in a list
public int remove(int i) {
    ListNode p = list;
    ListNode q = null;
    while (p != null && i != p.getInfo()) {
        q = p;
        p = p.getNext();
    }
    if (p == null)
        return -999;
    else return q == null ? removeFirst() : deleteAfter(q);
}


// Returns true if the item is found in the list
public boolean contains(int i) {
    ListNode p = list;
    while (p != null && i != p.getInfo())
        p = p.getNext();
    return p != null;
}


// Determines whether or not a list is empty
public boolean isEmpty() {
    return list == null;
}


// Removes all elements from a list
public void clear() {
    list = null;
    last = null;
}


// Returns the number of elements in the list
public int size() {
    int count = 0;
    ListNode p = list;
    while (p != null) {
        ++count;
        p = p.getNext();
    }
    return count;
}
```

```java
// Returns sum of the integers in the list
public int sumElements() {
    int sum = 0;
    ListNode p = list;

    while (p != null) {
        sum += p.getInfo();
        p = p.getNext();
    }
    return sum;
}


// Returns a reference to the node with the requested value
// Returns null otherwise
public ListNode select(int i) {
    ListNode p = list;
    while (p != null)
        if (p.getInfo() == i)
            return p;
        else
            p = p.getNext();
    return null;
}


// Makes a copy of a list
public ListLast copyList() {
    ListNode p = null;
    ListNode q = null; // to satisfy compiler;
    ListNode r = list;

    if (isEmpty())
        return null;
    ListLast newList = new ListLast();
    while (r != null) {
        p = new ListNode(r.getInfo());
        if (newList.isEmpty())
            newList.addFirst(p);
        else
            q.setNext(p);
        q = p;
        r = r.getNext();
    }
    newList.last = p;
    return newList;
}
```

```java
// Reverses a list
public void reverse() {
    ListNode p = list;
    ListNode q = null;
    ListNode r;

    while (p != null) {
        r = q;
        q = p;
        p = p.getNext();
        q.setNext(r);
    }
    last = list;
    list = q;
}
}
```

Object Linear Linked Lists

As with the case of stacks and queues, we usually write programs that use linear linked lists to manipulate objects rather than integers. Rather than writing a separate List class for each specific object we might want to manipulate, we're able to write a general `ObjectListNode` class and a general `ObjectList` class that will be able to manipulate objects of any type.

Remember that all objects in Java are said to be derived from the superclass `Object`. With the exception of the primitive types, `int`, `double`, `char`, or `boolean`, an object of any type may be stored in an object of type `Object`. Using an `Object` allows the programmer to define the features of a data structure without reference to a particular type, with the method using the data structure being responsible for properly interpreting the object placed on the data structure.

We rewrite our `ObjectListNode` class to manipulate Objects as follows:

```java
// ObjectListNode.java

public class ObjectListNode {
    private Object info;
    private ObjectListNode next;

    // Default ctor
    public ObjectListNode() {
        info = null;
        next = null;
    }

    // One-arg ctor
    public ObjectListNode (Object o) {
        info = o;
        next = null;
    }

    // Two-arg ctor
    public ObjectListNode (Object o, ObjectListNode p) {
        info = o;
        next = p;
    }
```

```java
    // Sets info field
    public void setInfo(Object o) {
        info = o;
    }

    // Returns object in info field
    public Object getInfo() {
        return info;
    }

    // Sets next field
    public void setNext(ObjectListNode p) {
        next = p;
    }

    // Returns object in info field
    public ObjectListNode getNext() {
        return next;
    }
}
```

We now rewrite our `ListLast` class as our `ObjectList` class as follows:

```java
// ObjectList.java

public class ObjectList {
    private ObjectListNode list;
    private ObjectListNode last;

    // Constructs an empty list
    public ObjectList() {
        list = null;
        last = null;
    }

    // Returns the first node in the list
    public ObjectListNode getFirstNode() {
        return list;
    }

    // Returns the last node in the list
    public ObjectListNode getLastNode() {
        return last;
    }
```

```java
// Returns the first item in the list
   public Object getFirst() {
       if (list == null) {
           System.out.println("Runtime Error: getFirst()");
           System.exit(1);
       }
       return list.getInfo();
   }

   // Returns the last item in the list
   public Object getLast() {
       if (list == null) {
           System.out.println("Runtime Error: getLast()");
           System.exit(1);
       }
       return last.getInfo();
   }

   // Adds an item to the front of a list
   public void addFirst(Object o) {
       ObjectListNode p = new ObjectListNode(o, list);
       if (list == null)
           last = p;
       list = p;
   }

   // Adds an item to the front of the list
   public void addFirst(ObjectListNode p) {
       if (p == null) {
           System.out.println("Runtime Error: addFirst()");
           System.exit(1);
       }
       p.setNext(list);
       if (list == null)
           last = p;
       list = p;
   }

   // Adds an item to the end of the list
   public void addLast(Object o) {
       ObjectListNode p = new ObjectListNode(o);
       if (list == null)
           list = p;
       else
           last.setNext(p);
       last = p;
   }
```

```java
// Adds an item to the end of the list
public void addLast(ObjectListNode p) {
    if (p == null) {
        System.out.println("Runtime Error: addLast()");
        System.exit(1);
    }
    p.setNext(null);
    if (list == null)
        list = p;
    else
        last.setNext(p);
    last = p;
}

// Removes the first item from the list
public Object removeFirst() {
    if (list == null) {
        System.out.println("Runtime Error: removeFirst()");
        System.exit(1);
    }
    ObjectListNode p = list;
    list = p.getNext();
    if (list == null)
        last = null;
    return p.getInfo();
}

// Removes the last item from the list
public Object removeLast() {
    if (list == null) {
        System.out.println("Runtime Error: removeLast()");
        System.exit(1);
    }
    ObjectListNode p = list;
    ObjectListNode q = null;
    while (p.getNext() != null) {
        q = p;
        p = p.getNext();
    }
    if (q == null) {
        list = null;
        last = null;
    }
    else {
        q.setNext(null);
        last = q;
    }
    return p.getInfo();
}
```

```java
// Inserts a node after the node referenced by p
public void insertAfter (ObjectListNode p, Object o) {
    if (list == null || p == null) {
        System.out.println("Runtime Error: insertAfter()");
        System.exit(1);
    }
    ObjectListNode q = new ObjectListNode(o, p.getNext());
    p.setNext(q);
    if (q.getNext() == null)
        last = q;
}

// Inserts a node after the node referenced by p
public void insertAfter(ObjectListNode p, ObjectListNode q) {
    if (list == null || p == null || q == null) {
        System.out.println("Runtime Error: insertAfter()");
        System.exit(1);
    }
    q.setNext(p.getNext());
    p.setNext(q);
    if (last.getNext() != null)
        last = q;
}

// Deletes the node after the node referenced by p
public Object deleteAfter(ObjectListNode p) {
    if (list == null || p == null || p.getNext() == null) {
        System.out.println("Runtime Error: deleteAfter()");
        System.exit(1);
    }
    ObjectListNode q = p.getNext();
    p.setNext(q.getNext());
    if (p.getNext() == null)
        last = p;
    return q.getInfo();
}

// Determines whether or not a list is empty
public boolean isEmpty() {
    return list == null;
}

// Removes all elements from a list
public void clear() {
    list = null;
    last = null;
}
```

```java
// Returns the number of elements in the list
    public int size() {
        int count = 0;
        ObjectListNode p = list;
        while (p != null) {
            ++count;
            p = p.getNext();
        }
        return count;
    }

    // Makes a copy of a list
    public ObjectList copyList() {
        ObjectListNode p = null;
        ObjectListNode q = null; // to satisfy compiler;
        ObjectListNode r = list;

        if (isEmpty())
            return null;
        ObjectList newList = new ObjectList();
        while (r != null) {
            p = new ObjectListNode(r.getInfo());
            if (newList.isEmpty())
                newList.addFirst(p);
            else
                q.setNext(p);
            q = p;
            r = r.getNext();
        }
        newList.last = p;
        return newList;
    }

    // Reverses a list
    public void reverse() {
        ObjectListNode p = list;
        ObjectListNode q = null;
        ObjectListNode r;

        while (p != null) {
            r = q;
            q = p;
            p = p.getNext();
            q.setNext(r);
        }
        last = list;
        list = q;
    }
}
```

Comparable Interface

If you look closely at the `ObjectList` class of Objects we recently developed, you'll find that we did not implement five methods from the original `ListLast` class of integers. The original five methods not implemented in the `ObjectList` class are shown below:

```java
// Inserts an item into its correct location within an ordered list
public void insert(int i) {
    ListNode p = list;
    ListNode q = null;
    while (p != null && p.getInfo() < i) {
        q = p;
        p = p.getNext();
    }
    if (q == null)
        addFirst(i);
    else {
        ListNode r = new ListNode(i);
        insertAfter(q, r);
    }
}

// Inserts an item into its correct location within an ordered list
public void insert(ListNode r) {
    ListNode p = list;
    ListNode q = null;
    while (p != null && r.getInfo() > p.getInfo()) {
        q = p;
        p = p.getNext();
    }
    if (q == null)
        addFirst(r);
    else
        insertAfter(q, r);
}
```

```java
// Removes the first occurrence of an item in a list
public int remove(int i) {
    ListNode p = list;
    ListNode q = null;
    while (p != null && p.getInfo() != i) {
        q = p;
        p = p.getNext();
    }
    if (p == null)
        return -1;
    else return q == null ? removeFirst() : deleteAfter(q);
}

// Returns true if the item is found in the list
public boolean contains(int i) {
    ListNode p = list;
    while (p != null && p.getInfo() != i) {
        p = p.getNext();
    return p != null;
}

// Returns a reference to the node with the requested value
// Returns null otherwise
public ListNode select(int i) {
    ListNode p = list;
    while (p != null)
        if (p.getInfo() == i)
            return p;
        else
            p = p.getNext();
    return null;
}
```

Can you see what each of these five methods has in common? Look closely at the line of code underlined in each method.

Each method is required to make a comparison of the contents of a node's `info` field with an integer being passed as a parameter. This comparison is necessary to perform one of the required tasks:

- Find the correct position in the list to insert the parameter.

- Remove the first occurrence of the parameter if it appears in the list.

- Determine whether or not the parameter is found in the list.

- Return a reference to the parameter if found in the list.

We're able to make this kind of direct comparison in each of the methods because we specifically built our `ListLast` class around the integer data type. Our linear linked list is a list of integers.

But in our new `ObjectListNode` and `ObjectList` classes that contain `Objects`, the classes do not know what type of objects will be stored in the `info` field of the nodes. What object would we pass in as a parameter to the `ObjectList` class's methods? What information would we base our comparisons upon? We do not have the answers to these questions and therefore we are unable to make a direct comparison in the methods of the `ObjectList` class. How, then, could we possibly write the above methods that require comparisons in the methods for our `ObjectList` class of Objects?

The solution is to create an entity that will interface with our `ObjectList` class and the class of objects that are being stored in the object linear linked list. For example, suppose we want our linear linked list to manipulate objects of a `Student` class. We can create an interface, `Comparable`, that could link a specific `compareTo()` method in the `Student` class with a more generalized comparison required in methods in the `ObjectList` class:

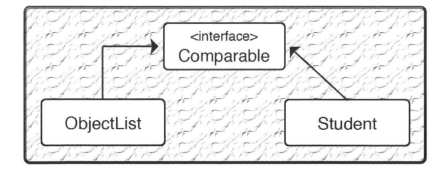

An interface, `Comparable`, might list a comparison method and its arguments but does not include any code for the method. A class, `Student`, is said to *implement* the interface if it supplies the definition of the methods specified in that interface.

Our declaration of the interface would look like this:

```
public interface Comparable {
    public int compareTo(Object o);
}
```

Note that an interface looks like a class declaration, except that it uses the keyword `interface`. The `Comparable` interface specifies one method that every subclass must implement: `compareTo()`.

We associate the `Student` class with the `Comparable` interface through the following declaration:

```
public class Student implements Comparable  {
```

We can then declare an instance variable, constructor, and accessor method for the `Student` class:

```
    private String name;

    public Student(String s) {
        name = s;
    }

    public String getName() {
        return name;
    }
```

Now the `Student` class must implement the `compareTo()` method declared in the interface that will compare the name of two `Student` objects:

```
    public int compareTo(Object o) {
        Student s = (Student) o;
        return name.compareTo(s.getName());
    }
}
```

The first line in the `compareTo()` method:

```
    Student s = (Student) o;
```

casts the `Object` argument into a `Student` object. The last line in the `compareTo()` method:

```
    return name.compareTo(s.getName());
```

uses the `compareTo()` method from the `String` class to compare the names of the `Student` object that invokes the method with the name of the `Student` object that is passed as a parameter to the method.

Note that we assume the objects contained in the linked lists are comparable, and therefore can be placed in some linear order. i.e., any object of the type is either less than, greater than, or equal to any other object of the type. The `compareTo()` method declared in the `Comparable` interface and implemented in the `Student` class returns a positive number if the object that invokes the `compareTo()` is greater than the parameter of the `compareTo()` in their linear order.

With this in mind, we can now implement the five methods from our original `ListLast` class as follows:

```
// Inserts an item into its correct location within an ordered list
public void insert(Object o) {
    ObjectListNode p = list;
    ObjectListNode q = null;
    while (p != null &&
            ((Comparable)o).compareTo(p.getInfo()) > 0) {
        q = p;
        p = p.getNext();
    }
    if (q == null)
        addFirst(o);
    else
        insertAfter(q, o);
}

// Inserts an item into its correct location within an ordered list
public void insert(ObjectListNode r) {
    ObjectListNode p = list;
    ObjectListNode q = null;
    while (p != null &&
            ((Comparable)r.getInfo()).compareTo(p.getInfo()) > 0) {
        q = p;
        p = p.getNext();
    }
    if (q == null)
        addFirst(r);
    else
        insertAfter(q, r);
}
```

```
// Removes and returns the first occurrence of the specified
// item in the list
public Object remove(Object o) {
    ListNode p = list;
    ListNode q = null;
    while (p != null &&
            ((Comparable)o).compareTo(p.getInfo()) != 0) {
        q= p;
        p = p.getNext();
    }
    if (p == null)
        return null;
    else return q == null ? removeFirst() : deleteAfter(q);
}


// Returns true if the list contains the specified item.
public boolean contains(Object o) {
    ListNode p = list;

    while (p != null &&
            ((Comparable)o).compareTo(p.getInfo()) != 0)
        p = p.getNext();
    return p != null;
}


// Returns a reference to the node with the requested value
// Returns null otherwise
public ListNode select(Object o) {
    ListNode p = list;
    while (p != null)
        if (((Comparable)o).compareTo(p.getInfo()) == 0)
            return p;
        else
            p = p.getNext();
    return null;
}
```

ObjectList Classes

```java
// ObjectListNode.java

public class ObjectListNode implements ObjectListNodeInterface {
    private Object info;
    private ObjectListNode next;

    // Default ctor
    public ObjectListNode() {
        info = null;
        next = null;
    }

    // One-arg ctor
    public ObjectListNode (Object o) {
        info = o;
        next = null;
    }

    // Two-arg ctor
    public ObjectListNode (Object o, ObjectListNode p) {
        info = o;
        next = p;
    }

    // Sets info field
    public void setInfo(Object o) {
        info = o;
    }

    // Returns item in info field
    public Object getInfo() {
        return info;
    }

    // Sets next field
    public void setNext(ObjectListNode p) {
        next = p;
    }

    // Returns item in info field
    public ObjectListNode getNext() {
        return next;
    }
}
```

```java
// ObjectList.java

public class ObjectList implements ObjectListInterface{
    private ObjectListNode list;
    private ObjectListNode last;

    // Constructs an empty list
    public ObjectList() {
        list = null;
        last = null;
    }

    // Returns a reference to the first node in the list
    public ObjectListNode getFirstNode() {
        return list;
    }

    // Returns a reference to the last node in the list
    public ObjectListNode getLastNode() {
        return last;
    }

    // Returns the first item in the list
    public Object getFirst() {
        if (list == null) {
            System.out.println("Runtime Error: getFirst()");
            System.exit(1);
        }
        return list.getInfo();
    }

    // Returns the last item in the list
    public Object getLast() {
        if (list == null) {
            System.out.println("Runtime Error: getLast()");
            System.exit(1);
        }
        return last.getInfo();
    }

    // Adds an item to the front of a list
    public void addFirst(Object o) {
        ObjectListNode p = new ObjectListNode(o, list);
        if (list == null)
            last = p;
        list = p;
    }
```

```java
// Adds an item to the front of the list
public void addFirst(ObjectListNode p) {
    if (p == null) {
        System.out.println("Runtime Error: addFirst()");
        System.exit(1);
    }
    p.setNext(list);
    if (list == null)
        last = p;
    list = p;
}

// Adds an item to the end of the list
public void addLast(Object o) {
    ObjectListNode p = new ObjectListNode(o);
    if (list == null)
        list = p;
    else
        last.setNext(p);
    last = p;
}

// Adds an item to the end of the list
public void addLast(ObjectListNode p) {
    if (p == null) {
        System.out.println("Runtime Error: addLast()");
        System.exit(1);
    }
    p.setNext(null);
    if (list == null)
        list = p;
    else
        last.setNext(p);
    last = p;
}

// Removes the first item from the list
public Object removeFirst() {
    if (list == null) {
        System.out.println("Runtime Error: removeFirst()");
        System.exit(1);
    }
    ObjectListNode p = list;
    list = p.getNext();
    if (list == null)
        last = null;
    return p.getInfo();
}
```

```java
// Removes the last item from the list
public Object removeLast() {
    if (list == null) {
        System.out.println("Runtime Error: removeLast()");
        System.exit(1);
    }
    ObjectListNode p = list;
    ObjectListNode q = null;
    while (p.getNext() != null) {
        q = p;
        p = p.getNext();
    }
    if (q == null) {
        list = null;
        last = null;
    }
    else {
        q.setNext(null);
        last = q;
    }
    return p.getInfo();
}

// Inserts a node after the node referenced by p
public void insertAfter (ObjectListNode p, Object o) {
    if (list == null || p == null) {
        System.out.println("Runtime Error: insertAfter()");
        System.exit(1);
    }
    ObjectListNode q = new ObjectListNode(o, p.getNext());
    p.setNext(q);
    if (q.getNext() == null)
        last = q;
}

// Inserts a node after the node referenced by p
public void insertAfter(ObjectListNode p, ObjectListNode q) {
    if (list == null || p == null || q == null) {
        System.out.println("Runtime Error: insertAfter()");
        System.exit(1);
    }
    q.setNext(p.getNext());
    p.setNext(q);
    if (last.getNext() != null)
        last = q;
}
```

```java
    // Deletes the node after the node referenced by p
    public Object deleteAfter(ObjectListNode p) {
        if (list == null || p == null || p.getNext() == null) {
            System.out.println("Runtime Error: deleteAfter()");
            System.exit(1);
        }
        ObjectListNode q = p.getNext();
        p.setNext(q.getNext());
        if (p.getNext() == null)
            last = p;
        return q.getInfo();
    }


    // Inserts an item into its correct location within an ordered list
    public void insert(Object o) {
        ObjectListNode p = list;
        ObjectListNode q = null;
        while (p != null && ((Comparable)o).compareTo(p.getInfo()) > 0)
        {

            q = p;
            p = p.getNext();
        }
        if (q == null)
            addFirst(o);
        else
            insertAfter(q, o);
    }


    // Inserts an item into its correct location within an ordered list
    public void insert(ObjectListNode r) {
        ObjectListNode p = list;
        ObjectListNode q = null;
        while (p != null &&
                ((Comparable)r.getInfo()).compareTo(p.getInfo()) > 0) {
            q = p;
            p = p.getNext();
        }
        if (q == null)
            addFirst(r);
        else
            insertAfter(q, r);
    }
```

```java
// Removes the first occurrence of an item in a list
public Object remove(Object o) {
    ObjectListNode p = list;
    ObjectListNode q = null;
    while (p != null && ((Comparable)o).compareTo(p.getInfo()) !=
                                                                 0) {

        q = p;
        p = p.getNext();
    }
    if (p == null)
        return null;
    else return q == null ? removeFirst() : deleteAfter(q);
}


// Returns true if the item is found in the list
public boolean contains(Object o) {
    ObjectListNode p = list;
    while (p != null && ((Comparable)o).compareTo(p.getInfo()) !=
                                                                0)

        p = p.getNext();
    return p != null;
}



// Returns a reference to the node with the requested value
// Returns null otherwise
public ObjectListNode select(Object o) {
    ObjectListNode p = list;
    while (p != null)
        if (((Comparable)o).compareTo(p.getInfo()) == 0)
            return p;
        else
            p = p.getNext();
    return null;
}


// Determines whether or not a list is empty
public boolean isEmpty() {
    return list == null;
}


// Removes all elements from a list
public void clear() {
    list = null;
    last = null;
}
```

```java
        // Returns the number of elements in the list
    public int size() {
        int count = 0;
        ObjectListNode p = list;
        while (p != null) {
            ++count;
            p = p.getNext();
        }
        return count;
    }


        // Makes a copy of a list
    public ObjectList copyList() {
        ObjectListNode p = null;
        ObjectListNode q = null; // to satisfy compiler;
        ObjectListNode r = list;

        if (isEmpty())
            return null;
        ObjectList newList = new ObjectList();
        while (r != null) {
            p = new ObjectListNode(r.getInfo());
            if (newList.isEmpty())
                newList.addFirst(p);
            else
                q.setNext(p);
            q = p;
            r = r.getNext();
        }
        newList.last = p;
        return newList;
    }

        // Reverses a list
    public void reverse() {
        ObjectListNode p = list;
        ObjectListNode q = null;
        ObjectListNode r;

        while (p != null) {
            r = q;
            q = p;
            p = p.getNext();
            q.setNext(r);
        }
        last = list;
        list = q;
    }
}
```

Time Complexity for Linear Linked Lists

	Average Case	Worst Case
Insert:	O(1)	O(1)
Delete:	O(1)	O(1)
Search:	O(n)	O(n)

Addition of Polynomials

In order to find a suitable representation for a polynomial (in one variable), we must distinguish between coefficients and exponents within each term of the polynomial. We shall first create a `Term` class whose objects contain a coefficient and exponent as shown below:

coefficient	exponent

These `Term` objects will be then attached to nodes in a linear linked list as follows:

coefficient	exponent	link to next term

So, for example:

$3X^2$ would be represented as:

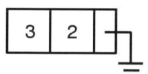

X^4 would be represented as:

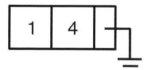

5 would be represented as:

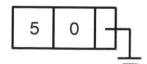

$3X^5 - 2X^3 + X^2 + 4$ would be represented as:

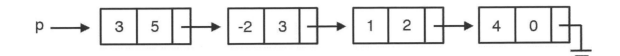

Polynomial Representation

Note the following three preconditions for representing a polynomial as a linear linked list:

Terms must be stored in order of decreasing exponent within the linear linked list.

No two terms may have the same exponent.

No term may have a zero coefficient.

Each node of the linear linked list will contain a `Term` object that represents one term of the polynomial. Shown below are the `Term` class declaration and constructors:

```
// Term.java
public class Term   {
    private int coeff;
    private int exp;


    // Creates a term with a coefficient and an exponent.
    public Term(int c, int e) {
        coeff = c;
        exp = e;
    }
}
```

Next we present methods to access the fields of the `Term` object:

```
    // Sets a value for the coefficient of the term.
    public void setCoeff(int c) {
        coeff = c;
    }

    // Returns the coefficient of the term.
    public int getCoeff() {
        return coeff;
    }

    // Sets a value for the exponent of the term.
    public void setExpon(int e) {
        exp = e;
    }

    // Returns the exponent of the term.
    public int getExpon() {
        return exp;
    }
}
```

Adding Two Polynomials

To add two polynomials together, we only must scan through them once each:

• If we find terms with the same exponent in the two polynomials, then we add the coefficients and copy the new term to the end of the `sum` polynomial; otherwise we copy the term with the larger exponent into the `sum` polynomial and continue.

• When we reach the end of one of the polynomials, we copy the remaining part of the other to the `sum` polynomial.

• We must be careful not to include terms with a 0 coefficient in the `sum` polynomial.

For example:

$$
\begin{array}{rcrcrcrcrcrcr}
6X^5 & + & 2X^4 & + & 3X^3 & & & + & 2x & & & & \\
+ & & & & & & & & & & & & \\
3X^5 & - & 2X^4 & & & - & 5X^2 & - & 8X & + & 7 & & \\
\hline
9X^5 & & & + & 3X^3 & - & 5X^2 & - & 6X & + & 7 & &
\end{array}
$$

Shown below is the `AddPolys` class declaration, class variable declaration, and class constructor:

```
// AddPolys.java
public class AddPolys {
    private ObjectList sum;

    // Constructs a new AddPoly list.
    public AddPolys() {
        sum = new ObjectList();
    }
```

At several locations in the addition algorithm, we must create a new term with given coefficient and exponent and place it at the end of the `sum` polynomial. This is accomplished by the `attach` method shown below:

```
    // Attaches a new term to the end of the sum list.
    private void attach(int coeff, int exp) {
        Term t = new Term(coeff, exp);
        sum.addLast(t);
    }
```

Shown below is the method, sumTwoPolys, which adds the two polynomials and creates a third sum polynomial that is also represented as a linear linked list:

```
// Adds two polynomial linked lists
public ObjectList sumTwoPolys(ObjectList list1, ObjectList list2) {
    ObjectListNode p = list1.getFirstNode();
    ObjectListNode q = list2.getFirstNode();

    while (p != null && q != null) {
        Term t1 = (Term) p.getInfo();
        Term t2 = (Term) q.getInfo();
        if (t1.getExpon() == t2.getExpon()) {
            int coeff = t1.getCoeff() + t2.getCoeff();
            if (coeff != 0)
                attach(coeff, t1.getExpon());
            p = p.getNext();
            q = q.getNext();
        }
        else if (t1.getExpon() > t2.getExpon()) {
            attach(t1.getCoeff(), t1.getExpon());
            p = p.getNext();
        }
        else {
            attach(t2.getCoeff(), t2.getExpon());
            q = q.getNext();
        }
    }
    while (p != null) {
        Term t1 = (Term) p.getInfo();
        attach(t1.getCoeff(), t1.getExpon());
        p = p.getNext();
    }
    while (q != null) {
        Term t2 = (Term) q.getInfo();
        attach(t2.getCoeff(), t2.getExpon());
        q = q.getNext();
    }
    return sum;
}
```

Other operations on polynomials can be programmed as methods of the same general nature as our method for addition.

For extra credit, see if you can do the following:

- Write a method that will input a sequence of coefficients and exponents and form them into a linked polynomial as described earlier.

- Write a method that will subtract two polynomials.

- Write a method that will compute the first, second, and third derivative of a polynomial.

- Write a method that will multiply a polynomial by a scalar.

- Write a method that, given a polynomial and an integer, evaluates the polynomial at that number.

- Write a method that will print a polynomial as a sequence of coefficients and exponents, arranged attractively.

Be sure to include an appropriate driver for your code and send all program output to `csis.txt` for submission.

Circular Linked Lists

One of the shortcomings of a linear linked list is that if we are given a reference p to a node in a linear linked list, we cannot easily reach any of the nodes that precede the node referenced by p.

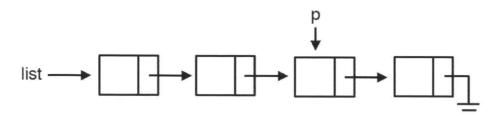

In a circular linked list, the next field in the last node in the list contains a reference back to the first node in the list rather than the `null` pointer. From any point in the circular list it is thus possible to easily reach any other point in the list. This can be useful when there is a need to access data in a circular (wrap-around) fashion.

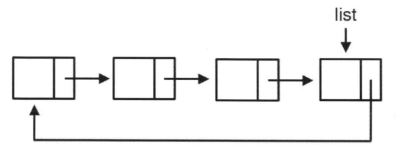

Note that a circular list has no natural first or last node. Therefore we have a convention that the external reference of a circular list references the last node in the list and the following node is therefore the first node of the list. This allows a single reference quick access to the last node in the list as well as to the first node in the list. Note that `list` references the last node and `list.getNext()` references the first node in the list. We then need only this one reference to add or to delete from either end of the list.

Circular linked lists are often used in the task maintenance of operating systems. The idea is that we are not bothered resetting a reference to the start of a list when we reach the end of the list. For example, suppose you select `File` menu in any program in Windows, then you press right arrow several times to reach the end menu `Help`. After you reach `Help` and you press right several times, you'll get to `File` menu again, even if you don't press the left arrow at all. The reference was able to simply loop back around.

Circular List Representation

Presented below are algorithms to manipulate circular linked lists. Once again, work through each algorithm, drawing pictures in each step to ensure their correctness.

```java
// CLL.java

public class CLL {
    private ObjectListNode list;

    // Constructs an empty circular linked list
    public CLL() {
        list = null;
    }

    // Adds the given element to the beginning of the circular list.
    public void addFirst(Object o) {
        ObjectListNode p = new ObjectListNode(o);
        if (list == null) {
            p.setNext(p);
            list = p;
        }
        else {
            p.setNext(list.getNext());
            list.setNext(p);
        }
    }

    // Appends the given element to the end of the circular list.
    public void addLast(Object o) {
        ObjectListNode p = new ObjectListNode(o);
        if (list == null)
            p.setNext(p);
        else {
            p.setNext(list.getNext());
            list.setNext(p);
        }
        list = p;
    }
```

```java
// Removes and returns the first element from the circular list
public Object removeFirst() {
    if (list == null) {
        System.out.println("Runtime Error: removeFront()");
        System.exit(1);
    }
    ObjectListNode p = list.getNext();
    if (p == list)
        list = null;
    else
        list.setNext(p.getNext());
    return p.getInfo();
}


// Removes and returns the last element from the circular list
public Object removeLast() {
    if (list == null) {
        System.out.println("Runtime Error: removeLast()");
        System.exit(1);
    }
    ObjectListNode p = list;
    ObjectListNode q = list;
    while (p.getNext() != list)
        p = p.getNext();
    if (p == list)
        list = null;
    else {
        p.setNext(list.getNext());
        list = p;
    }
    return q.getInfo();
}
}
```

Circular List Representation of Queues

It is easier to represent a queue as a circular linked list than as a linear linked list. In a linear linked list, the queue is specified by two references, one to the front and one to the rear of the list. In a circular list, the queue is specified by a single reference to the list.

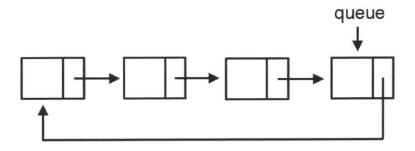

queue

Note that `queue` represents the rear of the queue and `queue.getNext()` represents the front of the queue.

Algorithms are presented below to show the representation of a queue. Please work through each algorithm, drawing pictures in each step to ensure their correctness. The `insert` operation should work with a queue that is either empty or non-empty, while the `remove` operation should work with a queue containing multiple elements or a single element.

```
// Queue.java - Queue represented as a circular linked list.

public class Queue {
    private ObjectListNode queue;

    // Constructs an empty queue
    public Queue() {
        queue = null;
    }

    // Inserts an item into a queue represented by a circular list.
    public void insert(Object o) {
        ObjectListNode p = new ObjectListNode(o);
        if (queue == null)
            p.setNext(p);
        else {
            p.setNext(queue.getNext());
            queue.setNext(p);
        }
        queue = p;
    }
```

```java
    // Removes an item from a queue represented by a circular list.
    public Object remove() {
        if (queue == null) {
            System.out.println("Runtime Error: Queue Underflow.");
            System.exit(1);
        }
        ObjectListNode p = queue.getNext();
        if (p == queue)
            queue = null;
        else
            queue.setNext(p.getNext());
        return p.getInfo();
    }
}
```

Doubly Linked Lists

In a singly linked list each node references the next node in the list:

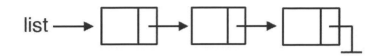

Thus to find a particular node, we traverse the node starting at the beginning of the list and visit each node in turn. A singly linked list can only be traversed in the direction in which the nodes are linked. Some operations are awkward with a singly linked list. For example, to remove an item, you may need to traverse the entire list to locate the item that came before the item you are removing in order to modify its `next` reference.

A doubly linked list, on the other hand, has two reference fields in each node, `next` and `back`.

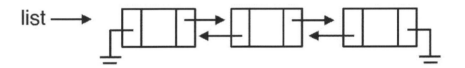

The `next` reference is used to traverse the list from left to right (that is, from beginning to end). The `back` reference is used back up to the left whenever that is desired. One can thus traverse a doubly linked list in both the forward and backward directions while using only one reference.

Note that the next field of the last node in the list as well as the back node of the first node in the list contains `null`.

The use of a doubly linked list can make coding simpler, for example, when writing a sequential search function to find a given node in the list, with the plan that we will use this to find the node after which to insert a new node. With a singly linked list we needed to return both a reference to the node found and a reference to the previous node. With a doubly linked list it suffices to return a reference to the matching node, since we can always follow its `back` field to access the previous node.

Additionally, we can delete a node in a doubly linked list given only a reference to the node to be deleted.

Shown below is the declaration of the Node class and Node class constructors:

```
public class DLLNode {
    private Object info;
    private DLLNode next;
    private DLLNode back;

    // Constructs an empty node.
    public DLLNode() {
        info = null;
        next = null;
        back = null;
    }

    // Constructs a node with an element in the info field.
    public DLLNode (Object o) {
        info = o;
        next = null;
        back = null;
    }

    // Constructs a node with an element in an info field and a
    // reference to a node in the next field and back field.
    public DLLNode (Object o, DLLNode p, DLLNode q) {
        info = o;
        next = p;
        back = q;
    }
```

We present the methods to access the fields of the DLLNode class:

```
    // Assigns an element to the info field of the node.
    public void setInfo(Object o) {
        info = o;
    }

    // Returns the element in the info field of the node.
    public Object getInfo() {
        return info;
    }

    // Sets DLLNode p to the next field of the node.
    public void setNext(DLLNode p) {
        next = p;
    }
```

```
    // Returns the next field of the node.
    public DLLNode getNext() {
        return next;
    }

    // Sets Node p to the back field of the node.
    public void setBack(DLLNode p) {
        back = p;
    }

    // Returns the back field of the node.
    public DLLNode getBack() {
        return back;
    }
}
```

The doubly linked list, DLL, class methods are presented below. Work through each algorithm, drawing pictures in each step to ensure their correctness.

```
// DLL.java

public class DLL {
    private DLLNode list;

    // Constructs an empty doubly linked list
    public DLL() {
        list = null;
    }

    // Removes the node in the double linked list referenced by p.
    public Object remove(DLLNode p) {
        if (p == null || list == null) {
            System.out.println("Runtime Error: remove()");
            System.exit(1);
        }
        DLLNode q = p.getBack();
        DLLNode r = p.getNext();
        if (q == null)
            list = r;
        else
            q.setNext(r);
        if (r != null)
            r.setBack(q);
        return p.getInfo();
    }
```

```java
// Insert a node to the left of the node referenced by p in a
// non-empty doubly linked list.
public void insertLeft(DLLNode p, Object o) {
    DLLNode r;

    if (list == null || p == null) {
        System.out.println("Runtime Error: insertLeft()");
        System.exit(1);
    }
    DLLNode q = new DLLNode(o);
    r = p.getBack();
    if (r != null)
        r.setNext(q);
    q.setBack(r);
    q.setNext(p);
    p.setBack(q);
    if (list == p)
        list = q;
}

// Insert a node to the right of the node referenced by p in a
// non-empty doubly linked list.
public void insertRight(DLLNode p, Object o) {
    DLLNode r;

    if (list == null || p == null) {
        System.out.println("Runtime Error: insertRight()");
        System.exit(1);
    }
    DLLNode q = new DLLNode(o);
    r = p.getNext();
    if (r != null)
        r.setBack(q);
    q.setNext(r);
    q.setBack(p);
    p.setNext(q);
}
}
```

Recursion in Linear Linked Lists

Iterative List Definition
A linear linked list is a list reference that is either `null` or that references a node that contains a reference that is either `null` or that references a node, …, that references a node that contains a `null` reference, denoting the end of the list.

Recursive List Definition
A linear linked list is a list reference which is either `null` or which references a node which contains a reference to a list.

The reason that recursive methods are so appropriate for linear linked lists is that the data structure is itself recursively defined. The definition of a node of a linear linked list below expresses the recursive nature of the data structure:

```
public class ObjectListNode {
    private Object info;
    private ObjectListNode next;
}
```

Note that an `ObjectListNode` is defined in terms of a reference to an `ObjectListNode`.

Rules for Recursion
1. Any problem you can solve recursively can be solved iteratively.

> Corollary: But you might not like to be the person with the job of writing the iterative solution.

2. Recursion tends to be more expensive in terms of machine resources.

3. When recursive solutions are employed, it is usually because they are easier to build and understand than corresponding iterative solutions.

> → In order to understand recursion, you must first understand recursion.

```java
// traverse.java - Iterative List Traversal
public void traverse() {
    ObjectListNode p = list;
    while (p != null) {
        System.out.println(p.getInfo());
        p = p.getNext();
    }
}


// rtraverse.java - Recursive list traversal
public void rtraverse(ObjectListNode list) {
    if (list != null) {
        System.out.println(list.getInfo());
        rtraverse(list.getNext());
    }
}


// btraverse.java - Iterative backwards list traversal
public void btraverse(ObjectListNode list) {
    ObjectStack s = new ObjectStack();

    while(list != null) {
        s.push(list);
        list = list.getNext();
    }
    while (!s.isEmpty()) {
        list = (ObjectListNode) s.pop();
        System.out.println(list.getInfo());
    }
}


// rbTraverse.java - Recursive backwards list traversal
public void rbtraverse(ObjectListNode list) {
    if (list != null) {
        rbtraverse(list.getNext());
        System.out.println(list.getInfo());
    }
}
```

```java
// countNodes.java - Iterative count the number of nodes in a list
public int countNodes(ObjectListNode p) {
    int count = 0;

    while (p != null) {
        ++count;
        p = p.getNext();
    }
    return count;
}


// rcountNodes.java - Recursive count the number of nodes in a list
public int rcountNodes(ObjectListNode p) {
    if (p == null)
        return 0;
    return 1 + rcountNodes(p.getNext());
}
```

❖ Written Homework: Linear Linked Lists

1. Write a pseudocode algorithm to perform each of the operations below. Be sure to draw pictures as you work through each algorithm. You cannot work on linked lists without drawing pictures and the homework will not be accepted without showing the pictures!

a) Determine the number of nodes in a list.

b) Determine the sum of the integers in a list.

c) Append a node to the end of a list.

d) Concatenate two lists.

e) Free all the nodes in a list.

f) Delete the last node from a list.

2. Select three methods in the `ObjectList` class to work through algorithmically. Describe any special cases or boundary conditions that might exist for each of the three methods selected. Be sure to draw pictures as you work through the methods. Remember that you cannot work on linked lists without drawing pictures. The homework will not be accepted without submitting the pictures!

3. Write a Java method with the signature:

```
public ObjectList intersect(ObjectList list1, ObjectList list2)
```

that accepts two unordered ObjectLists and returns a third ObjectList whose nodes contains the intersection of the two original ObjectLists. Note that the intersection of two lists is a new list containing the elements that the two lists have in common, without modifying the two original lists. Describe any boundary conditions that might exist. Be sure to draw pictures.

❖ Computer Lab: Payroll Processing

This assignment will focus on the manipulation of linear linked lists and their associated classes. Construct a Java program that will retrieve, update and manipulate a small payroll database. The payroll data (`payfile.txt`), along with two additional files (`hirefile.txt, firefile.txt`) required for this lab can be found in the appropriate class Canvas folder. The contents of each of the files can be found at the end of this lab.

Note that each line in the file, `payfile.txt`, contains a field for:

- `firstName`
- `lastName`
- `gender`
- `tenure`
- `rate`
- `salary`

Your program should perform each of the operations indicated below. Be sure to clearly label your output for each section and be sure to <u>properly format your output</u>. Note that all salaries should be shown to two decimal places and be sure to line up your decimal points in the table. Your program should send all output to a file called `csis.txt`. This output file will be submitted along with your source code for the lab.

a) Read each line of data from `payfile.txt,` place the data into an `Employee` object, and insert the `Employee` object onto the end of an `ObjectList`.

b) Output the contents of the info field of each `ObjectListNode` into an easily read table format with each field appropriately labeled.

c) Output the number of employees.

d) Output the first and last name of all women on the payroll.

e) Output the first and last names and salary of all weekly employees who make more than $35,000 per year and who have been with the company for at least five years.

f) Give a raise of $.75 per hour to all employees who are paid on an hourly basis and make less than $10.00 per hour; and give a raise of $50.00 per week to all employees who are paid on a weekly basis and make less than $350.00 per week. Be sure to output the first and last names and new salaries for each employee on the payroll who has received a raise.

g) Sort the nodes of the linked list into alphabetical order according to last/first name and print the first and last names and salaries for each employee on the payroll.

h) The file `hirefile.txt` contains data for three employees to be hired by the company. Insert each of the new employees into the correct location in the sorted linear linked list and print the first and last names for each employee on the payroll.

i) The file `firefile.txt` contains data for two employees to be fired by the company. Delete the corresponding nodes in the sorted linear linked list for each of the employees to be fired and print the first and last names for each employee on the payroll.

Here are the data files for the lab:

```
payfile.txt

Howard      Starr          M 8 H     30.00
Joan        Jacobus        F 9 W    925.00
David       Renn           M 3 H      4.75
Albert      Cahana         M 3 H     18.75
Douglas     Sheer          M 5 W    250.00
Shari       Buchman        F 9 W    325.00
Freda       Heller         F 1 H      7.50
Ricky       Mofsen         M 6 H     12.50
Jean        Brennan        F 6 H      5.40
Deborah     Starr          F 3 W   1000.00
Jamie       Michaels       F 8 W    150.00

hirefile.txt

Barry       Allen          M 0 H      6.75
Nina        Pinella        F 0 W    425.00
Lane        Wagger         M 0 W    725.00

firefile.txt

Jean        Brennan
Ricky       Mofsen
```

★ Payroll Lab Note 1: Classes

Be sure you use the `ObjectListNode` and `ObjectList` classes as well as the `Comparable` interface to allow you to make appropriate comparisons in the `ObjectList` class.

Your program should use at least the following classes:

```
ObjectListNode     Driver
ObjectList         Payroll
Employee
```

★ Payroll Lab Note 2: Sorting a Linear Linked List

Here's a simple algorithm to sort a linear linked list:

```
while (list != null)
    remove the first node
    insert node into newList
list = newList
```

★ Payroll Lab Note 3: Program Documentation

I've provided a document on the use of Javadoc that can be found in this link on Canvas:

```
Files | Java Review | Javadoc Program Documentation
```

In particular, note the following guidelines:

• Every class must have a Javadoc class comment.

• Every method must have a Javadoc method comment.

• Every method parameter must have an `@param` tag.
• Every method with a return statement must have an `@return` tag.

• Generate the HTML Javadoc documentation for your project and be sure to submit the folder that contains the Javadoc documentation in the zip archive when submitting the lab.

★ Payroll Lab Note 4: Interfaces

Each data structure in your project must implement an interface for that data structure. The interface files must be included in the zip archive for your code.

★ Payroll Lab Note 5: Class Diagram

Shown below is the class diagram for my solution to the linked list lab.

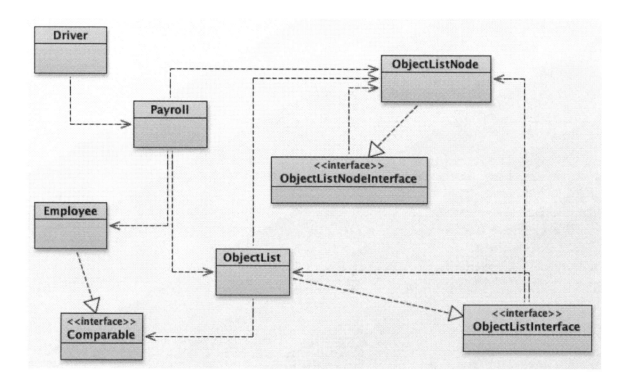

❖ Computer Lab: Calculating Very Large Factorials

This assignment will focus on the manipulation of linear linked lists. You are to write a Java program that queries the user for an integer, n, and returns the exact value of that integer's factorial, n!. The limit to the size of n can be quite large (up to 9,999), producing factorials containing hundreds and thousands of digits. Needless to say, our methodology will circumvent the inherent representation limitations of integers and longs in our programming languages.

The Storage of n!

Factorials will be stored in linear linked lists in which each node contains two fields. The first field, info, will hold an integer containing a value from 0 through 999. The second field, next, holds a reference to the next node in the linear linked list. To be certain that the nature of this storage plan is correctly conceptualized, depicted below are the representations of 10! and 15!:

```
10! = 3,628,800

 -------          -------          -------
|   3   |====> |  628  |====> |  800  |====X
 -------          -------          -------

15! = 1,307,674,368,000

 -------          -------          -------          -------          -------
|   1   |====> |  307  |====> |  674  |====> |  368  |====> |  000  |====X
 -------          -------          -------          -------          -------
```

Note that by storing only three digits per node, the placement of commas in the output is readily accomplished as just another action in stepping from one node to the next.

Multiplication

Suppose that the value of 15! is to be multiplied by 6. The value of 15!, stored in a linked list, is the multiplicand. The 6, stored as an ordinary scalar, is the multiplier. The multiplicand is always held in a linked list, and the multiplier is always a numeral between 0 and 9. The action consists of a sequence of individual multiplications where the number from a nodes info field is multiplied by the fixed multiplier. There are as many individual multiplications as there are nodes in the list holding the multiplicand.

The sequence of individual multiplications yields a sequence of individual products that have to be synthesized into the actual product of the full multiplicand times the multiplier. Realize that the actual product is to be stored in another linked list, identical in form to that of the multiplicand. This is accomplished by treating the thousands digit of each individual product as a "carry out" which is added to the units digit of the individual product from the node to the immediate left. This is perhaps more clearly seen through a concrete example. A diagram of the multiplication of 15! times 6 is shown below:

```
15! = 1,307,674,368,000

 -------       -------       -------       -------       -------
|   1   |====>|  307  |====>|  674  |====>|  368  |====>|  000  |====X
 -------       -------       -------       -------       -------


       1            307           674           368           000
     * 6          * 6           * 6           * 6           * 6
    ----          ----          ----          ----          ----
       6           1842          4044          2208          0|000


     + 1          + 4           + 2           + 0
    ----          ----          ----          ----
  0|007         1|846         4|046         2|208


15! * 6 = 7,846,046,208,000

 -------       -------       -------       -------       -------
|   7   |====>|  846  |====>|  046  |====>|  208  |====>|  000  |====X
 -------       -------       -------       -------       -------
```

A complication to be contended with when implementing this scheme for multiplication is that the individual multiplications have to start at the right-hand end of the multiplicand, which is stored at the rear of the list. In fact, it is necessary to proceed through the list taking the nodes in the reversed order. There are several ways to deal with this. One is to make the multiplicand's list doubly-linked, so that it is just as readily traversed from the rear to the front as from the front to the rear. Another approach is to store the 3-digit numbers in nodes, from front to rear, in the order in which they will need to be processed (instead of the order reflecting conventional representation):

```
15! = 1,307,674,368,000


 -------        -------        -------        -------        -------
| 000 |====> | 368 |====> | 674 |====> | 307 |====> | 001 |====X
 -------        -------        -------        -------        -------
```

A further complication entails extending the multiplication scheme so that it can deal with multiplications like 15! times 16, which is to say multiplications in which a factorial is multiplied by a number with two or more digits. The extension is directly analogous to the paper and pencil multiplication taught in grade school in which the digits in the multiplier are treated one-by-one. Just as each successive digit in the multiplier (i.e., the unit's digit, the ten's digit, the hundred's digit) requires another "round of multiplying" the multiplicand by a numeral (a number between 0 and 9) and another "intermediate product line", so it goes in the extension of the present multiplication scheme.

In implementing the multiplication of 15! times 16, first 15! would be multiplied times 6 and the result stored in a new linked list. Then, 15! would be multiplied times 1 (the numeral in the multiplier's tens place), and this result would be stored in a new linked list of its own. Next, the numerals in the linked list holding the product of 15! times 1 would be shifted one digit to the left, effecting a multiplication by ten to transform the 15! * 1 product to a 15! * 10 product. Lastly, the corresponding digits in the two "helping lists" would be added to give the final result. For example:

```
     15! * 16 =              1307674368000
                                     * 16
                             --------------
                              7846046208000
                              1307674368000
                             --------------
                             20922789888000


  -----      -----      -----      -----      -----
 |001|===>|307|===>|674|===>|368|===>|000|===X         15!
  -----      -----      -----      -----      -----
                                              * 16          * 16
 ------------------------------------------------------------


  -----      -----      -----      -----      -----
 |007|===>|846|===>|046|===>|208|===>|000|===X         15! * 6
  -----      -----      -----      -----      -----


  -----      -----      -----      -----      -----
 |001|===>|307|===>|674|===>|368|===>|000|===X         15! * 1
  -----      -----      -----      -----      -----


  -----      -----      -----      -----      -----
 |013|===>|076|===>|743|===>|680|===>|000|===X         15! * 10 (shifted)
  -----      -----      -----      -----      -----


  -----      -----      -----      -----      -----
 |007|===>|846|===>|046|===>|208|===>|000|===X         15! * 6 (recopied)
  -----      -----      -----      -----      ----

 +

  -----      -----      -----      -----      -----
 |013|===>|076|===>|743|===>|680|===>|000|===X         15! * 10 (recopied)
  -----      -----      -----      -----      -----

  0020      0|922      0|789      0|888      0|000      (sum before carry
                                                        out)

  +  0     +  0       +  0       +  0

  -----      -----      -----      -----      -----
 |020|===>|922|===>|789|===>|888|===>|000|===X         sum
  -----      -----      -----      -----      -----
```

Although the `15!` times `16` example just happens not to show this, provision has to be made for a node-to-node carry when adding the intermediate products in the "helping lists" to get the final result.

Because the program will have to support the multiplication of factorial multiplicands (e.g., `567!`) times three-digit numbers (e.g., `568`), or four-digit numbers, the idea embraced above will have to be enhanced to accommodate up to three or four intermediate products in three or four "helping lists".

General Computational Strategy

Supposed the user wished to calculate `15!`. 15! would be derived in the most straightforward of all possible ways, building it up from one factorial. One factorial, "hard wired" into the program as `1`, would be used as the basis for computing `2!`. Two factorial would be the basis for computing `3!`. This would continue until `14!` and this would be used as the basis for deriving `15!`.

Specification

The program will query the user for an integer, n, and return the exact value of that integer's factorial, $n!$. While there is no reason that there has to be a logical limit to the size of the n the program can handle, your program should be able to handle a number at least as high as `9,999!`.

Since $n!$ may be an integer hundreds or thousands of digits long, its display will spill across several lines. When this happens, print out $n!$ with the most significant digit at the left end of the top line and the units digit on the right-hand end of the number's lowest line. You should print a comma after every third digit (i.e., between the hundred's digit and the thousand's digit, between the hundred thousand's digit and the million's digit, etc.). Break lines at points where commas belong, and put the comma to the right of the number on the line being broken. This signifies that the number continues on the next line. Specifically, print no more than 45 digits per line. Your program should also output statistics on the following:

Number of digits in each factorial

Time, in milliseconds, taken by program to calculate $n!$. Here's a Java method that will be useful for this:

```
static long System.currentTimeMillis()
```

Your program should be run and produce output on the following data:

```
10, 98, 234, 567, 999, 5432, 9999
```

Note: This lab has nothing to do with factorials and the multiplication of numbers. By this I mean that I am NOT looking for a cleaner or more efficient approach to calculating factorials. The goal of this lab is to manipulate linear linked lists using dynamic storage allocation! You are required to implement the algorithm specified.

Be sure to include an appropriate driver for your code and send all program output to `csis.txt` for submission.

Chapter 8. Binary Trees

Introduction to Binary Trees
Binary Search Trees
Binary Tree Traversals – Part 1
Binary Expression Trees
Deletion of a Node from a Binary Search Tree
Binary Tree Representation in Java
Binary Tree Traversals – Part 2
Binary Tree Classes
Object Binary Tree Classes
Dictionary Compression (advanced/optional)
Huffman Code
Splay Trees
Priority Queues
Binary Heaps
Binary Heap Implementation of Priority Queues
BinaryHeap Class
❖ Written Homework: Binary Trees
❖ Computer Lab: Binary Trees and Hashing
❖ Computer Lab: Huffman Codes
❖ Computer Lab: Morse Code

Introduction to Binary Trees

A binary tree is a finite set of elements that is either empty or contains a single element called the *root* of the tree and whose remaining elements are partitioned into two disjoint subsets, each of which is itself a binary tree. These two subsets are called the *left and right subtrees* of the original tree. Each element of a binary tree is called a *node* of the tree.

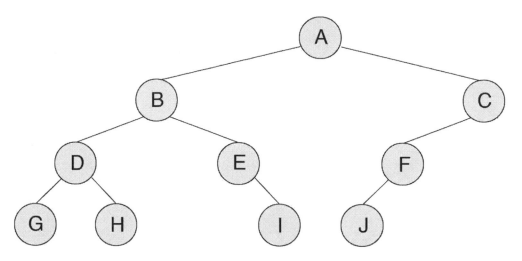

- The binary tree above consists of 10 nodes.

- The tree is rooted at node A.

- The left subtree is rooted at node B.

- The right subtree is rooted at node C.

- Node A is the parent of nodes B and C.

- Node B is the parent of nodes D and E. Node C is the parent of node F.

- Nodes B and C are children of node A. Node B is the left child and node C is the right child of node A.

- Node D is the left child and node E is the right child of node B.

- Node A is the ancestor of nodes B, C, D, E, F, G, H, I and J.

- Nodes B, C, D, E, F, G, H, I and J are descendants of node A.

- Node C is the ancestor of nodes F and J.

- Nodes F and J are descendants of node C.

- Nodes B and C are siblings. Nodes D and E are siblings. Nodes G and H are siblings.

- The absence of a branch indicates an empty subtree. For example, the right subtree of the binary tree rooted at C is empty. The left subtree of the binary tree rooted at E is empty. The right subtree of the tree rooted at F is empty.

- The binary trees rooted at G, H, I and J have empty left and right subtrees. Nodes with empty left and right subtrees (i.e., nodes that have no children) are called *leaves* of the binary tree.

Examples of Binary Trees

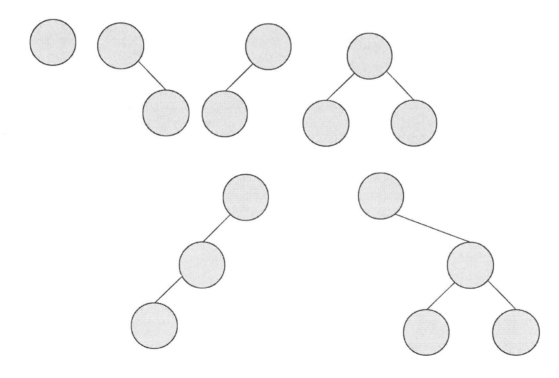

Examples of Incorrect Binary Trees
The following are not binary trees. Can you see why?

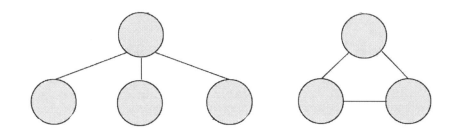

The Level of a Node of a Binary Tree
The level of a node of a binary tree is equal to zero if the node is the root of the binary tree. If the node is not the root then the level of the node is equal to the level of the parent node plus 1.

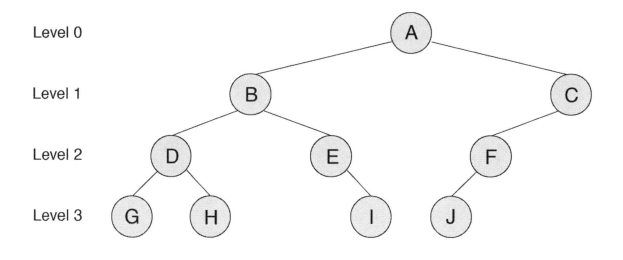

Level 0

Level 1

Level 2

Level 3

The Level of a Binary Tree

The level n of a binary tree is equal to the level of the leaf with the greatest level. The level of the above tree is therefore equal to 3.

Complete Binary Tree of Level n

A complete binary tree of level n is a binary tree in which every level $< n$ is completely filled. All leaves at level n appear towards the left of the tree. Complete binary trees are used to implement binary heaps and will be soon be discussed in greater detail.

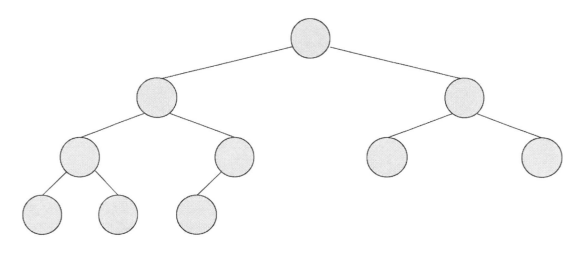

Perfect Binary Tree of Level n

A perfect binary tree of level n is one in which each node of level n is a leaf and in which each node of level less than n has non-empty left and right subtrees.

- Perfect binary tree of level 3:

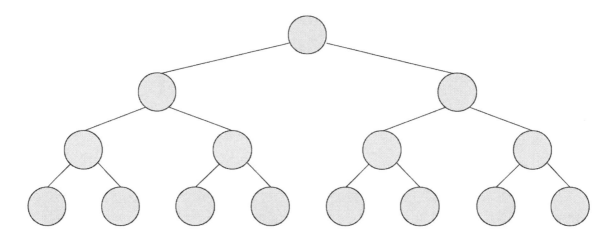

- Perfect binary tree of level 2:

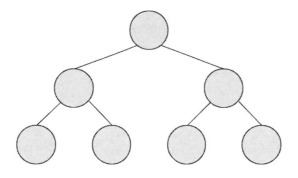

- Perfect binary tree of level 1:

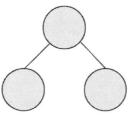

- Perfect binary tree of level 0:

Let's count the number of nodes in a perfect binary tree:

Level	Nodes
0	1
1	3
2	7
3	15
n	$2^{n+1} - 1$

Provided the tree maintains a full shape, the path length from root to leaf, or the height of the tree, will be at most:

$\log_2 n + 1$

where n is the total number of nodes in the tree.

Therefore, if $n = 1024$, the linked list may require as many as 1024 comparisons to make an insertion. But because $\log_2 1024 = 10$, the full binary tree method will require at most 11 comparisons.

This difference becomes even more dramatic as n gets larger. For an ordered list with 1,000,000 entries, a linked list may require that many comparisons whereas a perfect binary trees would require a mere 20 comparisons as:

$\log_2 1000000 = 20.$

Binary Search Trees

Binary search trees are good for storing information you must search through.

> A binary search tree is a binary tree such that each node is greater than any node in its left subtree and less than any node in its right subtree. In other words, a binary search tree is a binary tree that is organized in such a way that each parent is greater than its left child and less than its right child.

Of course, all of this implies that the data items in the tree nodes can be ordered by some sort of comparison. For numbers this can obviously be done. For strings, alphabetical ordering is often used. For records of data, a comparison based on a particular field (the key field) is often used.

The binary tree shown below is an example of a binary search tree:

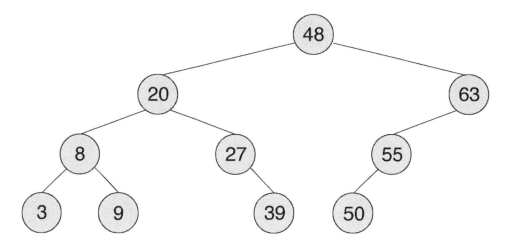

Note that every left child of a parent node is less than the parent node and every right child of a parent node is greater than the parent node.

Searching Through a Binary Search Tree

It is possible to locate a node of the binary search tree by starting at the root and preceding along a search path switching to a nodes left or right subtree by a decision based on inspection of that nodes data value.

For example, let's search the binary search tree below for the data value **9**:

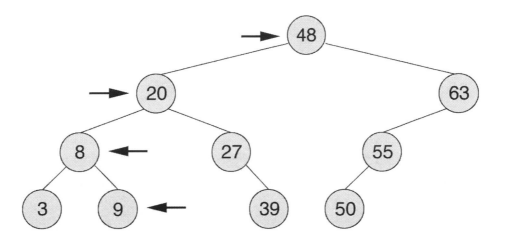

- Starting at the root we find that $9 < 48$ so we move to the left subtree.

- $9 < 20$ - We again move to the left subtree.

- $9 > 8$ - We move to the right subtree.

- $9 = 9$ - We've found the node that contains our data value

Binary Search Tree Height

The height of a binary search tree clearly depends on the tree's shape. In fact, searching through a binary search tree takes a time proportional to the average height of the tree.

We find that n elements may be organized in a binary tree of a height as little as $\log_2 n$. Therefore a search among n items may be performed with as few as $\log_2 n$ comparisons if the tree is perfectly balanced.

Building a Binary Search Tree
Let's go through the steps of building a binary search tree given the data values:

6 - 4 - 8 - 7 - 5 - 9 - 3

• Read data value 6:
The first data value 6 becomes the root of the binary search tree.

6

• Read data value 4:
4 < 6 so 4 becomes the left child of 6.

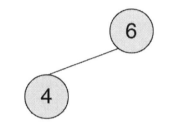

• Read data value 8:
8 > 6 so 8 becomes the right child of 6.

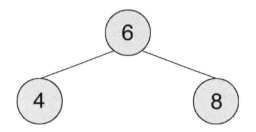

• Read data value 7:

7 > 6 but 7 < 8 so 7 becomes a left child of 8.

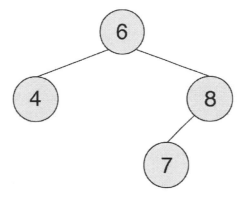

• Read data value 5:

5 < 6 but 5 > 4 so 5 becomes a right child of 4.

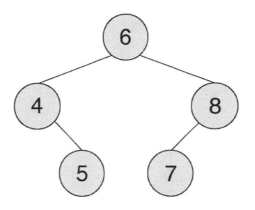

• Read data value 9:

9 > 6 and 9 > 8 so 9 becomes a right child of 8.

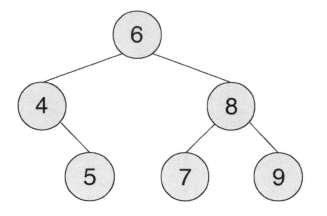

• Read data value 3:

3 < 6 and 3 < 4 so 3 becomes a left child of 4.

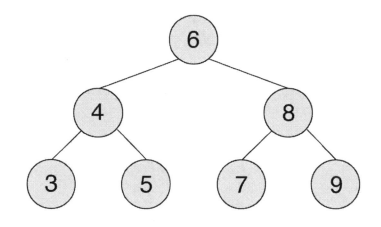

Now that we've built the binary search tree, let's search for the data value 9:

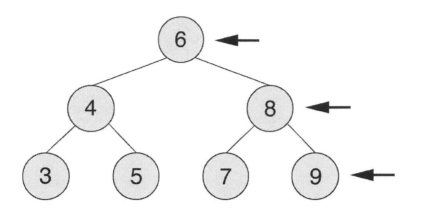

Note that it takes 3 comparisons to find our data value, whereas it would have taken 7 comparisons to find the data value is the data were stored within a linear linked list.

Binary Search Tree Examples
Build a binary search tree with the following data values:

- 6 – 8 – 3 – 4 – 9 – 7 – 1 – 2 – 5

- 4 – 6 – 8 – 3 – 5 – 9 – 7 – 1 - 2

- 1 – 2 – 3 – 4 – 5 – 6 – 7 – 8 – 9

Note that the tree produced by this last sequence of data values is referred to as a degenerate tree. Its shape is that of a linear linked list and its search time is that of a sequential search.

Binary Tree Traversals – Part 1

Traversing a binary tree means passing through the tree enumerating each if its nodes, i.e., visiting each of the nodes of a binary tree. Visiting a node of a binary tree allows us to process each of the nodes' data value, or perhaps just printing out its data value.

There are several well-known ways to traverse a binary tree. We will look at three of them:

• **Preorder Traversal**

Visit the root.
Traverse the left subtree in preorder.
Traverse the right subtree in preorder.

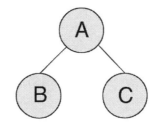

A preorder traversal of the above tree visits the nodes in the following order:

A - B - C

• Inorder Traversal

> Traverse the left subtree in inorder.
> Visit the root.
> Traverse the right subtree in inorder.

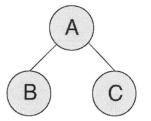

An inorder traversal of the above tree visits the nodes in the following order:

```
B - A - C
```

• Postorder Traversal

> Traverse the left subtree in postorder.
> Traverse the right subtree in postorder.
> Visit the root.

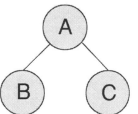

A postorder traversal of the above tree visits the nodes in the following order:

```
B - C - A
```

Note the recursive nature of these traversal definitions.

Walking the Tree

A simple procedure to perform tree traversals is to *walk the tree*.

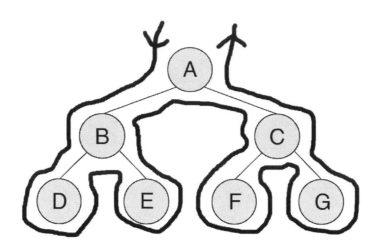

If we walk the tree and visit each node on the left, we perform a preorder traversal. If we walk the tree and visit each node on the bottom, we perform an inorder traversal. If we walk the tree and visit each node on the right, we perform a postorder traversal.

Exercises

1. Perform preorder, inorder, and postorder traversals of the following tree:

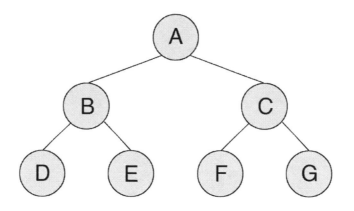

Preorder: A – B – D – E – C – F – G

Inorder: D – B – E – A – F – C – G

Postorder: D – E – B – F – G – C – A

2. Perform preorder, inorder, and postorder traversals of the following tree:

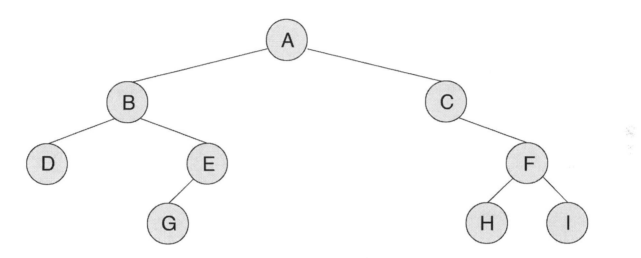

Preorder: A – B – D – E – G – C – F – H – I

Inorder: D – B – G – E – A – C – H – F - I

Postorder: D – G – E – B – H – I – F – C – A

3. Perform preorder, inorder, and postorder traversals of the following tree:

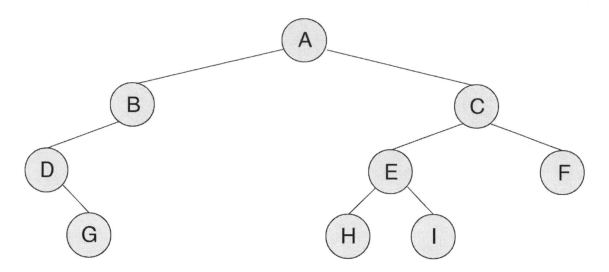

Preorder: A – B – D – G – C – E – H – I - F

Inorder: D – G – B – A – H – E – I – C - F

Postorder: G – D – B – H – I – E – F – C – A

4. Given a list of numbers in an input file, perform the operations below.

2 – 3 – 8 – 4 – 6 – 9 – 1 – 5 – 7

• Build a binary search tree from the input data.

• Perform an inorder traversal of the binary search tree.

After completing this last exercise you should discover something VERY interesting regarding an inorder traversal of a binary search tree. If you have not made this discovery after completing this exercise, try the exercise a second time.

Binary Expression Trees

When we write an expression in infix notation, we must depend on some operator precedence scheme and the use of parentheses to describe an expression precisely. We can use a binary tree to represent an expression without the need for parentheses or rules of precedence.

Given the tree below:

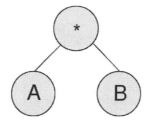

The root contains an operator that is to be applied to the two operands as left and right subtrees.

- a node representing an operator has two non-empty subtrees

- a node representing an operand has two empty subtrees

Given the following infix expression:

```
(8 - 3) * (4 + 1)
```

we can build a binary expression tree as follows:

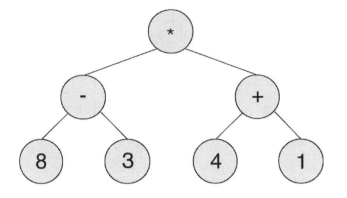

Here the root contains an operator that is to be applied to the results of evaluating the expression represented by the left and right subtrees.

Note that the level of the nodes in the tree indicates the relative precedence of evaluation implicitly. Operations at higher levels of the tree are evaluated later than those below them. The operation at the root is always the last operation to be performed.

Binary Expression Tree Examples

- A + B * C

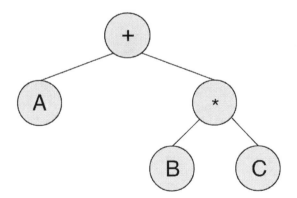

- (A + B) * C

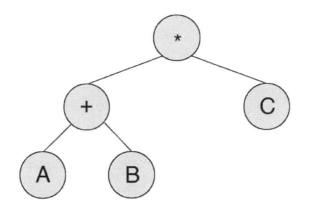

- A + (B - C) * D ^ E

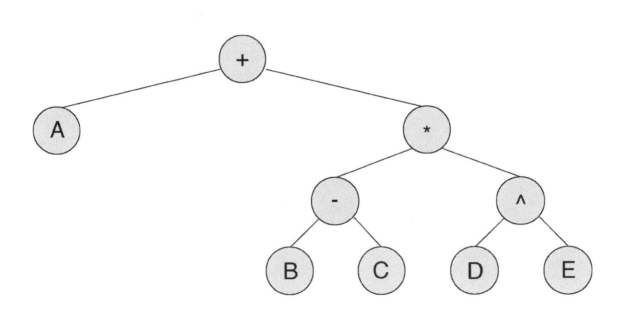

Traversing Binary Expression Trees

What happens when these binary trees expression are traversed?

• Traversing such a tree in preorder means that the operator (the root) will precede its two operands (the subtrees). Therefore, a preorder traversal should yield the prefix form of the expression.

• Traversing such a binary tree in postorder places the operator after its two operands. Therefore, a postorder traversal produces the postfix form of the expression.

What happens when such binary trees are traversed in inorder?

• Since the root (operator) is visited after the nodes of the left subtree and before the nodes of the right subtree (the two operands), we might expect an inorder traversal to yield the infix form of the expression.

However, the binary tree does not contain parentheses since the ordering of the operations is implied by the structure of the tree. Therefore, an expression whose infix form requires parentheses to override explicitly the conventional precedence rules cannot be retrieved by a simple inorder traversal.

Deletion of a Node from a Binary Search Tree

1. Delete a leaf (a node with no children) in a binary search tree.
We need only replace the reference to the node to be deleted by **null** and dispose of the unnecessary node.

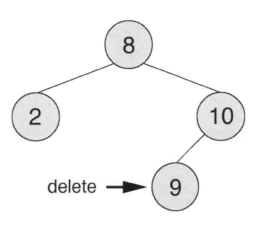

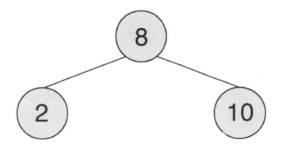

2. Delete a node with only one child in a binary search tree.

To delete a node with only one child, it is necessary to adjust the reference from the parent of the node to be deleted to the child of the node we intend to delete.

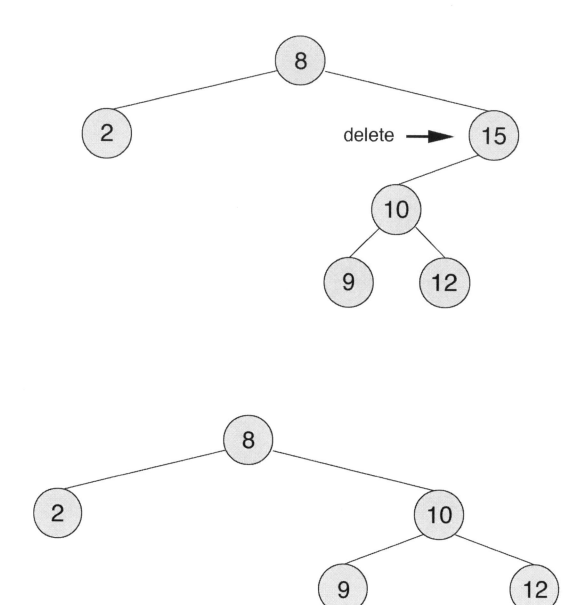

3. Delete node with two children (i.e. two subtrees) in a binary search tree.
What if the node to be deleted has both left and right subtrees. To which of the subtrees should the parent of the deleted item reference? What is to be done with the other subtree? This is the most complicated case since we cannot make the parent of the deleted node reference both of the deleted node's children.

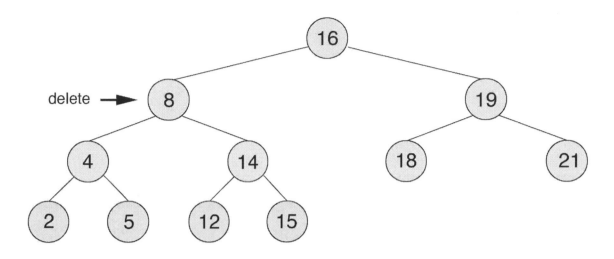

Step one of our solution will be to attach the right subtree in place of the deleted node:

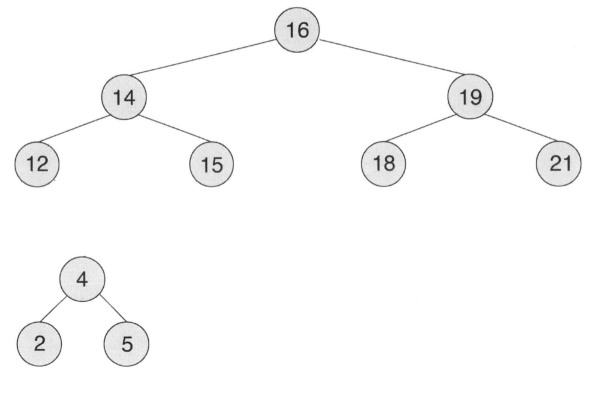

But what do we do with the left subtree?

Step two of our solution will be to attach the left subtree to an appropriate node of the right subtree. But to which node of the right subtree should the former left subtree be attached?

Since every number in the left subtree precedes every other number of the right subtree, it must be as far to the left as possible. This point can be found by taking left branches until an empty left subtree is found.

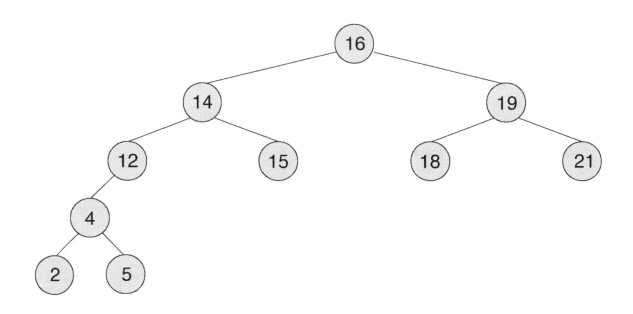

However, there are problems associated with this solution. Do you see how the size or height of the tree has increased? We can make this a bit more dramatic with the following example:

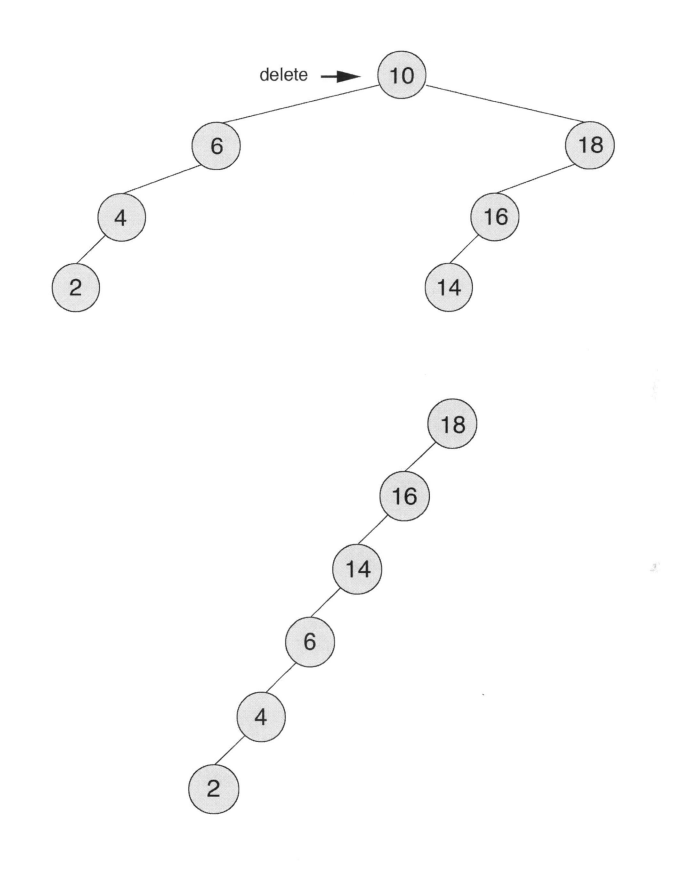

Note that the height of the tree is dramatically increased. Therefore the time required for a later search can subsequently increase even though the total size (total number of nodes) of the tree has decreased.

Better Solution to Delete a Node with Two Children (subtrees)
The inorder successor of the node we want to delete will take the place of the deleted node. The inorder successor, node 12, of the node we want to delete, node 11, is the next node in the tree we would traverse in an inorder traversal of the binary search tree after the node we want to delete.

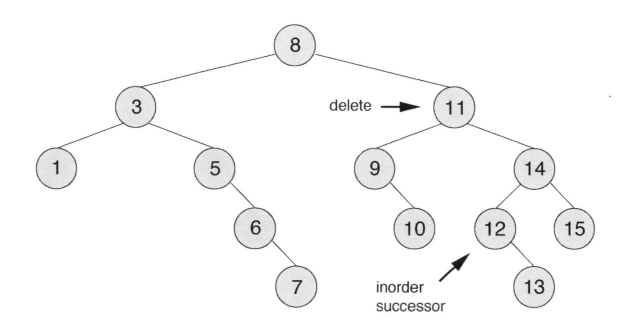

Note that the inorder successor cannot have a left subtree since a left descendant would be the inorder successor of the node we were going to delete.

So the inorder successor of the node we want to delete, node 11, is the next node we would visit in an inorder traversal, namely node 12. Therefore node 12 will take the place of the deleted node and node 12's right child will replace node 12:

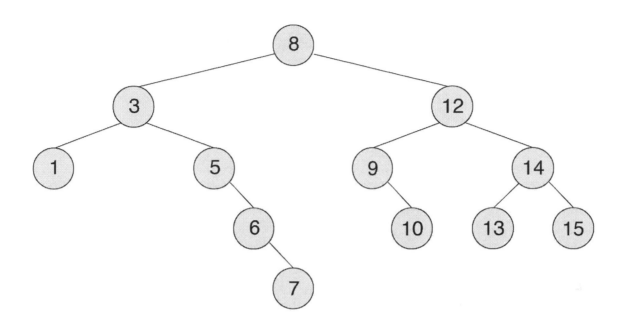

Note that the height of the tree has not changed!

Time Complexity for Binary Search Trees

	Average Case	Worst Case
Insert:	O(log n)	O(n)
Delete:	O(log n)	O(n)
Search:	O(log n)	O(n)

Binary Tree Representation in Java

To represent a node of a binary tree, we create a `TreeNode` class with the following instance variables:

- `info` - information portion of the node
- `left` - reference to the root of the left subtree of the binary tree
- `right` – reference to the root of the right subtree of the binary tree

```
public class TreeNode {
    private int info;
    private TreeNode left;
    private TreeNode right;
```

The left and right fields of a `TreeNode` are references to the roots of its left and right subtrees, respectively. Our newly defined tree node is shown below:

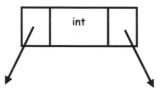

Using our new node representation, a perfect binary tree of level 2 looks like this:

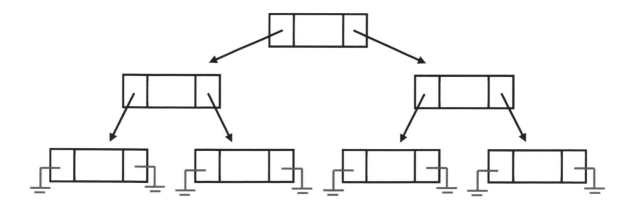

Two constructors are presented for the `TreeNode` class:

```
public TreeNode() {
    info = 0;
    left = null;
    right = null;
}

public TreeNode (int i) {
    info = i;
    left = null;
    right = null;
}
```

We implement the following primitive operations as accessor methods for the `TreeNode` class:

```
    public void setInfo(int i) {
        info = i;
    }

    public int getInfo() {
        return info;
    }

    public void setLeft(TreeNode p) {
        left = p;
    }

    public TreeNode getLeft() {
        return left;
    }

    public void setRight(TreeNode p) {
        right = p;
    }

    public TreeNode getRight() {
        return right;
    }
}
```

BinaryTree Class

We implement the `BinaryTree` class declaration and constructor as follows:

```
public class BinaryTree {
    private TreeNode root;

    public BinaryTree() {
        root = null;
    }
```

We utilize an accessor method to return the root of a binary tree:

```
    public TreeNode getRoot() {
        return root;
    }
```

The `setLeftChild()` and `setRightChild()` methods give a left and right child to a parent node.

```
    public void setLeftChild(TreeNode parent, TreeNode r) {
        if (parent == null || parent.getLeft() != null) {
            System.out.println("Runtime Error: setLeftChild()");
            System.exit(1);
        }
        parent.setLeft(r);
    }

    public void setRightChild(TreeNode parent, TreeNode r) {
        if (parent == null || parent.getRight() != null) {
            System.out.println("Runtime Error: setRightChild()");
            System.exit(1);
        }
        parent.setRight(r);
    }
```

We present a method to insert a node into its correct position in a binary search tree:

```
public void insertBST(int i) {
    TreeNode p, q;
    TreeNode r = new TreeNode(i);
    if (root == null)
        root = r;
    else {
        p = root;
        q = root;
        while (q != null) {
            p = q;
            if (r.getInfo() < p.getInfo())
                q = p.getLeft();
            else
                q = p.getRight();
        }
        if (r.getInfo() < p.getInfo())
            setLeftChild(p, r);
        else
            setRightChild(p, r);
    }
}
```

We also present a method to search a binary search tree for a data value. Note that the return value for this method is a pointer to the appropriate TreeNode if the data value is found. Otherwise null is returned.

```
public TreeNode searchBST(int i) {
    TreeNode p;

    if (root != null) {
        p = root;
        while (p != null) {
            if (i < p.getInfo())
                p = p.getLeft();
            else if (i > p.getInfo())
                p = p.getRight();
            else
                return p;
        }
    }
    return null;
}
```

Binary Tree Traversals – Part 2

There are generally three techniques used to traverse binary trees:

> - recursion
> - stacks
> - threads

Recursive Tree Traversals

Recursive routines to traverse binary trees mirror the traversal definitions previously presented. The parameter to each routine is a reference to the root node of a binary tree.

Preorder Traversal of a Binary Tree

> - visit the root
> - traverse the left subtree in preorder
> - traverse the right subtree in preorder

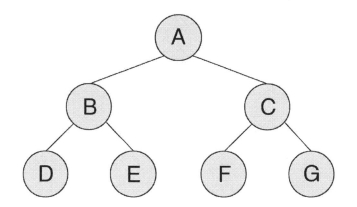

Preorder traversal of this tree yields: A B D E C F G

```
// preorderTraversal.java

public void preTrav(TreeNode tree) {
    if (tree != null) {
        System.out.println(tree.getInfo());
        preTrav(tree.getLeft());
        preTrav(tree.getRight());
    }
}
```

Inorder Traversal of a Binary Tree

- traverse the left subtree in inorder
- visit the root
- traverse the right subtree in inorder

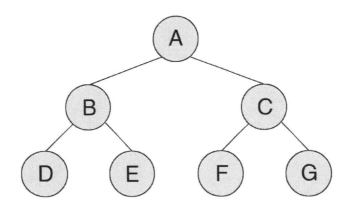

Inorder traversal of this tree yields: D B E A F C G

```
// inorderTraversal.java

public void inTrav(TreeNode tree) {
    if (tree != null) {
        inTrav(tree.getLeft());
        System.out.println(tree.getInfo());
        inTrav(tree.getRight());
    }
}
```

Postorder Traversal of a Binary Tree

- traverse the left subtree in postorder
- traverse the right subtree in postorder
- visit the root

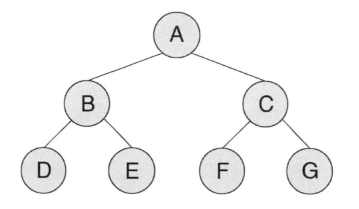

Postorder traversal of this tree yields: D E B F G C A

```
// postorderTraversal.java

public void postTrav(TreeNode tree) {
    if (tree != null) {
        postTrav(tree.getLeft());
        postTrav(tree.getRight());
        System.out.println(tree.getInfo());
    }
}
```

It is left as an exercise to work through the recursive descent and recursive ascent for each of the recursive traversal algorithms.

Iterative Binary Tree Traversals

More efficient non-recursive routines could be written to perform these traversals that explicitly perform the necessary stacking and unstacking operations. However, the algorithms are not quite as elegant!

Inorder traversal of binary trees using stacks (no recursion):

```java
// Inorder traversal using integer stack

public void inTravStack(TreeNode tree) {
    Stack s = new Stack();
    TreeNode p;

    p = tree;
    do {
        while (p != null) {
            s.push(p);
            p = p.getLeft();
        }
        if (!s.isEmpty()) {
            p = s.pop();
            System.out.println(p.getInfo());
            p = p.getRight();
        }
    } while (!s.isEmpty() || p != null)
}
```

It is left as an exercise to work through the stacking and unstacking of the iterative traversal algorithm.

Threaded Binary Tree Traversals

Threads are a type of additional reference added to each node that typically references a nodes inorder successor. Threaded traversal algorithms are beyond the scope of this class.

```java
// TreeNode.java

public class TreeNode {
    private int info;
    private TreeNode left;
    private TreeNode right;

    public TreeNode() {
        info = 0;
        left = null;
        right = null;
    }

    public TreeNode (int i) {
        info = i;
        left = null;
        right = null;
    }

    public void setInfo(int i) {
        info = i;
    }

    public int getInfo() {
        return info;
    }

    public void setLeft(TreeNode p) {
        left = p;
    }

    public TreeNode getLeft() {
        return left;
    }

    public void setRight(TreeNode p) {
        right = p;
    }

    public TreeNode getRight() {
        return right;
    }
}
```

```
public class BinaryTree {
    private TreeNode root;

    public BinaryTree() {
        root = null;
    }

    public TreeNode getRoot() {
        return root;
    }

    public void setLeftChild(TreeNode parent, TreeNode r) {
        if (parent == null || parent.getLeft() != null) {
            System.out.println("Runtime Error: setLeftChild()");
            System.exit(1);
        }
        parent.setLeft(r);
    }

    public void setRightChild(TreeNode parent, TreeNode r) {
        if (parent == null || parent.getRight() != null) {
            System.out.println("Runtime Error: setRightChild()");
            System.exit(1);
        }
        parent.setRight(r);
    }

    public void insertBST(int i) {
        TreeNode p, q;
        TreeNode r = new TreeNode(i);
        if (root == null)
            root = r;
        else {
            p = root;
            q = root;
            while (q != null) {
                p = q;
                if (r.getInfo() < p.getInfo())
                    q = p.getLeft();
                else
                    q = p.getRight();
            }
            if (r.getInfo() < p.getInfo())
                setLeftChild(p, r);
            else
                setRightChild(p, r);
        }
    }
```

```java
    public TreeNode searchBST(int i) {
        TreeNode p;

        If (root != null) {
            p = root;
            while (p != null) {
                if (i < p.getInfo())
                    p = p.getLeft();
                else if (i > p.getInfo())
                    p = p.getRight();
                else
                    return p;
            }
        }
        return null;
    }

    public void preTrav(TreeNode tree) {
        if (tree != null) {
            System.out.println(tree.getInfo());
            preTrav(tree.getLeft());
            preTrav(tree.getRight());
        }
    }

    public void inTrav(TreeNode tree) {
        if (tree != null) {
            inTrav(tree.getLeft());
            System.out.println(tree.getInfo());
            inTrav(tree.getRight());
        }
    }

    public void postTrav(TreeNode tree) {
        if (tree != null) {
            postTrav(tree.getLeft());
            postTrav(tree.getRight());
            System.out.println(tree.getInfo());
        }
    }
}
```

```java
// ObjectTreeNode.java

public class ObjectTreeNode implements ObjectTreeNodeInterface {
    private Object info;
    private ObjectTreeNode left;
    private ObjectTreeNode right;

    public ObjectTreeNode() {
        info = null;
        left = null;
        right = null;
    }

    public ObjectTreeNode (Object o) {
        info = o;
        left = null;
        right = null;
    }

    public void setInfo(Object o) {
        info = o;
    }

    public Object getInfo() {
        return info;
    }

    public void setLeft(ObjectTreeNode p) {
        left = p;
    }

    public ObjectTreeNode getLeft() {
        return left;
    }

    public void setRight(ObjectTreeNode p) {
        right = p;
    }

    public ObjectTreeNode getRight() {
        return right;
    }
}
```

```java
// ObjectTreeNodeInterface.java

public interface ObjectTreeNodeInterface {
    public void setInfo(Object o);
    public Object getInfo();
    public void setLeft(ObjectTreeNode p);
    public ObjectTreeNode getLeft();
    public void setRight(ObjectTreeNode p);
    public ObjectTreeNode getRight();
}


// ObjectBinaryTree.java

public class ObjectBinaryTree implements ObjectBinaryTreeInterface {
    private ObjectTreeNode root;

    public ObjectBinaryTree() {
        root = null;
    }

    public ObjectTreeNode getRoot() {
        return root;
    }

    public void setLeftChild(ObjectTreeNode parent, ObjectTreeNode r) {
        if (parent == null || parent.getLeft() != null) {
            System.out.println("Runtime Error: setLeftChild()");
            System.exit(1);
        }
        parent.setLeft(r);
    }

    public void setRightChild(ObjectTreeNode parent, ObjectTreeNode r){
        if (parent == null || parent.getRight() != null) {
            System.out.println("Runtime Error: setRightChild()");
            System.exit(1);
        }
        parent.setRight(r);
    }
```

```
    public void insertBST(Object o) {
        ObjectTreeNode p, q;

        ObjectTreeNode r = new ObjectTreeNode(o);
        if (root == null)
            root = r;
        else {
            p = root;
            q = root;
            while (q != null) {
                p = q;
                if
(((TreeComparable)(r.getInfo()))).compareTo((TreeComparable)(p.getInfo()
)) < 0 )
                    q = p.getLeft();
                else
                    q = p.getRight();
            }
            if
(((TreeComparable)(r.getInfo()))).compareTo((TreeComparable)(p.getInfo()
)) < 0)
                setLeftChild(p, r);
            else
                setRightChild(p, r);
        }
    }
```

insertBSTDup() will insert an object into a binary search tree and will take specific action on duplicate objects being inserted into the binary search tree. The specific action taken will be defined within the operate() method implemented in the class of objects being inserted into the binary search tree. As with the compareTo() method, the operate() method must be declared in the TreeComparable interface.

```
public void insertBSTDup(Object o) {
    ObjectTreeNode p, q;

    ObjectTreeNode r = new ObjectTreeNode(o);
    if (root == null)                        .
        root = r;
    else {
        p = root;
        q = root;
        while (q != null &&
((TreeComparable)(r.getInfo())).compareTo((TreeComparable)(p.getInfo())
) != 0) {
            p = q;
            if
(((TreeComparable)(r.getInfo())).compareTo((TreeComparable)(p.getInfo()
)) < 0)
                q = p.getLeft();
            else
                q = p.getRight();
        }
        if
(((TreeComparable)(r.getInfo())).compareTo((TreeComparable)(p.getInfo()
)) < 0)
            setLeftChild(p, r);
        else if
(((TreeComparable)(r.getInfo())).compareTo((TreeComparable)(p.getInfo()
)) > 0)
            setRightChild(p, r);
        else
((TreeComparable)(p.getInfo())).operate((TreeComparable)(r.getInfo()));
    }
}
```

In our search BST method below, note that the return value for this method is a pointer to the appropriate `ObjectTreeNode` if the data value is found. Otherwise `null` is returned.

```java
    public ObjectTreeNode searchBST(Object o) {
        ObjectTreeNode p;

        ObjectTreeNode r = new ObjectTreeNode(o);
        if(root != null) {
            p = root;
            while (p != null) {
                if
((((TreeComparable)(r.getInfo()))).compareTo((TreeComparable)(p.getInfo()
)) < 0)
                        p = p.getLeft();
                else if
((((TreeComparable)(r.getInfo()))).compareTo((TreeComparable)(p.getInfo()
)) > 0)
                        p = p.getRight();
                else
                    return p;
            }
        }
        return null;
    }
```

What does it mean to visit the root of a traversal method? Previously, we simply output the integer contents of the `info` field. But as we are now working with objects, we need to specify a `visit()` method that will take appropriate action. Like the `compareTo()` and `operate()` methods, the `visit()` method must be declared in the `TreeComparable` interface and defined within the class of objects being inserted into the binary search tree.

```
public void preTrav(ObjectTreeNode tree) {
    if (tree != null) {
        ((TreeComparable)tree.getInfo()).visit();
        preTrav(tree.getLeft());
        preTrav(tree.getRight());
    }
}

public void inTrav(ObjectTreeNode tree) {
    if (tree != null) {
        inTrav(tree.getLeft());
        ((TreeComparable)tree.getInfo()).visit();
        inTrav(tree.getRight());
    }
}

public void postTrav(ObjectTreeNode tree) {
    if (tree != null) {
        postTrav(tree.getLeft());
        postTrav(tree.getRight());
        ((TreeComparable)tree.getInfo()).visit();
    }
}
```

```
// Deletion of a node of a BST

public void delete(Object o) {
        ObjectTreeNode s, t, v;
        boolean found = false;

        ObjectTreeNode r = new ObjectTreeNode(o);
        ObjectTreeNode p = root;
        ObjectTreeNode q = null;
        // Search for the node with info key, set p to point to
           that node and set q to point to its parent, if any.
        while (p != null && !found) {
            if
(((TreeComparable)(r.getInfo())).compareTo((TreeComparable)(p.getInfo()
)) == 0)
                    found = true;
            else {
                q = p;
                if
(((TreeComparable)(r.getInfo())).compareTo((TreeComparable)(p.getInfo()
)) < 0)
                    p = p.getLeft();
                else
                    p = p.getRight();
            }
        }
        if (found) {
            // Set v to point to the node that will replace the node
            // that p points to.
            if (p.getLeft() == null)
                v = p.getRight();
            else if (p.getRight() == null)
                v = p.getLeft();
            else {
                // the node that p points to has two children;
                // set v to the inorder successor of p;
                // set t to the parent of v
                t = p;
                v = p.getRight();
                s = v.getLeft();   // s is the left child of v
                while (s != null) {
                    t = v;
                    v = s;
                    s = v.getLeft();
                }
```

```
                    // At this point, v is the inorder successor of p
                    if (t != p) {
                        // p is not the parent of v and v = t.getLeft()
                        t.setLeft(v.getRight());
                        // Remove the node that v points to from its
                        // current position to take the place of the
                        // node that p points to.
                        v.setRight(p.getRight());
                    }
                    v.setLeft(p.getLeft());
                }
                // Insert the node that v points to into the position
                // formally occupied by the node that p points to
                if (q == null)
                    // The node that p points to was the root of the tree
                    root = v;
                else if (p == q.getLeft())
                    q.setLeft(v);
                else q.setRight(v);
            }
        }
```

```
// ObjectBinaryTreeInterface.java

public interface ObjectBinaryTreeInterface {
    public ObjectTreeNode getRoot();
    public void setLeftChild(ObjectTreeNode parent, ObjectTreeNode r);
    public void setRightChild(ObjectTreeNode parent, ObjectTreeNode r);
    public void insertBST(Object o);
    public void insertBSTDuplicate(Object o);
    public ObjectTreeNode searchBST(Object o);
    public void preTrav(ObjectTreeNode tree);
    public void inTrav(ObjectTreeNode tree);
    public void postTrav(ObjectTreeNode tree);
}
```

Finally, we have our `TreeComparable` interface:

```
public interface TreeComparable {
    public int compareTo(Object o);
    public void operate(Object o);
    public void visit();
}
```

Huffman Code

A dictionary is normally represented using a fixed alphabet where each character is represented by a fixed-length bit string (e.g. a byte). A statistical encoding scheme takes advantage of the probabilities of occurrence of single characters such that short codes can be used to represent frequently occurring characters while longer codes are used to represent less frequently encountered characters.

The statistical encoding process can be used to minimize the average code length of the encoded data in a manner similar to that in which Morse selected the dot and dash representations of characters. His scheme used a single dot to represent the letter E, which is the most frequently encountered letter in the English language, while longer strings of dots and dashes were used to represent characters that appear less frequently.

Huffman coding is such a statistical data compression technique that takes advantage of the relative probability of occurrence of individual characters such that shorter codes can be used to represent frequently occurring characters while larger codes are used to represent less frequently encountered characters. The effect is to reduce the average code length used to represent the symbols of the alphabet.

The Huffman Tree

The Huffman code can be developed through the development of a tree structure. First, the symbols in our alphabet are listed in descending order of frequency of occurrence:

Code	Character	Probability of Occurrence
	c1	0.50
	c2	0.15
	c3	0.12
	c4	0.10
	c5	0.09
	c6	0.04

Next, the tree combines the two lowest probabilities, 0.09 and 0.04 of characters $c5$ and $c6$, into a node that represents the combined probability of that pair, 0.13.

Code	Character	Probability of Occurrence	
	c1	0.50	
	c2	0.15	
	c3	0.12	
	c4	0.10	
	c5	0.09 ------	
		|-0.13--	
	c6	0.04 ------	

Then the next pair of lowest probabilities, in this case, those of characters c_3 and c_4, is combined into a node of probability 0.22.

Code	Character	Probability of Occurrence		
	c1	0.50		
	c2	0.15		
	c3	0.12 ------		
		|		
		|-0.22--		
		|		
	c4	0.10 ------		
	c5	0.09 ------		
		|		
		|-0.13--		
		|		
	c6	0.04 ------		

The next two nodes of lowest probability numbers are 0.13 (the combined $c5$ and $c6$ nodes) and 0.15, the probability of $c2$. This pair joins into a node with a combined probability of 0.28.

Code	Character	Probability of Occurrence
	c1	0.50
	c2	0.15
	c3	0.12
	c4	0.10
	c5	0.09
	c6	0.04

```
c2    0.15 ----------------
                          |
                          |
                          |
c3    0.12 ------         |
                |         |
                |-0.22--| |
                |         |
c4    0.10 ------         |
                          |-0.28-
                          |
                          |
c5    0.09 ------         |
                |         |
                |-0.13--|
                |
c6    0.04 ------
```

The next two lowest probability nodes are with numbers 0.28 and 0.22. This pair joins into a node with a combined probability of 0.50.

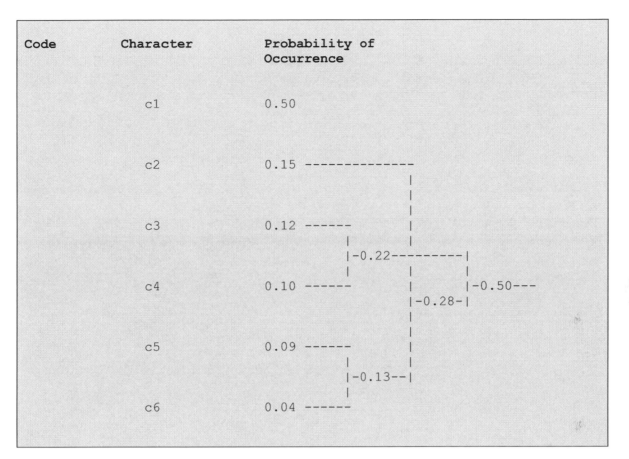

```
Code            Character         Probability of
                                  Occurrence


                   c1             0.50



                   c2             0.15 ---------------
                                                     |
                                                     |
                                                     |
                   c3             0.12 ------         |
                                          |          |
                                          |-0.22---------|
                                          |          |   |
                   c4             0.10 ------         |   |-0.50---
                                                 |-0.28-|
                                                     |
                                                     |
                   c5             0.09 ------         |
                                          |          |
                                          |-0.13--|
                                          |
                   c6             0.04 ------
```

The tree is then completed, by combining the remaining two pairs (0.50 and 0.50), to a node with a combined probability of 1.0 (unity). This final master node represents the probability of occurrence of all six characters in the character set.

```
Code          Character          Probability of
                                 Occurrence


              c1                 0.50 --------------------------------|
                                                                     |
                                                                     |
                                                                     |
              c2                 0.15 ---------------                |
                                                    |                |--1.0
                                                    |                |
                                                    |                |
              c3                 0.12 ------         |                |
                                       |             |                |
                                       |-0.22--------|                |
                                       |             |        |       |
              c4                 0.10 ------          |        |-0.50---|
                                                     |-0.28-|
                                                     |
                                                     |
              c5                 0.09 ------          |
                                       |             |
                                       |-0.13--|
                                       |
              c6                 0.04 ------
```

We have now built a Huffman tree (lying on its side) that can be used to obtain the Huffman codes and compress data. To derive the Huffman code for each character we must first assign binary 0s and 1s to every segment emanating from each node.

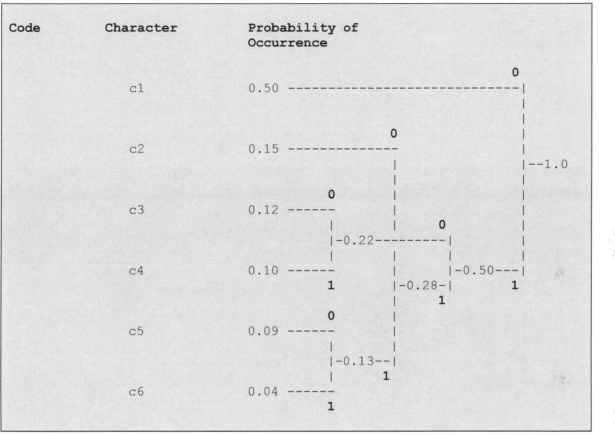

The final step to derive the Huffman code for each character is to trace the Huffman tree from the root (the generated symbol with probability 1) to each character symbol, and assign to each lower branch 1, and to each upper branch 0.

```
Code        Character          Probability of
                               Occurrence

                                                                          0
0           c1                 0.50  ------------------------------|
                                                                         |
                                                                         |
                                                        0                |
110         c2                 0.15  --------------                     |
                                                   |                     |--1.0
                                                   |                     |
                                  0                |                     |
100         c3                 0.12  ------        |                     |
                                        |          |        0            |
                                        |-0.22-----------|                |
                                        |          |        |            |
101         c4                 0.10  ------        |        |-0.50---|
                                       1           |-0.28-|          1
                                                   |        1
                                  0                |
1110        c5                 0.09  ------        |
                                        |          |
                                        |-0.13--|
                                        |        1
1111        c6                 0.04  ------
                                       1
```

Prefix Property

Note that the code for one letter cannot be the prefix of the code of another letter. For example, if the code for a symbol x, c(x), were a prefix of the code of a symbol y, c(y), then when c(x) is encountered, it is unclear whether c(x) represents the symbol x or whether it is the first part of c(y).

In other words, no short code is duplicated as the beginning of a longer code. This means that if one character is represented by the bit combination 100, then 10001 cannot be the code for another letter as 100 is a prefix of 10001. This prefix property of Huffman codes is a crucial property since in scanning the bit stream from left to right the decoding algorithm would interpret the five bits as the 100 bit configuration character followed by perhaps a 01 bit configuration character.

The Huffman tree created above can be redrawn as follows. Note that a 0 appears at every left branch and a 1 at every right branch.

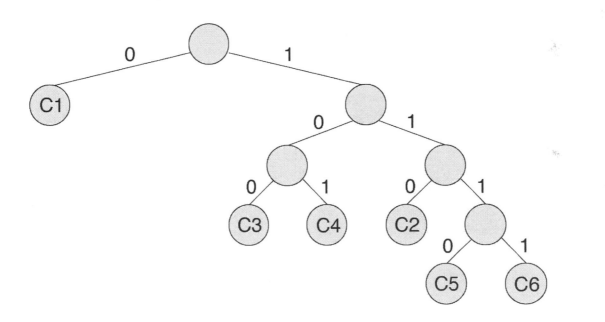

It turns out that encoding data using a Huffman tree is a description of traversing the tree. To calculate the code for a character, we begin at the root and output a 0 when you take a left branch and a 1 when you take a right branch. Repeat until you reach the letter you're encoding, which will always be a leaf (can you explain why).

Encoding a Message

Suppose we wanted to encode the message:

```
c5   c1   c1   c3   c6   c2
```

We would encode $c5$ by starting at the root and them moving to the right branch (1), to the right branch (1), to the right branch (1), and finally to the left branch (0). Note that we stop when we reach the character we wish to encode. So the Huffman code for $c5$ is: 1110. Other characters are thus encoded in a similar fashion.

The final encoding of the character string shown above looks like this:

```
1110001001111110
```

Decoding a Message

A key property of the Huffman code is that it can be instantaneously decoded as the coded bits in the compressed data stream are encountered. This is due to the fact that no code value is the prefix of another. As a result, one can always distinguish successive code values without resorting to delimiters or length codes. However, the loss of a single bit may affect the decoding of all subsequent code values unless decoding is resynchronized in some way.

The compressed data stream:

```
1110001001111110
```

can be decoded by reading the data from left to right, traversing the tree starting at the root, and moving to the left branch when a 0 is encountered and moving to the right branch when a 1 is encountered. Encountering a leaf would represent the corresponding character that's been encoded.

```
Encoded message    1110    0    0    100    1111    110
                    |       |    |    |      |       |
                    |       |    |    |      |       |
Decoded Message     c5      c1   c1   c3     c6      c2
```

Average Bit Length

The average number of bits used to encode each character can be calculated by multiplying the Huffman code lengths (which are inversely proportional to the log of the frequency of the character) by their probability of occurrence. Thus, the code uses:

```
    1 * 0.50
+   3 * 0.15
+   3 * 0.12
+   3 * 0.10
+   4 * 0.09
+   4 * 0.04
```

or 2.13 bits per character.

Another Example

Shown below are the probability of occurrence for letters in a sample 50,000 word dictionary and the actual Huffman codes produced for each letter in the dictionary.

Letter	Probability	Code
e	0.114	100
i	0.084	110
a	0.081	0010
s	0.073	0000
n	0.072	0001
r	0.072	0110
t	0.068	0100
o	0.064	0101
l	0.055	1110
c	0.042	00110
d	0.039	00111
u	0.033	01110
m	0.030	10110
p	0.029	10100
g	0.027	10101
h	0.025	11110
b	0.020	011110
y	0.018	101110
f	0.014	101111
v	0.011	111110
k	0.010	111111
w	0.009	0111110
z	0.003	011111100
x	0.003	011111101
j	0.002	011111110
q	0.002	011111111

We can calculate the average number of bits used to encode each character by multiplying the Huffman Code lengths by their probability of occurrence. Thus, the code uses:

```
3 * 0.114 + 3 * 0.084 + 4 * 0.081 + 4 * 0.073 +
4 * 0.072 + 4 * 0.072 + 4 * 0.068 + 4 * 0.064 +
4 * 0.055 + 5 * 0.042 + 5 * 0.039 + 5 * 0.033 +
5 * 0.030 + 5 * 0.029 + 5 * 0.027 + 5 * 0.025 +
6 * 0.020 + 6 * 0.018 + 6 * 0.014 + 6 * 0.011 +
6 * 0.010 + 7 * 0.009 + 9 * 0.003 + 9 * 0.003 +
9 * 0.002 + 9 * 0.002
```

or 4.25 bits per character; a compression of 46.88%.

Huffman Code Summary

The Huffman encoding scheme pays off only with a skewed character distribution. If all characters appear with the same frequency, the Huffman tree would be perfectly balanced and therefore all characters would require the same number of bits to encode. Therefore no compression would take place. Normally, however, the characters don't appear with the same frequency, so you can compress the file.

Not only does the above scenario produce no net savings, but it actually produces a net loss. If you recall, the Huffman tree is absolutely necessary to decode the data. So not only do you have to transmit the compressed data, but you also must transmit the Huffman tree with the data you're decoding. In the worst case, not only is the data the same size, but you have the added overhead of the Huffman tree. In this case, your file actually gets larger! Therefore your file must be compressed enough to offset the size of the Huffman tree before you can gain from this algorithm.

Splay Trees

A binary search tree is an efficient data structure for searching, inserting or deleting data items. The time requirements for each of these operations is, on average, O(log n). However, as previously discussed, the shape of a binary search tree is completely determined by the order in which the data items are inserted into the tree. A worst-case scenario for building a binary search tree would be when the data items arrive in, or almost in, alphabetical order. This would create a very unbalanced tree whose search time would be that of a linear linked list, O(n).

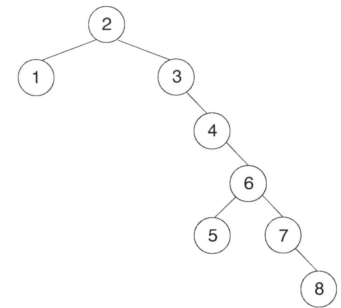

A splay tree is a *self-adjusting* binary search tree that guarantees an average time of O(log n) for any sequence of operations. Although a single operation can have a worst case of O(n), any sequence of operations is guaranteed to behave as if each operation in the sequence exhibited logarithmic behavior, O(log n). This means that you can have a few operations that are very slow. However, most of the operations will be so much faster that they will balance out in the end and you will always get average O(log n) time or better.

Splay trees are designed to give fast access to data items that have been most recently accessed. So if your program is working with a large amount of data, but there's a small number of data items that get accessed over and over again, those data items are going to be accessed much more quickly than the data items that don't get accessed very often. In fact, each of those data items will be accessed in O(1) time, which is actually faster than in an ordinary binary search tree.

Splay Tree Rotations

There are two basic rotations that are performed on a splay tree, a *left rotation* and a *right rotation.*

➡ Rotate Left

Shown below is a tree with node X and parent node P. Note that A, B and C are subtrees such that:

- all data items in subtree A are less than P
- all data items in subtree B are greater than P but less than X
- all data items in subtree C are greater than X

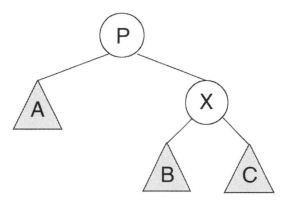

A rotate left operation on node X would move node X up one level in the tree by making node P the left child of node X. Subtree A would remain the left child of node P and subtree C would remain the right child of node X. However, subtree B would now become the right child of node P. Note that all data items in subtree B are greater than P but less than X.

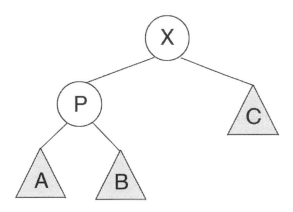

➔Rotate Right
Shown below is a tree with node X and parent node P. Note that A, B and C are subtrees such that:

- all data items in subtree A are less than X
- all data items in subtree B are greater than X but less than P
- all data items in subtree C are greater than P

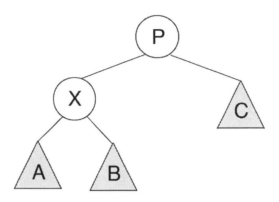

A rotate right operation on node X would move node X up one level in the tree by making node P the right child of node X. Subtree A would remain the left child of node X and subtree C would remain the right child of node P. However, subtree B would now become the left child of node P. Note that all data items in subtree B are greater than X but less than P.

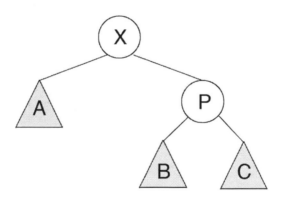

We're going to build our algorithms for rebalancing splay trees entirely out of these two rotations.

Rotation 1: Zig-Zag
A zig-zag rotation is used when the node that we're splaying up to the root is the *left child of a right* child or the *right child of a left child*:

Example: Node X is the left child of a right child:

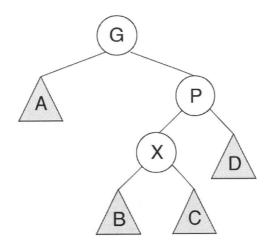

Note that node X is the left child of node P (parent node), and node P is the right child of node G (grandparent node). Note that A, B, C, and D are considered subtrees of the tree. The splay occurs in two steps. The first step is to rotate node X up through its parent, node P, using a rotate right operation:

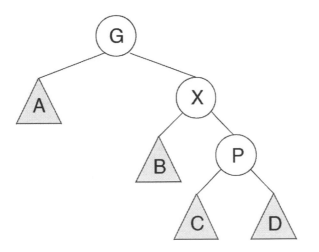

Subtree C, previously a right subtree of node X, is now a left subtree of node P. In both cases, all data items in subtree C is greater than X and less than P.

Next we rotate node X up through what used to be its grandparent, node G, using a rotate left operation:

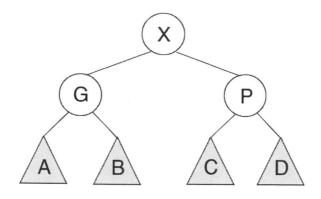

Subtree B, previously a left subtree of node X, is now a right subtree of node G. In both cases, all data items in subtree B is greater than G and less than X. Note that node X has moved two levels up the tree.

Example: Node X is the right child of a left child:

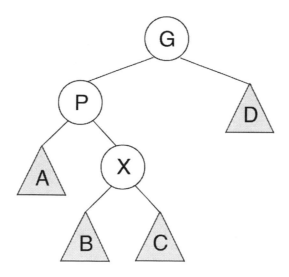

Note that node X is the right child of node P (parent node), and node P is the left child of node G (grandparent node).

Once again the splay occurs in two steps. The first step is to rotate node X up through its parent, node P, using a rotate left operation:

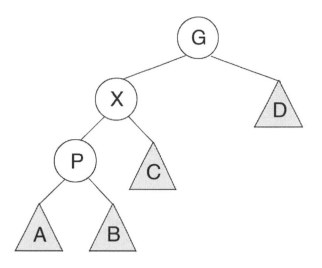

Subtree B, previously a left subtree of node X, is now a right subtree of node P. In both cases, all data items in subtree B are greater than P and less than X.

Next we rotate node X up through what used to be its grandparent, node G, using a rotate right operation:

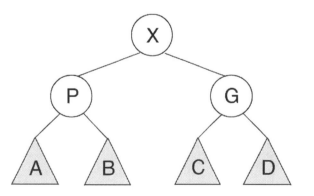

Subtree C, previously a right subtree of node X, is now a left subtree of node G. In both cases, all data items in subtree C is greater than X and less than G. Note that node X has moved up two levels in the tree.

Rotation 2: Zig-Zig
A zig-zig rotation is used when the node that we're splaying up to the root is the *left child of a left* child or the *right child of a right child*:

Example: Node X is the left child of a left child:

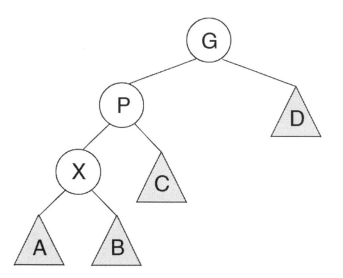

Note that node X is the left child of node P and node P is the left child of node G. Again the splay occurs in two steps. But in this case, *we first splay the parent node P up through the grandparent node using a rotate right operation*:

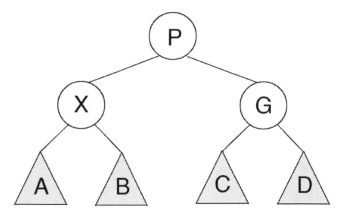

Subtree C, previously a right subtree of node P, is now a left subtree of node G. In both cases, all data items in subtree C is greater than P and less than G.

Then we splay node X up through its parent, node P, using a rotate right operation.

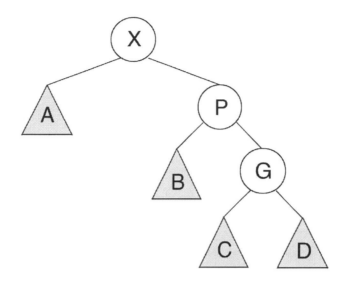

Subtree B, previously a right subtree of node X, is now a left subtree of node P. In both cases, all data items in subtree B is greater than X and less than P. It's very important to note that the order of rotation is reversed for a zig-zig rotation.

Example: Node X is the right child of a right child:

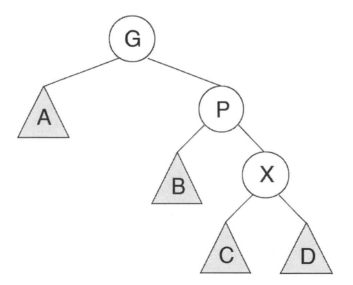

In this example, node X is the right child of node P and node P is the right child of node G.

Once again the splay occurs in two steps. First we splay the parent, node P, up through the grandparent, node G, using a rotate left operation:

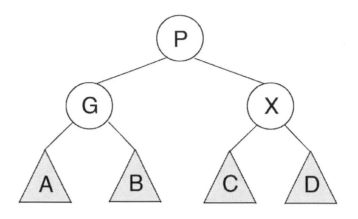

Then we splay node X up through its parent, node P, using a rotate left operation:

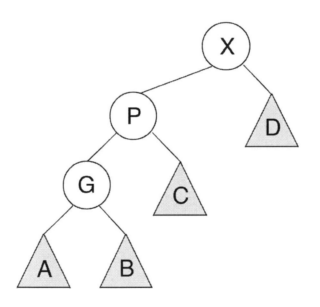

Once again, in each case, node X has moved two levels up the tree.

Rotation 3: Zig
A zig rotation is used when the node that we're splaying is the child of the root.

Example: Node X is the left child of root node P:

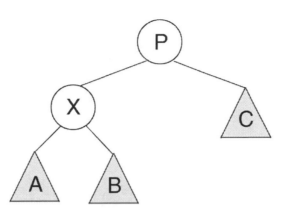

The splay occurs in a single step by rotating node X up through its parent, node P, using a rotate right operation:

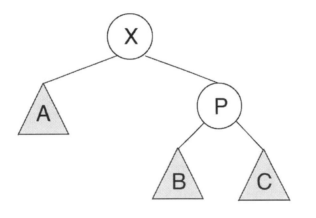

Example: Node X is the right child of root node P:

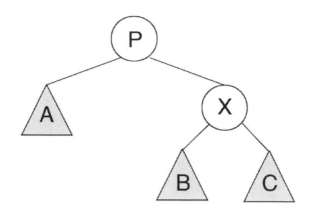

Again, the splay occurs in a single step by rotating node X up through its parent, node P, using a rotate left operation:

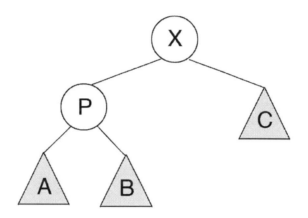

Splay Tree Algorithm

The splay operation on a node X is as follows:

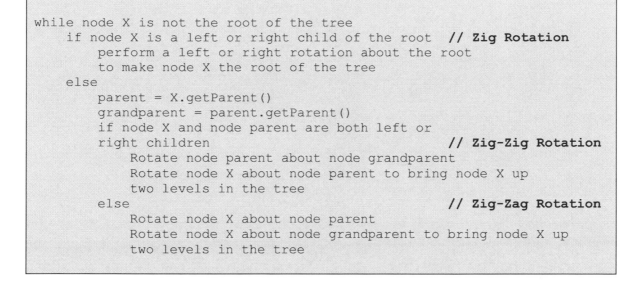

```
while node X is not the root of the tree
    if node X is a left or right child of the root    // Zig Rotation
        perform a left or right rotation about the root
        to make node X the root of the tree
    else
        parent = X.getParent()
        grandparent = parent.getParent()
        if node X and node parent are both left or
        right children                                // Zig-Zig Rotation
            Rotate node parent about node grandparent
            Rotate node X about node parent to bring node X up
            two levels in the tree
        else                                          // Zig-Zag Rotation
            Rotate node X about node parent
            Rotate node X about node grandparent to bring node X up
            two levels in the tree
```

Splay Tree Primitive Operations

There are four fundamental splay tree operations: `splay()`, `search()`, `insert()` and `delete()`.

• Splay()

The `splay()` operation moves a node X to the root of the tree using zig-zag, zig-zig, and zig rotations. In addition to moving node X to the root of the tree, the height of the tree may be shortened. Since the time to access a node in a binary tree is proportional to the depth of the accessed node, moving frequently accessed items toward the root will allow for much faster access, typically `O(1)`.

• Search()

The `search()` operation follows the same steps as the `search()` operation of a binary search tree. If the `search()` operation in a splay tree is successful, then the node that has been found is splayed to the root of the tree using a series of zig-zag, zig-zig, and zig rotations. If the `search()` operation is unsuccessful, then we splay the node where the search ended to the root.

Example Successful Search: `search(6)`

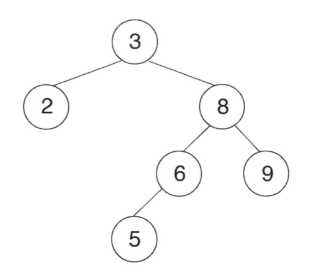

A search of the splay tree finds node 6, which then gets splayed to the root of the tree. Since node 6 is the left child of a right child we perform a zig-zag operation on the node.

First we rotate right node 6 around its parent, node 8.

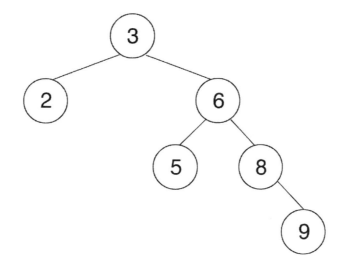

Then we left rotate node 6 around what was its grandparent, node 3.

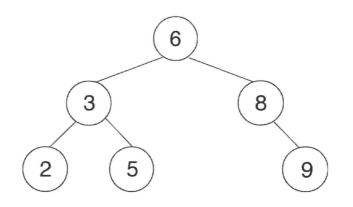

Example Unsuccessful Search: `search(4)`

Searching down the tree for node 4 finds that the node does not appear in the tree. The last node visited in the search, node 5, then gets splayed to the root.

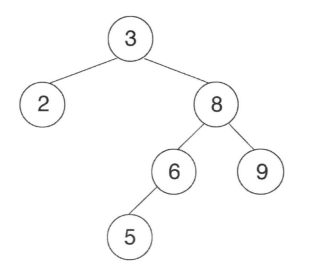

As node 5 is the left child of a left child, we perform a zig-zig rotation. First we right rotate node 5's parent, node 6, around its grandparent, node 8.

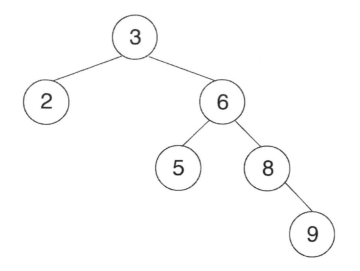

Then we right rotate node 5 around its parent, node 6.

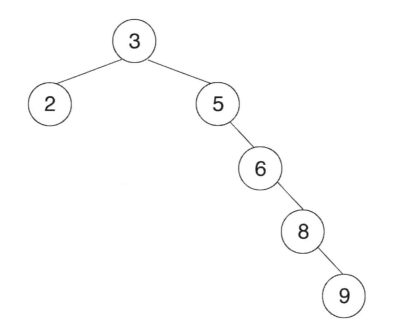

As node 5 is now the child of the root, we perform a zig rotation and left rotate node 5 through the root.

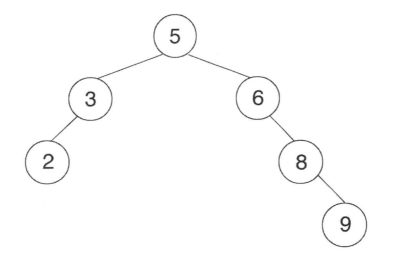

• Insert()

The `insert()` operation of a splay tree follows the same steps as the `insert()` operation in a binary search tree. Once a node has been inserted into its correct location within the splay tree, the node then gets splayed up to the root through a series of zig-zag, zig-zig, and zig rotations.

Example: `insert(7)`

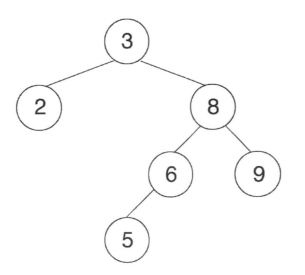

We insert 7 into its correct location within the splay tree.

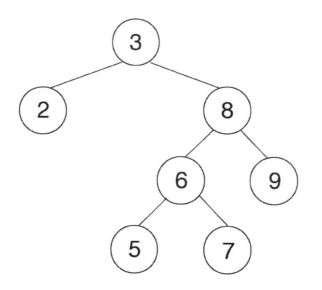

We must now splay node 7 to the root of the tree.

Since node 7 is the right child of a left child we must perform a zig-zag operation. First we left rotate node 7 through its parent, node 6.

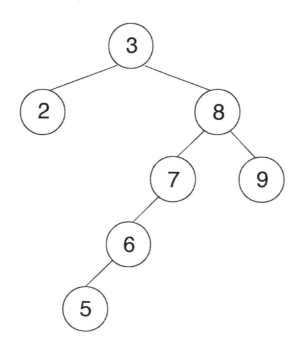

Then we right rotate node 7 through what was its grandparent, node 8.

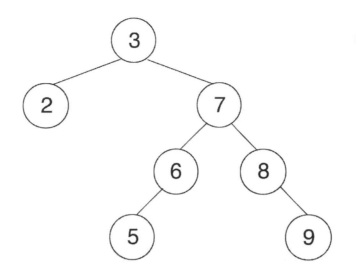

As node 7 is now the child of the root, we perform a zig rotation and left rotate node 7 through the root.

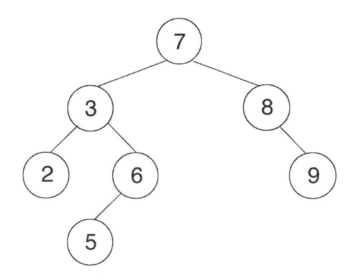

Delete()
The `delete()` operation is the same for a `delete()` operation in a binary search tree. If the node to be deleted is either a leaf or has one subtree, once the node has been deleted, the *parent* of the deleted node gets splayed up to the root through a series of zig-zag, zig-zig, and zig rotations. If the node to be

deleted has two subtrees, the node gets replaced with its inorder successor and the parent of the inorder successor gets splayed up to the root. If the item to be deleted is not found in the tree, then we splay the node where the search ended to the root.

Example Successful Delete: `delete(3)`

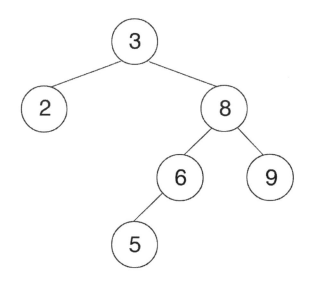

The node to delete, node 3, has two children. Therefore, its inorder successor, node 5, will take its place.

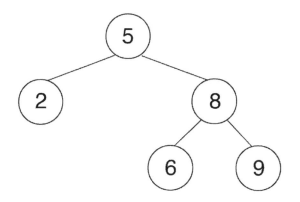

Next, the parent of the inorder successor, node 6, must be splayed to the root. As node 6 is the left child of a right child, we perform a zig-zag rotation. First we right rotate node 6 through its parent, node 8.

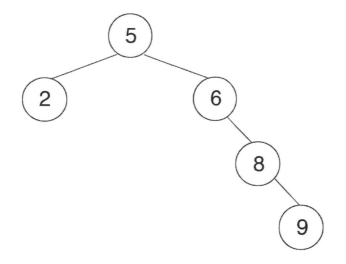

Then we left rotate node 6 through what was its grandparent, node 5.

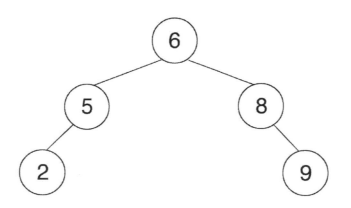

Example Unsuccessful Delete: `delete(7)`

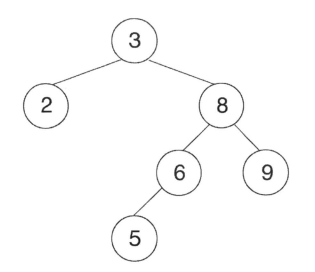

As we search the tree to delete node 7, we find that node 7 is not in the tree. The last node visited in the search for node 7 was node 6. Therefore, node 6 must get splayed to the root of the tree.

Since node 6 is the left child of a right child, we perform a zig-zag rotation. First we right rotate node 6 through its parent, node 8.

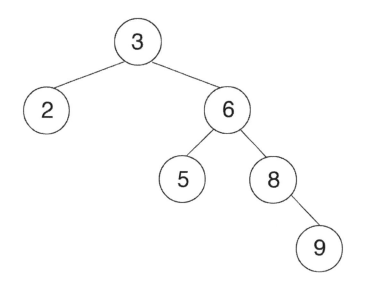

Then we left rotate node 6 through what was its grandparent, node 3.

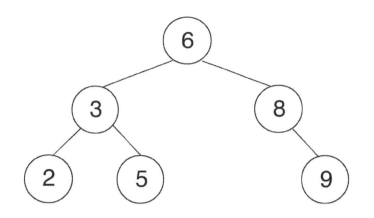

The self-adjusting nature of a splay tree allows the most frequently accessed data items to splay to the root allowing for very fast access. This property has made splay trees one of the most widely used data structures invented in the last 25 years. Splay trees are used in operating systems (Linux kernel), compilers (GCC and GNU), web caching proxies (Squid), switching and routing equipment (Fore Systems), text editors (sed), and data compression. Splay trees are also used to implement `malloc()`, the dynamic memory allocation system in Unix.

Time Complexity for Splay Trees (Amortized Time)

	Average Case	Worst Case
Insert:	O(log n)	O(log n)
Delete:	O(log n)	O(log n)
Search:	O(log n)	O(log n)

Exercise 1

Given the splay tree below, perform a `search(8)` operation and show the splay tree that results.

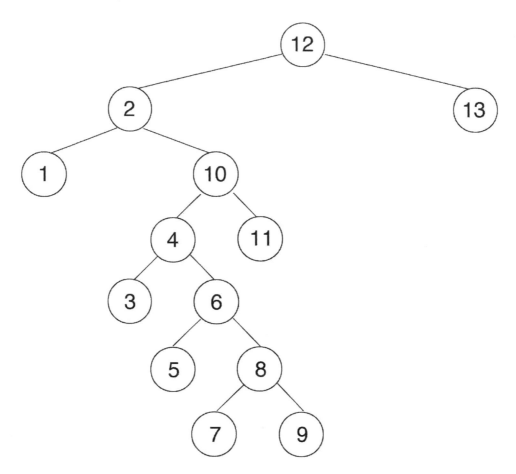

Exercise 2
On the original splay tree shown above, perform a `delete(4)` operation and show the splay tree that results.

Priority Queues

A *priority queue* is a data structure that collects data items and processes or removes the data item that contains the highest priority. For example, a printer that receives many jobs might want to prioritize the jobs submitted and print the shorter documents before the longer documents. A priority queue would allow this prioritization as opposed to enforcing a strictly FIFO queue. An operating system's job scheduling policy might utilize priority queues to determine which process will be assigned the CPU when it becomes available.

We have previously defined a stack as a LIFO (last-in-first-out) data structure in which items are inserted and removed from the top of the stack. Likewise, we have previously defined a queue as a FIFO (first-in-first-out) data structure in which items are inserted into the rear of the queue and removed from the front of the queue. In fact, both stacks and queues can really be thought of as specializations of priority queues.

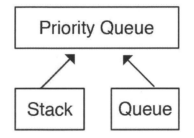

In this context, the essential difference between a stack and a queue is the way in which we prioritize the next item to be removed from each data structure. In a stack, the item that has been in the priority queue the shortest amount of time has priority and gets removed first. In a queue, the item that has been in the priority queue the longest amount of time has priority and gets removed first. In each case, the prioritization is based upon length of time in the data structure. So stacks and queues are both specializations of priority queues.

Priority queues support three basic primitive operations:

`pq.insert()`
Adds a new item to priority queue `pq`.

`x = pq.remove()`
Removes and returns the item in the priority queue `pq` with the greatest priority.

`x = pq.max()`
Returns the item in priority queue `pq` with the greatest priority, without modifying the priority queue.

Binary Heaps

The binary heap is used to implement the primitive operations of the priority queue. A *binary heap* is an ordering of a complete binary tree such that every node is larger than its immediate successor, i.e., every node has higher prioritization than its immediate successor. In other words, each parent node is greater than (or equal to) the nodes of its children. This ensures that the root is the largest value in the heap.

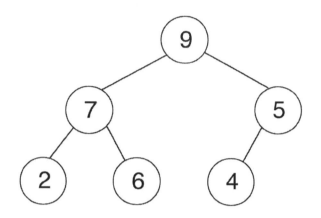

Note that each leaf is a heap in its own right and every subtree is also a heap. Also note that a heap is not necessarily a binary search tree.

We have previously defined a complete binary tree of level n as a perfect binary tree through level $n-1$ (i.e., every row at level $n-1$ is full), and leaf nodes at level n (the bottom row) are all situated in the tree to the left. Due to this compact structure of a complete binary tree, we can easily represent the complete binary tree sequentially within an array by placing tree nodes in the array level-by-level.

As long as we do not lose the relationship between the parent and child nodes, we can store the above binary heap in array A as follows:

9	7	5	2	6	4
A(1)	A(2)	A(3)	A(4)	A(5)	A(6)

This ordering of the nodes of a binary heap within an array is called the *canonical numbering* of its nodes:

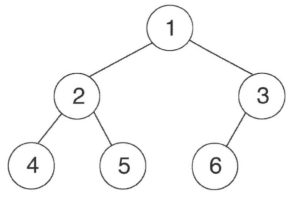

The relationship between tree nodes and array elements is shown below:

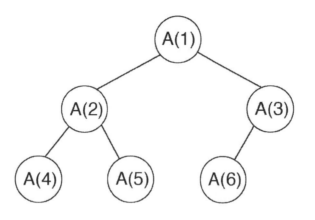

The two children of the node with value 7 (canonical node 2) are the node with value 2 (canonical node 4) and the node with value 6 (canonical node 5).

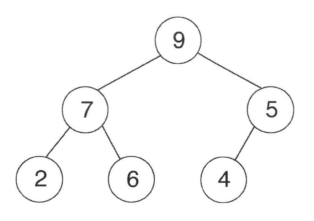

The canonical number of the left child is twice that of the parent node and the canonical number of the right child is twice plus 1 that of the parent node.

In general, if the canonical number of a parent node is `i`:

- the canonical number of the left child is `2*i`

- the canonical number of the right child is `2*i+1`

Therefore:

- The left child of `A(i)` is at `A(2i)`, if it exists.

- The right child of `A(i)` is at `A(2i+1)`, if it exists.

Additionally, given the canonical number of a node in a tree, the canonical number of its parent can easily be found:

- The canonical number of the parent of left child at `A(i)` is `A(i/2)`.

- The canonical number of the parent of right child at `A(i)` is also `A(i/2)` due to integer division.

Utilizing canonical numbering of the nodes of the binary tree, we can therefore store the binary heap within an array while maintaining the relationship among the nodes of the binary heap data structure.

Heap Property

If we have a binary heap stored in an array, node `i` has the *heap property* if:

```
A(i) >= A(2i)

and

A(i) >= A(2i+1)
```

whenever `A(2i)` and `A(2i+1)` exists. In other words, node `i` must be at least as great as the nodes of its children.

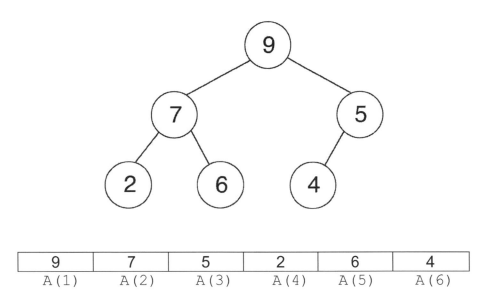

9	7	5	2	6	4
A(1)	A(2)	A(3)	A(4)	A(5)	A(6)

For example, node `A(2) = 7` has the heap property because 7 > 2, `A(2) > A(4)`, and 7 > 6, `A(2) > A(5)`. This tree, or data structure, is called a *heap* if every node has the heap property.

Almost Heap

If every node except the root has the heap property, the data structure is called an *almost heap*. Here's an example of an almost heap:

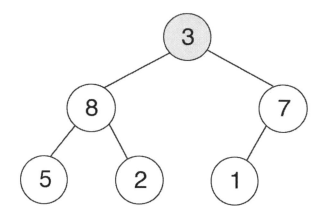

Note that every node has the heap property except for the root. We can convert an almost heap into a heap by allowing the root of the tree to *sift down* to its correct location within the tree. This is accomplished by swapping the root with its largest child:

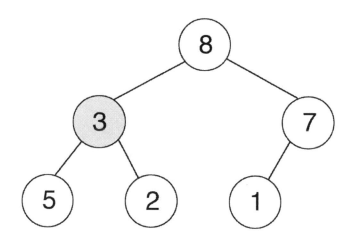

Note that now every node has the heap property except for the node with value 3. In fact, the tree rooted at 3 is an almost heap. So to convert that almost heap into a heap we allow the root of that subtree to sift down to its correct location within the tree by swapping it with its largest child:

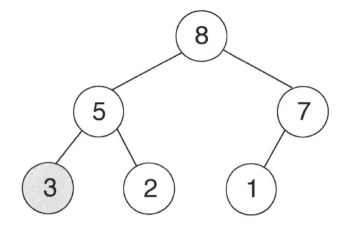

Now every node in the tree has the heap property and we have thus created a binary heap!

Binary Heap Implementation of Priority Queues

Binary Heap Insert Operation
The technique to insert an item into a binary heap is as follows:

> Insert the new item into the first free array location, i.e., the item becomes the rightmost leaf at the lowest level of the tree. Note that we always leave the 0th element of the array empty.
>
> While the new item is not at the root of the tree and the new item is greater than its parent
>
> > Swap the new item with its parent. This allows the new item to rise up to its proper level in the binary heap.

For example, given the binary heap shown below:

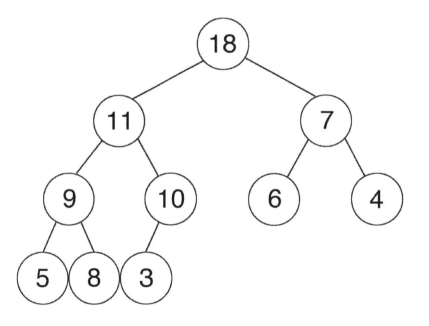

we place the new item 22 into the lowest level of the tree as the rightmost leaf. This new item will be placed in the heap at canonical number 11. Note that if the lowest level of the binary heap were full, then we would start a new level and insert the new item as a leaf at the far left. In our array implementation of the binary heap, the new item would be placed at the first free location in the array, excluding array location 0.

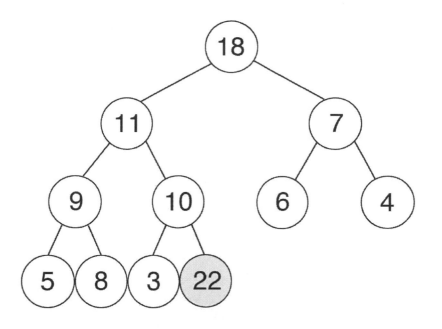

Note that this newly inserted item is not in its proper location within the tree as it's greater than its parent. So we swap the new item with its parent to allow the new item to rise up to its proper level in the binary heap.

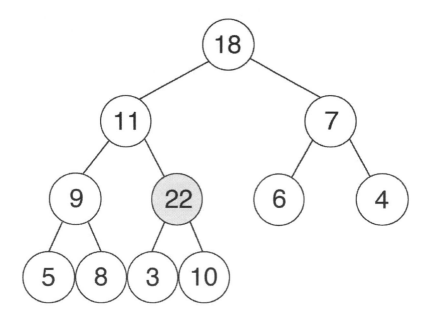

Once again, this newly inserted item is not in its proper location within the tree as it's greater than its parent. So we swap the new item with its parent to allow it to move up an additional level.

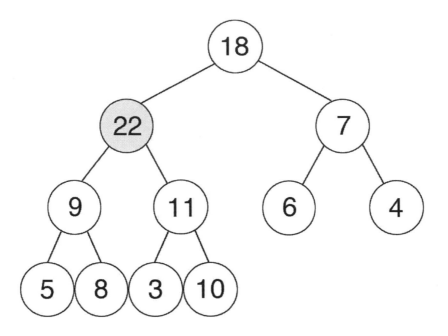

Finally, the new item is still larger than its parent so we swap the new item with its parent to allow the new item to become the root of the tree, thereby creating a heap.

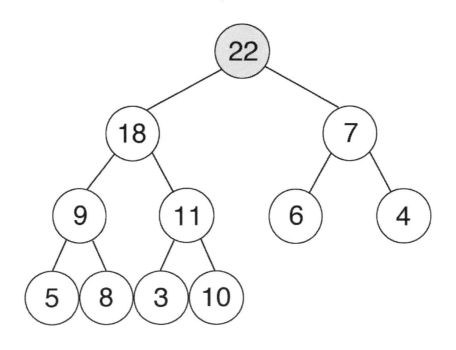

Our method to insert an item into a binary heap is shown below. Note that `count` is declared as a class variable and represents the number of items currently in the binary heap.

```
public void insert(int x) {
    if (count == item.length-1)
        resize(2 * item.length);
    item[++count] = x;
    riseUp();
}

private void riseUp() {
    int i = count;

    while (i > 1 && item[i] > item[i/2]) {
        int temp = item[i];
        item[i] = item[i/2];
        item[i/2] = temp;
        i = i/2;
    }
}
```

Binary Heap Delete Operation

The largest item in the heap is always found at the root of the tree, or at index 1 in the array. We delete the largest item by replacing the root with the last item in the array, i.e., the rightmost node in the lowest level of the tree. We then allow the new root to sift down the heap until it reaches it proper location within the heap.

The algorithm to delete an item from a binary heap is as follows:

Extract the 1st element of the array and move the last array element (rightmost leaf at lowest level) into the first array position, i.e., the root of the tree. Once again, we exclude array location 0.

We now have an almost heap. Allow the item at the root to sift down to its proper position as follows:

While the item is not a leaf and the item is smaller than either of its children

    Swap the root with its largest child.

For example, we want to delete the largest value from the initial binary heap shown below. The largest value is located at the root of the tree.

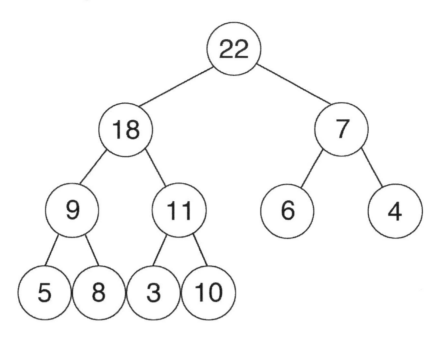

We extract and remove the largest value and move the rightmost leaf at the lowest level, i.e., the last item in the array, to the root of the tree.

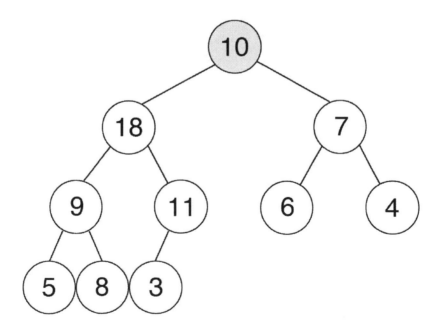

While the item is smaller than either of its children and the item is not a leaf, we swap the item with its largest child.

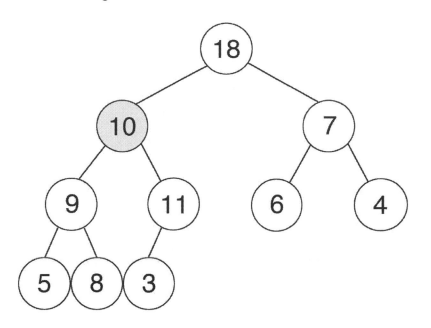

Once again the item is smaller than one of its children so we swap it with the largest child.

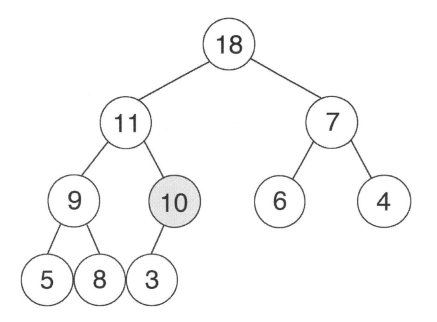

The item has now reached its proper level in the tree and we have recreated our binary heap!

Our method to delete an item from a binary heap is shown below. Once again `count` represents the number of elements currently in the binary heap.

```
public int delete() {
    int large = item[1];
    if (isEmpty()) {
        System.out.println("Binary Heap Underflow.");
        System.exit(1);
    }
    item[1] = item[count--];
    siftDown();
    if (count == item.length/4)
        resize(item.length/2);
    return large;
}

private void siftDown() {
    int i = 1;
    int max, temp;
    boolean isMaxHeap = false;

    while (i*2 <= count && !isMaxHeap) {
        if (i*2 == count || item[i*2] > item[i*2+1])
            max = i*2;
        else
            max = i*2+1;
        if (item[max] > item[i]) {
            temp = item[max];
            item[max] = item[i];
            item[i] = temp;
            i = max;
        }
        else
            isMaxHeap = true;
    }
}
```

Binary Heap Max Operation

The `max()` operation simply returns the largest item in the binary heap without modifying the heap. The largest item will always be found at the root of the tree and therefore we simply return the first element of the array.

```
public int max() {
    if (isEmpty()) {
        System.out.println("Binary Heap Underflow.");
        System.exit(1);
    }
    return item[1];
}
```

Exercise

Perform the following operations on an initially empty priority queue, `pq`, implemented as a binary heap. Show the resultant array.

pq.insert(5);
pq.insert(6);
pq.insert(2);
pq.delete();
pq.insert(7);
pq.insert(1);
pq.insert(4);
pq.delete();
pq.insert(8);
pq.insert(3);
pq.insert(9);
pq.delete();

Time Complexity of Priority Queues Implemented as Binary Heaps

Our implementation of the priority queue will utilize a binary heap that will provide no more than $O(\log n)$ time for insert and delete operation in the worst case as the heap is always rebuilt in $O(\log n)$ time. However, we show below the worst case time for insert and delete as $O(n)$ due to the potential resizing of the underlying array.

Time Complexity for Priority Queues Implemented as Binary Heap

	Average Case	Worst Case
Insert:	$O(\log n)$	$O(n)$
Delete:	$O(\log n)$	$O(n)$
Max:	$O(1)$	$O(1)$

```
public class BinaryHeap {
    private int[] item;
    private int count;

    public BinaryHeap() {
        item = new int[1];
        count = 0;
    }

    public void insert(int x) {
        if (count == item.length-1)
            resize(2 * item.length);
        item[++count] = x;
        riseUp();
    }

    private void riseUp() {
        int i = count;

        while (i > 1 && item[i] > item[i/2]) {
            int temp = item[i];
            item[i] = item[i/2];
            item[i/2] = temp;
            i = i/2;
        }
    }

    public int remove() {
        int large = item[1];
        if (isEmpty()) {
            System.out.println("Binary Heap Underflow.");
            System.exit(1);
        }
        item[1] = item[count--];
        siftDown();
        if (count == item.length/4)
            resize(item.length/2);
        return large;
    }
}
```

```java
    private void siftDown() {
        int i = 1;
        int max, temp;
        boolean isMaxHeap = false;

        while (i*2 <= count && !isMaxHeap) {
            if (i*2 == count || item[i*2] > item[i*2+1])
                max = i*2;
            else
                max = i*2+1;
            if (item[max] > item[i]) {
                temp = item[max];
                item[max] = item[i];
                item[i] = temp;
                i = max;
            }
            else
                isMaxHeap = true;
        }
    }

    public int max() {
        if (isEmpty()) {
            System.out.println("Binary Heap Underflow.");
            System.exit(1);
        }
        return item[1];
    }

    public boolean isEmpty() {
        return count == 0;
    }

    private void resize(int size) {
        int[] temp = new int[size];
        for (int i = 1; i <= count; i++)
            temp[i] = item[i];
        item = temp;
    }
}
```

❖ Written Homework: Binary Trees

1. Draw a perfect binary tree of level 3.

2. How many nodes are there in a perfect binary tree of level n?

3. How many ancestors does a node at level n in a binary tree have?

4. What is the maximum number of nodes in a binary tree of level n?

5. What is the maximum number of leaves in a binary tree of level n?

6. What is the maximum number of nodes in a perfect binary tree with n leaves?

7. Write a recursive definition for the height (or level) of a binary tree.

8. Show the binary search tree that gets produced after the following insertions into an initially empty tree:

```
10 - 20 - 25 - 15 - 45 - 40 - 50 - 35 - 30
```

9. Traverse the binary tree below in preorder, inorder, and postorder.

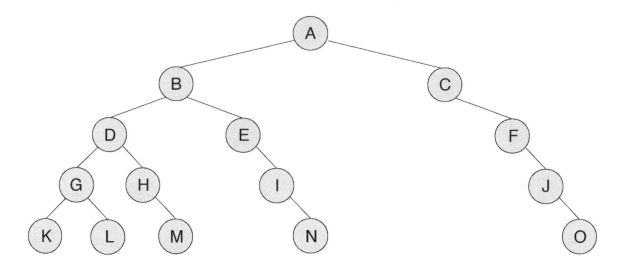

10. Show the binary search tree that results after 12 is removed from the tree below:

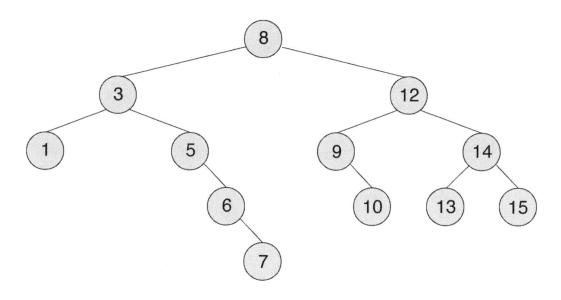

11. Given the probability of occurrence of the characters below, create a Huffman Tree and show the Huffman code that results for each character. Also calculate the average number of bits per character.

```
c1    0.40

c2    0.25

c3    0.15

c4    0.10

c5    0.08

c6    0.02
```

12. Show the splay tree that results from the insertion of the following numbers into an initially empty tree. Be sure to show your work.

```
7 - 3 - 9 - 1 - 4 - 2 - 6 - 8 - 5
```

13. Show the splay tree that results from the search(6) operation of the tree from question 12. Be sure to show your work.

14. Show the splay tree that results from the remove(4) operation of the tree from question 13. Be sure to show your work.

15. Show the binary search tree that results from the insertion of the following numbers into an initially empty tree. Be sure to show your work.

```
1 - 2 - 3 - 4 - 5 - 6 - 7
```

16. Show the splay tree that results from the insertion of the following numbers into an initially empty tree. Be sure to show your work.

```
1 - 2 - 3 - 4 - 5 - 6 - 7
```

17. Show the splay tree that results from a `search(1)` operation on the splay tree from question 16. Be sure to show your work.

18. Based upon the resultant trees from questions 15 – 17, what conclusions can you draw regarding the self-adjusting nature of a splay tree versus a binary search tree?

19. Show the binary heap that results from the insertion of the following numbers into an initially empty heap. Be sure to show your work.

```
10 - 20 - 25 - 15 - 45 - 40 - 50 - 35 - 30
```

20. Show the binary heap that results from a `remove()` operation performed on the heap in question 19. Be sure to show your work.

21. Show the heap from question 20 as an array.

22. Describe the use of the following methods from the `ObjectBinaryTree` class:

```
compareTo()
operate()
visit()
```

❖ Computer Lab: Binary Tree and Hashing

Web search engines are programs that search webpages for specified keywords and returns a list of relevant webpages where the keywords were found. The two main tasks for search engines are *matching* and *ranking*. The matching phase determines which webpages match a query and the ranking phase determines the relevance of each of the matches. Note that search queries can produce thousands or millions of hits (matches) and a search engine must be capable of picking the most relevant results (ranking).

The concept of an *index* is the most fundamental idea behind any search engine. The index for a search engine works the same way as a book's index. The "pages" of the book are now webpages and search engines assign a different page number to every single page on the web. The search engine builds up an index by first making a list of all the words that appear in any page, making a note of the page number in which each word appears, and then sorts that list in alphabetical order. So if a query is made on the word "computer", the search engine can quickly jump to the entry for "computer" in the word list and extract the pages for that entry.

Rather than build an index for webpages, this lab will build an index, or a *cross-reference listing*, for text-based documents. The lab will display the number of times each word appears in the document, the line numbers in which each word appears and the position of each word in the line. The lab will also allow us to query the document for specific words and will display the number of times the word appears in the document, the line numbers in which the word appears and the position of the word in the line.

At the outset we do not know how many different words are in the text, nor do we know in how many different lines a word may appear. Our approach will be to use an object binary search tree whose nodes provide for the following fields:

- a `Word` object

- two references to the left and right children of the current node

Note that while the `ObjectTreeNode` class is built to hold a generic `Object`, you'll be creating a `Word` class whose objects will be placed in the `ObjectTreeNode`s of the object binary search tree.

Each `Word` object should provide for the following fields:

- a `String` for the word to be stored. Note that a word is defined as any sequence of characters separated by a blank, tab, or newline. Punctuation at the end of a word should be removed. Therefore, is a hyphen considered a word? Words should not be case sensitive.

- an `int` to count the number of times the word appears in the text

- a reference to an object linear linked list in which each object contains the line number in which the current word can be found as well as the position of the word on the line. <u>Note that we're counting word-by-word position here and not character-by character position.</u>

Here is a listing of the classes and interfaces that you will want to include in your project:

```
Xref              ObjectBinaryTree            ObjectList
Word              ObjectBinaryTreeInterface   ObjectListInterface
LinePosition      ObjectTreeNode              ObjectListNode
Hash              ObjectTreeNodeInterface     ObjectListNodeInterface
Query             TreeComparable              Comparable
```

Specifically, your program should perform the following operations:

- Input text from a file, `getty.txt`, and output each line of text prefixed by a line number.

- Output a well-formatted cross-referenced listing alphabetically by performing an inorder traversal of the binary search tree. Each word, the number of times each word appears in the text, the line number(s), in ascending order, in which each word is found, as well as the position the word appears on each line should be output. Here's a look at the recommended output format:

```
our      2    1-7     11-10
people   3    20-11   21-1    21-4
perish   1    21-7
```

• Allow the user of the program to perform run-time queries and perform a search for the following words:

dedicate	men	resolve	vain
devotion	not	soldier	war
gave	people	us	

For each word searched, output the word, the number of times the word appears in the text, the line numbers in which the word appears and the position the word appears on each line.

To make this cross-reference table as simple and as useful as possible, we will not include all the words of the text in the index. The following words should be omitted:

a	have	that
after	in	the
all	is	their
and	it	there
because	its	to
every	now	was
for	of	were
from	on	which
had	so	with

To accomplish this task, we shall store each of the above words in a hash table of size 37 that resolves collisions by linear probing or chaining. After the hash table is created, we can select each word from the text, get its hash, and determine whether or not it appears in the hash table. If the word does appear in the hash table, we should simply ignore it; otherwise, we should store the word in the binary search tree, incrementing the counter which keeps track of the number of times the word appears, and attaching a new node to the linear linked list which contains the line number in which the word appears along with its position within the line. Note that the line numbers stored in the linear linked list should be kept in increasing order for eventual output.

You may place the 27 unimportant words into a text file, read the words into your program, and hash the words into their proper location within the hash table. Note that these 27 unimportant words placed into the hash table are not the same as the `Word` objects that will be placed into the binary search tree!

Note that the hash table should be created before reading any data from the `getty.txt` file. The hash function signature should be as shown below and the hash function should be completely self-contained (i.e., does not utilize any class variables or class constants.)

```
private int getHash(String s);
```

All hash functions created for this lab should use a mathematical calculation to return a value within the range of the hash table size. Conditional type statements should not be used. Also, be sure to use the required hash function signature as shown above. To confirm your hash collision numbers, I will execute your hash function within my code.

If you are using linear probing to resolve collisions, you should output the number of hash function collisions, the number of resolution collisions, as well as the total number of collisions. The total number of collisions should be ten or less.

If you are using chaining to resolve collisions, your hash function should return five or fewer collisions and you should output the total number of collisions, the average chain size to two decimal places, as well as the maximum chain size. Note that you should not count null lists when you are calculating the average chain size.

Be sure to create your own `Hash` class rather than use the `Hash` class built into the Java library. Your hash function should use a mathematical calculation to return a value within the range of the hash table size. Conditional type statements should not be used.

For extra credit, develop a *perfect hash function*. For extra, extra credit, develop a *minimal perfect hash function*.

The following should be added to your program's output:

- a description of your hash function

- a display of the hash table including array indices of each item in the hash table

- the load factor of the hash table

Be sure all output is sent to the terminal window as well as the `csis.txt` output file. Shown below are the contents of `getty.txt`.

```
Four score and seven years ago our fathers brought forth, upon this
continent, a new nation, conceived in liberty, and dedicated to the
proposition that all men are created equal. Now we are engaged in a
great civil war, testing whether that nation, or any nation, so
conceived, and so dedicated, can long endure. We are met here on a
great battlefield of that war. We have come to dedicate a portion of
it as a final resting place for those who here gave their lives that
that nation might live. It is altogether fitting and proper that we
should do this. But in a larger sense we can not dedicate - we can not
consecrate - we can not hallow this ground. The brave men, living and
dead, who struggled here, have consecrated it far above our poor power
to add or detract. The world will little note, nor long remember, what
we say here, but can never forget what they did here. It is for us, the
living, rather to be dedicated here to the unfinished work which they
have, thus far, so nobly carried on. It is rather for us to be here
dedicated to the great task remaining before us that from these honored
dead we take increased devotion to that cause for which they here gave
the last full measure of devotion - that we here highly resolve that
these dead shall not have died in vain; that this nation shall have a
new birth of freedom; and that this government of the people, by the
people, for the people, shall not perish from the earth.
```

★ Note 1: Methods

The user-defined `operate()` method, invoked from `insertBSTDup()`, will increment the word count and add the line number and position to a node of a linked list.

The user-defined `visit()` method, invoked from `inTrav()`, will output the word, along with the number of times the word was found as well as the line numbers and positions of each word found.

★ Note 2: Interfaces

We use a TreeComparable interface for the tree lab to distinguish from the Comparable interface in the list lab as there might be a need for both interfaces.

Each data structure in your project must implement an interface for that data structure. The interface files must be included in the zip archive for your code.

❖ Computer Lab: Huffman Codes

When storing or transmitting large amounts of text, it frequently pays to look for ways to compress the text into a smaller number of bits. The time needed to transmit a certain message is proportional to the number of bits in the message. By compacting the data to be sent, transmission times can be reduced. Furthermore, compacted data requires fewer bits to store.

One way of compressing text is to eliminate the restriction that all character codes must be the same length. If the codes for common letters such as "e" and "t" were shorter than the codes for rare letters such as "q" and "x", the total number of bits needed to store or transmit the text would be decreased. Such a coding scheme is called a frequency-dependent code or Huffman Code.

This method can only be used if the probability of occurrence of each character is known at the time the code is designed. A code based on the probabilities for English text may not be optimum for Java programs, and it will be far from optimum for transmitting messages in Hungarian or Polish. What follows is an example of a frequency distribution for English text from a particular computer textbook:

A	-	6.22	J	-	0.06	S	-	5.81
B	-	1.32	K	-	0.31	T	-	7.68
C	-	3.11	L	-	3.07	U	-	2.27
D	-	2.97	M	-	2.48	V	-	0.70
E	-	10.53	N	-	5.73	W	-	1.13
F	-	1.68	O	-	6.06	X	-	0.25
G	-	1.65	P	-	1.89	Y	-	1.07
H	-	3.63	Q	-	0.10	Z	-	0.06
I	-	6.14	R	-	5.87	SPACE	-	18.21

Utilizing the Huffman algorithm with the above frequency distribution for the letters of the alphabet we might produce the following Huffman Code:

```
A   -   0010           J   -   00000011      S   -   1010
B   -   110010         K   -   00000010      T   -   1110
C   -   10011          L   -   10000         U   -   10001
D   -   1101           M   -   10010         V   -   110011
E   -   1111           N   -   0011          W   -   110000
F   -   000011         O   -   0001          X   -   00000001
G   -   110001         P   -   000010        Y   -   000001
H   -   1011           Q   -   000000001     Z   -   000000000
I   -   0111           R   -   0110          SPACE  -   010
```

Note that the shortest codes are assigned to the most common characters, whereas the longest codes are assigned to relatively infrequently occurring characters. Also note that the code for one letter is not a prefix of the code of another letter. For instance, if the code for a symbol X, C(X), were a prefix of the code of a symbol Y, C(Y), then when C(X) is encountered, it is unclear whether C(X) represents the symbol X or whether it is the first part of C(Y).

Your assignment is to construct a binary tree based upon the data given in the Huffman Code above. Then, utilizing this tree, you are to decode the message stored in the file: codefile.txt.

It is important to understand that each piece of data, each character in our alphabet, will reside in a leaf of the binary tree. The path that you take to get to each particular leaf depends upon the binary digit you are processing at each moment. A "0" might take you to a nodes left child while a "1" might take you to a nodes right child. When you arrive at a leaf, the character in its info field represents the current character of the text that should then be output.

All program output should be saved in a file called csis.txt

❖ Computer Lab: Morse Code

Write a program that constructs the international Morse Code tree from the table below and allows users to enter a code message of dots, dashes, and separators. The output of the message is the decoded message.

```
A .-          H ....        O ---          V ...-
B -...         I ..          P .--.          W -..-
C -.-.         J .---        Q --.-          X -..-
D -..          K -.-        R .-.           Y -.-
E .           L .-..        S ...           Z --..
F ..-.         M --          T -
G --.          N -.          U ..-
```

All program output should be saved in a file called csis.txt

Chapter 9. Searching

Introduction to Searching

We've seen in our previous discussions of trees, lists, queues, and stacks, that these data structures are designed to store information, which should be retrieved for frequent usage. Information retrieval is one of the interesting issues in computer science. The challenge of information retrieval includes the efficiency of storage usage, as well as the speed of the search algorithm, which is important for fast retrieval.

Searching is the process of retrieving a record of data from a structure or from a database, which may contain hundreds or even several millions of records. The storage structure of these records is the essential factor, which affects the speed of search. However, a good searching strategy also influences the speed, even on the same underlying storage structure.

Searching is often the most time-consuming part of many computer programs. There are a variety methods, or algorithms, used to search for a data item, depending on how much data there is to look through, what kind of data it is, what type of structure the data is stored in, and even where the data is stored - inside computer memory or on some external medium. Because the substitution of one search algorithm for another can sometimes lead to a dramatic increase in computing speed, every computer scientist should be familiar with a variety of search algorithms and be able to select the best one to use in a given situation. In this section, we will investigate the performance of three searching algorithms and the data structures which they use:

- Linear search
- Binary search
- Hashing

Linear Search

The simplest search strategy is the linear or sequential search. The linear search is usually performed on unordered arrays. It starts at the beginning of the array, checks every element in order, until it either finds the data item it is looking for or until it reaches the end of the array, in which case the data item is not found in the array. Note that the comparison in the linear search can be on a single key of the data item, or on a compounded key that includes several search criteria.

```
// linearSearch.java - returns the index in the array of data item
// found returns -1 if data item not in array

public int linearSearch(int[] list, int max, int key) {
    for (int i = 0; i < max; ++i)
        if (list[i] == key)
            return i;
    return -1;
}
```

Let's examine how long it will take to find a data item matching a key in the unsorted array. Although we might be interested in the:

- average time
- worst-case time
- best possible time

we will generally be most concerned with the worst-case time, as calculations based on worst-case times can lead to guaranteed performance predictions. Conveniently, the worst-case times are generally easier to calculate than average times.

To simplify analysis and comparison of algorithms, we look for a dominant operation and count the number of times that dominant operation has to be performed. In the case of searching, the dominant operation is the comparison.

If there are n items in our array, it is obvious that in the worst case when there is no item in the array with the desired key, then n comparisons of the key with the data items in the array will have to be made. In the best case we'll find our data item on the first comparison. In the average case we'll find our data item in (1 + n) / 2 or approximately n/2 comparisons.

Therefore, an array of 100 data items requires an average of 50 comparisons for a successful search. If we were to double the number of data items we had to search through, the number of comparisons would also double and therefore the run-time of our algorithm would double. We say that the number of comparisons is proportional to the number of data items n in the array. Accordingly, the search time of the algorithm is proportional to the number of data items n in the array. An array of 1000 data items takes 10 times longer to search than an array of 100 data items.

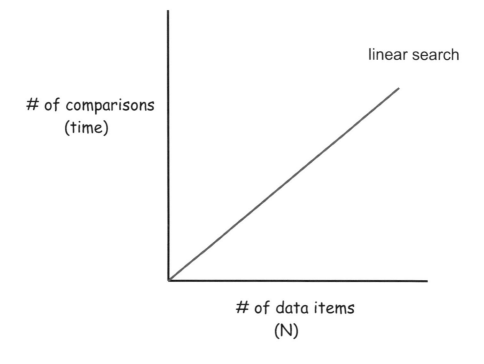

Binary Search

As we saw earlier, the linear search algorithm is simple and convenient for small problems, but if the array is large and/or requires many repeated searches, it makes good sense to have a more efficient algorithm for searching an array.

The binary search algorithm works only on a sorted array. It selects the *median* (middle) element in the array and compares its value to that of the target value. Because the array is known to be sorted, if the target value is less than the middle value, then the target must be in the first half of the array. Likewise if the value of the target item is greater than that of the middle value in the array, it is known that the target lies in the second half of the array. In either case we can, in effect, "toss out" one half of the search space with only one comparison.

Now, knowing that the target must be in one half of the array or the other, the binary search examines the median value of the half in which the target must reside. The algorithm thus narrows the search area by half at each step until it has either found the target data or the search fails.

The algorithm is easy to remember if you think about a child's guessing game. Imagine I told you that I am thinking of a number between 1 and 1000 and asked you to guess the number. Each time you guessed I would tell you "higher" or "lower." Of course you would begin by guessing 500, then either 250 or 750 depending on my response. You would continue to refine your choice until you got the number correct.

Given a sorted array of items, say:

```
     ------------------------------------
     | 12 | 29 | 30 | 32 | 35 | 49 |
     ------------------------------------
       0    1    2    3    4    5

     low                   high
     index                 index
```

Suppose we wish to search for the position of an element equal to `key`. We will search the array that begins at some low index and ends at some high index. In our case the low index of the effective array to be searched is 0 and the high index is 5. We can find the approximate midway index by integer division (`low + high`) `/ 2`, i.e. 2. We compare our value, `key` with the element at index 2. If they are equal, we have found what we were looking for; the index is 2.

Otherwise, if `key` is greater than the item at this index, our new effective search array has a low index value of 3 and the high index remains unchanged at 5. If `key` is less than the element, the new effective search array has a high index of 1 and the low index remains at 0. The process repeats until the item is found, or there are no elements in the effective search array. The terminating condition is found when the low index exceeds the high index.

The binary search algorithm is implemented below:

```java
// binarySearch.java - Assumes array is in sorted order.
// Returns index of the location of the key in the array.
// Retuns -1 if not found.

public int binarySearch(int[] list, int max, int key) {
    int mid;

    int i = 0;
    int j = max-1;
    while (i <= j) {
        mid = (i + j) / 2;
        if (list[mid] > key)
            j = mid - 1;
        else if (list[mid] < key)
            i = mid + 1;
        else return mid;
    }
    return -1;
}
```

Recursive Binary Search

The recursive version of the binary search algorithm requires more than just the original array and a value to search. It also needs to know what part of the array is going to be searched, i.e., the subscripts that determine where the "sub-array" starts and where it ends.

The definition first looks to see if the search area to look through is empty, i.e., has the left index crossed the right index, $i > j$. It then determines whether the key is in the left half or right half of the array and makes the appropriate recursive call. If you look closely at the code below, you'll see that this recursive implementation of binary search uses tail-end recursion!

```
// recursiveBinarySearch.java - Assumes array is in sorted order.
// Returns index of the location of the key in the array.
// Retuns -1 if not found.

public int recursiveBinarySearch(int[] list, int i, int j, int key) {
    if (i > j)
        return -1;
    int mid = (i + j) / 2;
    if (list[mid] > key)
        return recursiveBinarySearch(list, i, mid-1, key);
    else if (list[mid] < key)
        return recursiveBinarySearch(list, mid+1, j, key);
    else
        return mid;
}
```

Analysis of Binary Search

Why use a binary search when a linear search is easier to code? The answer lies in the efficiency of the search. With a linear search, if you double the size of a list, you could potentially take twice as much time to find an item. With a binary search, doubling the size of the list merely adds one more item to look at. Each time you look with a binary search, you eliminate half of the remaining list items as possible matches.

For example, suppose we're given a search space of 1,000,000 data elements. Sequential search would take about 500,000 searches or comparisons on the average. If we were to double the search space to 2,000,000 data items, the number of comparisons would double to 1,000,000 and therefore our search time would effectively double. Binary search, on the other hand, would only require about 20 searches through a search space of 1,000,000 data items and doubling this data size to 2,000,000 would only increase the number of comparisons by 1. Binary search is indeed a powerful search algorithm!

So we say that binary search on an array takes approximately $\log_2 n$ comparisons because at each test you can "throw out" one-half of the search space. We can divide a set of n items in half at most $\log_2 n$ times. Thus the running time of a binary search is proportional to $\log_2 n$ and we say this is a $\log n$ algorithm.

It is noteworthy that for very small arrays a linear search can prove faster than a binary search. However as the size of the array to be searched increases, the binary search is the clear victor in terms of number of comparisons and therefore overall speed. Thus at large values of n, $\log n$ is much smaller than n;

consequently a `log n` algorithm (binary search) is much faster than an algorithm whose time is proportional to `n` (linear search).

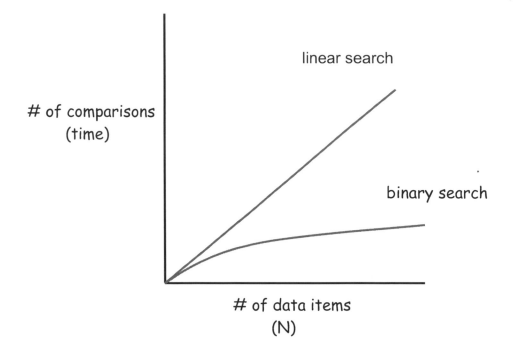

Still, the binary search has some drawbacks. First of all, it requires that the data to be searched be in sorted order. If there is even one element out of order in the data being searched it can throw off the entire process. When presented with a set of unsorted data the efficient programmer must decide whether to sort the data and apply a binary search or simply apply the less-efficient linear search. Even the best sorting algorithm is a complicated process. Is the cost of sorting the data is worth the increase in search speed gained with the binary search? If you are searching only once, it is probably better to do a linear search in most cases.

Once the data is sorted it can also prove very expensive to add or delete items. In a sorted array, for instance, such operations require a shift of array elements to open or close a "hole" in the array. This is an expensive operation, as it requires, in worst case, $log_2 n$ comparisons and n data movements. We'll explore this further in our section on sorting algorithms.

Introduction to Hashing

In the search methods examined so far, we've searched for a given key by rummaging amongst the table entries according to some systematic policy such as:

• running through elements in order (sequential search)
• eliminating half the elements each time we do a comparison (binary search)

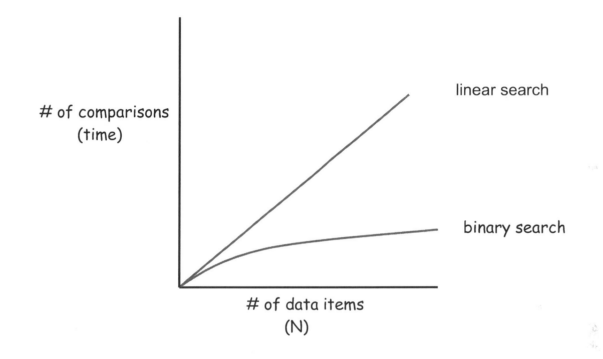

Is it possible to design a search of constant time performance, i.e. , one that takes the same search time to find any element in a group of elements of any size? Whether we have 1,000 data elements or 1,000,000 data elements to search through, can we design a search technique that will find out data item in one, or two, or perhaps three comparisons?

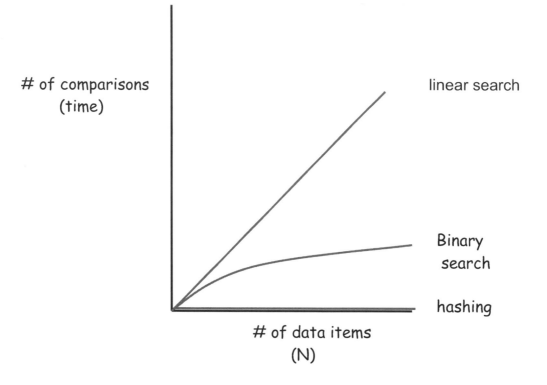

# of comparisons
(time)

linear search

Binary
search

hashing

# of data items
(N)

This constant time search algorithm is not impossible in theory. Consider a college that uses its student's social security numbers as primary lookup keys. Here we have a situation in which the range of possible keys `(000-00-0000` to `999-99-9999` or one billion) is vastly larger than the number of elements to be stored (perhaps 25,000 students). We could then map each student to its unique slot in the array using each students social security number as the index into the table.

This technique would be trivial to add, delete, and search out students, but would be very expensive in terms of space. It would not make sense, in this case, to allocate an array of one billion storage locations just to ensure that the 25,000 records will be in a perfectly unique and predictable location in the array. Using students names as keys would be even worse, since there's typically no way to use a string as an array subscript (besides, students may have identical names.)

Let's scale our problem down in size and consider a fairly small company, perhaps with 50-60 employees. Rather than use an employee's social security number as an index into an array to do a lookup, we're going to use the last two digits of an employee's social security number as the index into an array to do a lookup. The following employee social security numbers:

```
467-39-5236
814-95-6001
776-38-4735
```

will be mapped into a 100-element table as follows:

```
                    KEY          RECORD
              ----------------------------
    0       |                |          |
              ----------------------------
    1       |  814-95-6001   |          |
              ----------------------------
    2       |                |          |
              ----------------------------
    3       |                |          |
              ----------------------------
    :       |                |          |
              ----------------------------
   35       |  776-38-4735   |          |
              ----------------------------
   36       |  467-39-5236   |          |
              ----------------------------
   37       |                |          |
              ----------------------------
   38       |                |          |
              ----------------------------
    :       |                |          |
              ----------------------------
   96       |                |          |
              ----------------------------
   97       |                |          |
              ----------------------------
   98       |                |          |
              ----------------------------
   99       |                |          |
              ----------------------------
```

Note that the records are ordered in the array with respect to some function that is performed on the key value (social security number) to produce an array index into the table. The function is used to determine where in the array a record is to be stored and the function is used as a method of accessing the record.

The function is referred to as a *hash function* (h) that transforms a *key* into a *table index*. If h is a hash function and key is a key, then h(key) is called the *hash of the key* and is the index at which a record with key key should be placed. It's the purpose of the hash function to take a key and reduce it to an index within a limited range. In this example, the hash function is:

```
h(key) = key % 100
```

where % represents the modulus operator. This hash function produces an index between $0 - 99$ and therefore covers the entire set of indices in the hash table. We can generalize our hash function to:

```
h(key) = key % tablesize
```

where `tablesize` represents the number of elements in the hash table.

So hashing is a searching technique used to improve data access times by locating the desired item after one look. Rather than sorting the data according to a key, hashing computes the location of the data from the key. It computes an index value from the key of the desired record. At that index value, the record is stored and retrieved.

Hash Collisions

When inserting items into a hash table, it sometimes happens that an item to be inserted hashes to the same location as an item already in the table. This is referred to as a *collision*. Our hash function does not guarantee unique addresses!

Ideally, no two keys should hash to the same address. But suppose two keys, `key1` and `key2` are such that:

```
h(key1) = h(key2)
```

Then when a record with key `key1` is entered into the table, it is inserted at position `h(key1)`. But when `key2` is hashed, the position obtained is the same as where the record with key `key1` is stored. This attempt to store two records in the same table location is referred to as a *hash collision* or *hash clash*.

Given our previous hash function:

```
h(key) = key % tablesize
```

and our previous 100-element hash table:

```
                    KEY          RECORD
            ----------------------------------
      0     |              |              |
            ----------------------------------
      1     | 814-95-6001  |              |
            ----------------------------------
      2     |              |              |
            ----------------------------------
      3     |              |              |
            ----------------------------------
      :     |              |              |
            ----------------------------------
      35    | 776-38-4735  |              |
            ----------------------------------
      36    | 467-39-5236  |              |
            ----------------------------------
      37    |              |              |
            ----------------------------------
      38    |              |              |
            ----------------------------------
      :     |              |              |
            ----------------------------------
      96    |              |              |
            ----------------------------------
      97    |              |              |
            ----------------------------------
      98    |              |              |
            ----------------------------------
      99    |              |              |
            ----------------------------------
```

A hash collision would occur if a record with key `159-48-7636` were attempted to be added to the table. This key would hash to location `36`, which is taken by a record with key `467-39-5236`.

The problem of avoiding these collisions is the biggest challenge in designing a good hash function. A good hash function minimizes collisions by spreading the records uniformly throughout the table. That's why it's desirable to have the array size larger than the number of actual records. The larger the range of the hash function, the less likely it is that two keys will yield the same hash value.

One possible way to avoid this collision would be to increase the size of the hash table to 1,000 and make our hash function:

```
h(key) = key % 1000
```

The distribution of keys in the new hash table would now look like this:

```
                    Key          Record
              -------------------------------
    0       |              |              |
              -------------------------------
    1       | 814-95-6001  |              |
              -------------------------------
    2       |              |              |
              -------------------------------
    3       |              |              |
              -------------------------------
    :       |              |              |
              -------------------------------
   234      |              |              |
              -------------------------------
   235      |              |              |
              -------------------------------
   236      | 467-39-5236  |              |
              -------------------------------
    :       |              |              |
              -------------------------------
   635      |              |              |
              -------------------------------
   636      | 159-48-7636  |              |
              -------------------------------
    :       |              |              |
              -------------------------------
    :       |              |              |
              -------------------------------
   735      | 776-38-4735  |              |
              -------------------------------
   736      |              |              |
              -------------------------------
    :       |              |              |
              -------------------------------
   997      |              |              |
              -------------------------------
   998      |              |              |
              -------------------------------
   999      |              |              |
              -------------------------------
```

We no longer have a collision, but it's at the cost of added storage for the hash table! However, keep in mind that no matter how large we make our hash table, there is always the possibility of collisions, and therefore we must always devise a collision resolution policy for finding a record containing a given key amongst those whose keys collide at the same location. The three collision resolution policies that we'll look at are:

- Linear probing
- Rehashing
- Chaining

Linear Probing

A collision is a failed attempt to insert an item into a table because there is already an item in the slot the new item has hashed to. Once a space in the table is occupied, no other item can be placed there unless the existing item is deleted first. *Collision resolution techniques* are used to offset the effects of collisions. Should a collision occur, these techniques look for another place in the table for an item to be stored.

The simplest collision resolution policy is called *linear probing*. When there is a collision (when we hash to a place in the table that is already occupied with an item whose key is not the same as the search key), then we just check the next position in the table. It is customary to refer to such a check (determining whether or not a given table position holds an item with key equal to the search key) as a probe.

Linear probing is characterized by identifying three possible outcomes of a probe:

> • If the table position contains an item whose key matches the search key, then we have a search hit.
>
> • If the table position is empty, then we have a search miss.
>
> • Otherwise (if the table position contains an item whose key does not match the search key) we just probe the table position with the next higher index, continuing (wrapping back to the beginning of the table if we reach the end) until either the search key or an empty table position is found.

If an item containing the search key is to be inserted following an unsuccessful search, then we put it into the empty table space that terminated the search.

For example, given the hash function:

```
H(key) = key % TABLESIZE;
```

Insert the sequence of keys: 5, 24, 22, 16, 11, 28, 31, 47

```
 0      ------
       |      |
        ------
 1     |      |
        ------
 2     |  28  |
        ------
 3     |  16  |
        ------
 4     |      |
        ------
 5     |  5   |
        ------
 6     |  31  |
        ------
 7     |      |
        ------
 8     |  47  |
        ------
 9     |  22  |
        ------
10     |      |
        ------
11     |  24  |
        ------
12     |  11  |
        ------
```

Note that we store the colliding element into the next available space in the table. Searching is done the same way. If the computer address does not contain the desired record, we use linear probing and check the next address or record.

This linear probing strategy, however, does not always work well if the hash function does not evenly distribute the data items, because the data tend to clump together as the table fills up (primary clustering), leading to long stretches of occupied slots separated by sparsely occupied stretches.

For example, given the same hash function:

```
h(key) = key % TABLESIZE
```

Insert this sequence of keys: 5, 24, 22, 16, 11, 28, 31, 29

```
            ------
   0       |      |
            ------
   1       |      |
            ------
   2       | 28  |
            ------
   3       | 16  |
            ------
   4       | 29  |
            ------
   5       |  5  |
            ------
   6       | 31  |
            ------
   7       |      |
            ------
   8       |      |
            ------
   9       | 22  |
            ------
  10       |      |
            ------
  11       | 24  |
            ------
  12       | 11  |
            ------
```

If another key to be inserted into the hash table hashes to address 2, 3, 4, 5, 6, it will be placed into table location 7. So primary clustering occurs when the hashing function does not spread the addresses uniformly throughout the address range. If several keys hash to the same address we could get bogged down into a sequential search that is too costly.

The main problem with linear probing is the expense of inserting and searching for elements involved in collisions. This is not significant when the table is relatively empty, but becomes more and more important as the table fills up. The determining factor for search times is not the total number of elements but how full the table is. This is measured by what is referred to as the load factor, which is calculated as n/t, where n equals the number of keys in the table and t equals the hash table size.

Insertions to these locations tend to be slower as do lookups of the data stored there. This is because we are getting away from our goal of checking one location and finding our data item. The number of rehashes needed should be kept as small as possible.

For best performance, the hash table's load factor should never increase beyond 80%. Otherwise the time required to deal with collisions, which rises very sharply when the hash table is almost full, will outweigh any decrease in running time obtained by using a random-access data structure.

How do we delete a key from a hash table built with linear probing? We cannot just remove it, because items that were inserted later might have skipped over that item, so searches for those items would terminate prematurely at the hole left by the deleted item. Our solution to implement deletion is to replace the deleted key with a sentinel key that can serve as a placeholder for searches but can be identified and reused for insertions.

Rehashing

Another collision resolution policy called *rehashing* or *secondary hashing*, applies another hash function to the key after finding an occupied position (a collision), to figure out where in the hash table to place the new data value.

For example, given the same hash function:

```
h(key) = key % TABLESIZE
```

and the rehash function:

```
rh(key) = key * key % TABLESIZE
```

we insert this sequence of keys as follows:

```
5, 24, 22, 16, 11, 28, 31, 12
```

```
         ------
  0    |      |
         ------
  1    |  12  |
         ------
  2    |  28  |
         ------
  3    |  16  |
         ------
  4    |  11  |
         ------
  5    |   5  |
         ------
  6    |      |
         ------
  7    |      |
         ------
  8    |      |
         ------
  9    |  22  |
         ------
 10    |      |
         ------
 11    |  24  |
         ------
 12    |  31  |
         ------
```

So we must write two functions:

• a hash function, h(key), that takes a key as an argument and returns a value that is an index into the hash table's array

• a rehash function, rh(key), that provides an alternative index (derived from the key) when a collision has occurred.

Note that there are two constraints on these functions:

• Since `h(key)` will be invoked very frequently, it should be simple and fast.

• Since hash tables work best when the collision rate is low, `h(key)` and `rh(key)` should "randomize" the keys. In other words, the values they produce should not conform to any pattern that may characterize the keys.

Finally, note that the collision resolution policy of linear probing is a special case of rehashing.

```
rh(key) = (key + 1) % TABLESIZE
```

When an item hashes to a location that is already in use, the rehash function then tells us to try the next location in the table, unless it's off the end of the table, in which case the rehash function sends us back to the start of the table at index 0.

Chaining

Perhaps the most widely used method for handling collisions is called chaining. Chaining implements the hash table, not as an array of elements, but as an array of singly linked lists of elements. The hash function is applied to the key to determine which of these lists the new element should be added to. In the event of a collision, one simply puts all of the elements that hash to the same array subscript into the same list, often called a *bucket*.

In contrast to linear probing and rehashing (secondary hashing), this method has the advantage that it can, if necessary, accommodate more elements than there are positions in the array. However, as the average size of the lists grow longer, there will be a progressive degradation in performance as the linear search down the lists begin to occupy a larger fraction of time.

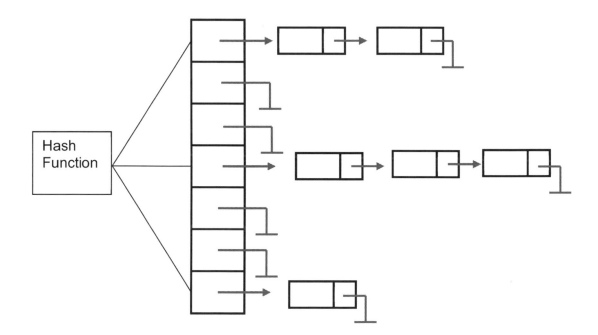

Assume the hash function:

```
h(key) = key % 7
```

Let's insert the following data items into the hash table using chaining as our collision resolution policy:

```
3 - 10 - 4 - 6 - 13
```

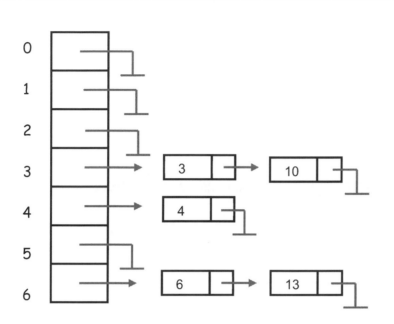

So we keep a linked list of all records whose keys hash into the same value. Again note that the positions in the hash table hold not actual data items but holds pointers to linked lists of all records that have hashed to that point.

To search for a given record, first apply the hash function to the key, then search the chain for the bucket indicated by the hash address. Deleting a node from a table that is constructed by hashing and chaining involves simply removing a node from a linked list.

The main disadvantage of chaining is the extra space that is required for header table and pointers. The initial array in chaining is usually smaller and we can allocate as many nodes as we need. But if the lists become too long, the whole purpose of hashing, direct addressing and resultant search efficiency, is defeated.

Hash Functions

One problem that we must address is the computation of the hash function that transforms keys into table addresses. This arithmetic computation is normally simple to implement, but we must proceed with caution to avoid various subtle pitfalls.

If we have a table that can hold n items, then we need a function that transforms keys into integers in the range 0 to $n-1$. The important issues to consider when choosing a hash function are:

> - The hash function should be simple to implement and easy to compute.
>
> - The hash function should avoid collisions by mapping keys to table addresses in a uniform and random manner.
>
> - A good hash function gives an average-case lookup that is a small constant, independent of the number of search keys.

Choice of Hash Function

In practice, unless we know something about the keys chosen, we cannot guarantee that there will not be collisions. However, in certain applications we have some specific knowledge about the keys that we can exploit to reduce the likelihood of a collision. For example, if the keys in our application are telephone numbers, and we know that the telephone numbers are all likely to be from the same geographic area, then it makes little sense to consider the area codes in the hash function as the area codes are all likely to be the same.

Perhaps the simplest of all the methods of hashing an integer `key` is to divide `key` by n and then to use the remainder modulus n. This is called the *division method of hashing*. In this case, the hash function is:

```
h(key) = key mod N
```

Generally, this approach is quite good for just about any value of n. However, in certain situations some extra care is needed in the selection of a suitable value for n.

For example, it is often convenient to make n an even number. But this means that h(key) is even if key is even; and h(key) is odd if key is odd. If all possible keys are equally probable, then this is not a problem. However if, say, even keys are more likely than odd keys, the function h(key) = key mod n will not spread the hashed values of those keys evenly.

Similarly, it is often tempting to let n be a power of two. For example, $n = 2^k$ for some integer $k > 1$. In this case, the hash function:

```
h(key) = key mod 2^k
```

simply extracts the bottom k bits of the binary representation of key. While this hash function is quite easy to compute, it is not a desirable function because it does not depend on all the bits in the binary representation of key. For these reasons n is often chosen to be a prime number.

For example, suppose there is a bias in the way the keys are created that makes it more likely for a key to be a multiple of some small constant, say two or three. Then making n a prime increases the likelihood that those keys are spread out evenly. Also, if n is a prime number, the division of key by that prime number depends on all the bits of key, not just the bottom k bits, for some small constant k.

Prime Numbers are Good Things

Suppose we wanted to hash check totals by the dollar value in pennies mod 1000. What happens?

```
$25.99 ==> 599
$45.99 ==> 599
$65.99 ==> 599
```

Note that prices tend to be clumped by similar last digits, so we get clustering. If we instead use a different prime number, these clusters will get broken. In general, it is a good idea to use prime modulus for hash table size, since it is less likely the data will be multiples of large primes as opposed to small primes.

Also note:

- The last k digits of `key`: `h(key) = key mod` 10^k

- The last k bits of `key`: `h[key] = key mod` 2^k

String Hashing

To hash a string, we can just add the characters together as in the following:

```java
// hash.java - Maps a string of characters to a number in range
0 to TABLESIZE-1

public int hash(String s) {
    final private int TABLESIZE = 97;
    int sum = 0;

    for (int i = 0; i < s.length(); i++)
        sum += (int)s.charAt(i);
    return sum % TABLESIZE;
}
```

We could also use a hash function that multiplies all the individual digits in the key together, and takes the remainder after dividing the resulting number by the table size.

Folding

A folding method is sometimes used to hash integers. Here the key is chopped into two or more parts and the parts recombined in some easy manner. For example, suppose the keys are 9 digit longs, such as:

```
542981703
```

We chop this into 3 equal-length pieces and add them together:

```
542 + 981 + 703
```

taking the:

```
sum % tablesize
```

to cut the answer down to size. So the sum of three parts of the key is divided by the table size. The remainder is the hash key.

Let's fold the key:

```
123456789
```

into a hash table of ten locations ($0 - 9$), i.e., we are given:

```
key = 123456789
```

and the `tablesize` is equal to 10. Since we can break `key` into three parts any way we want to, we will break it up evenly:

```
a = 123
b = 456
c = 789
```

Therefore,

```
h(123456789) = (123 + 456 + 789) % 10
             = 1368 % 10
             = 8
```

So `123456789` is inserted into the hash table at address `8`.

Another version of the folding method breaks the key into several pieces and exclusive-or's (`XOR`) the pieces together to form the hash address.

For example, let's devise a hash function to produce an index between 0 and 255 (note that it takes 8 bits to represent the 256 index values as $2^8 = 256$). The internal representation of the key is a string of 32 bits:

```
key = 618403 = 00000000000010010110111110100011
```

The folding algorithm proceeds as follows:

• Break the key into 4 strings of 8 bits each:

```
00000000 00001001 01101111 10100011
```

• Exclusive-or the first and last bit strings:

```
        00000000
XOR 10100011
        10100011
```

• Exclusive-or the two middle bit strings:

```
        00001001
XOR 01101111
        01100110
```

• Exclusive-or the results of the previous two steps to produce the 8-bit index into the array:

```
        10100011
XOR 01100110
        11000101 = 197
```

Therefore key 618403 is placed into the hash table at index 197.

Perfect Hash Functions

Recently, one active area of research in computer science has been devising algorithms to find hash functions that are tailored to specific values, in the sense that among those particular values no collisions whatever will take place. A hash function that produces no collisions is referred to as a *perfect hash function*.

The perfect hash function maps each key to a distinct integer within some range and enables us to build a hash table that allows a search in only one lookup. For instance, one might design such a function for Java's reserved words and predefined identifiers, so that, when a compiler's symbol table is implemented as a hash table, these frequently occurring strings will not cause unnecessary collisions.

Minimal Perfect Hash Functions

A minimal perfect hash function maps the set of actual key values to the hash table without any collisions, and does so using a table that has only as many slots as there are key values to be hashed. Minimal perfect hash functions totally avoid the problem of wasted space in a hash table and wasted time in performing table lookups.

Minimal perfect hash functions are widely used for memory efficient storage and fast retrieval of items from static sets, such as words in natural languages, reserved words in programming languages or interactive systems, universal resource locations (URLs) in Web search engines, or item sets in data mining techniques.

Time Complexity for Hash Tables

	Average Case	Worst Case
Insert:	O(1)	O(n)
Delete:	O(1)	O(n)
Max:	O(n)	O(n)
Search:	O(n)	O(n)

1. Define the following terms:

    a) hash table
    b) hash function
    c) perfect hash function

2.   a) What is a collision?
    b) Explain three ways of handling collisions (a program is not needed; a clear brief explanation suffices).

3. Consider a hashing scheme that uses linear probing to resolve collisions.

    a) Design an algorithm (no code necessary) to delete an item from the hash table.

    b) What precautions do you need to take to make it work properly?

4. Given the following data:

    $$25 - 42 - 96 - 101 - 102 - 162 - 197$$

    a) Construct a hash table using the hash function, h(key) = key mod tablesize, where the size of the table is 11. Use the rehash function, rh(key) = (key + 3) mod tablesize to resolve collisions.

    b) Construct a second hash table using the same hash function as above, but use chaining to resolve collisions.

Chapter 10. Sorting

Introduction to Sorting

Sorting is the process of rearranging data items in some order and can be performed in many ways. Over time, several methods have been devised to sort information following specific algorithms. We're going to look at three categories of sorting techniques:

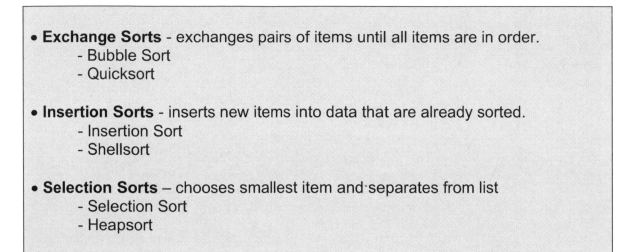

- **Exchange Sorts** - exchanges pairs of items until all items are in order.
  - Bubble Sort
  - Quicksort

- **Insertion Sorts** - inserts new items into data that are already sorted.
  - Insertion Sort
  - Shellsort

- **Selection Sorts** – chooses smallest item and separates from list
  - Selection Sort
  - Heapsort

Most sorting algorithms will fall in the category of $O(n^2)$ sorts (primitive or naïve sorts) and $O(n\ log\ n)$ sorts (advanced or sophisticated sorts). What's the difference between the two? For an $O(n^2)$ sort, multiplying the data size by 100 will multiply the sorting time by a factor 10,000 (100 * 100). For an $O(n\ log\ n)$ sort, multiplying the data size by 100 will multiply the sorting time by less than 200 (100 * $\log_2$ 100).

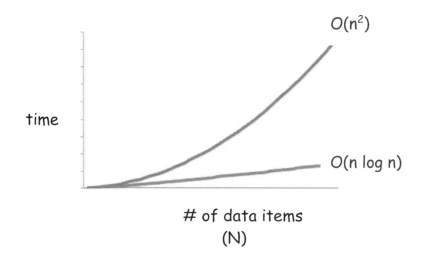

So in considering the time necessary to sort a file of size N, we're not concerned with actual time units, as these will vary from one machine to another, from one program to another, and from one set of data to another. Rather, we are interested in the *change* in the amount of time required to sort a file induced by a change in the file size N.

As we look at sorting algorithms, we're going to be concerned with the following:

Best Case
Assume the input, data, etc. are arranged in the most advantageous order for the algorithm, i.e., causes the execution of the fewest number of instructions.

Worst Case
Assumes the input, data, etc. are arranged in the most disadvantageous order for the algorithm, i.e., causes the execution of the largest number of statements.

Average Case
Determines the average of the running times over all possible permutations of the input data

Bubble Sort

The bubble sort makes repeated passes through an array, each time shifting the smallest item to the left end of the array. We start with the first item in the array and compare it to every other item in the array, exchanging items each time it finds a smaller item. The result is that the smallest items "bubble" to the top (left end) of the array. When we have performed these series of operations for each array position, the array is sorted.

Bubble Sort Example

Shown below is the bubble sort. The array location in this shade is the location that will receive the next smallest data item from the unsorted portion of the array. The number in this shade is the current number we're looking at. The numbers with a dash after them are the sorted array elements.

We begin with an unsorted array of data elements:

9	3	5	2	7

Our first pass seeks to find the smallest data item in the array and place it in the first array location.

9	3	5	2	7

3 < 9 so we swap the values in their respective array locations:

3	9	5	2	7

3	9	5	2	7

3	9	5	2	7

2 < 3 so we swap the values in their respective array locations:

2	9	5	3	7

2	9	5	3	7

At the end of the 1st pass, the smallest data item has "bubbled" to the top of the array:

| 2 - | 9 | 5 | 3 | 7 |

We begin the 2nd pass to find the next smallest data item in the unsorted portion of the array and place it in the 2nd array location:

| 2 - | 9 | 5 | 3 | 7 |

5 < 9 so we swap the values in their respective array locations:

| 2 - | 5 | 9 | 3 | 7 |

| 2 - | 5 | 9 | 3 | 7 |

3 < 5 so we swap the values in their respective array locations:

| 2 - | 3 | 9 | 5 | 7 |

| 2 - | 3 | 9 | 5 | 7 |

At the end of the 2nd pass, the next smallest data item has been placed in the sorted portion of the array:

| 2 - | 3 - | 9 | 5 | 7 |

We begin the 3rd pass to find the next smallest data item in the unsorted portion of the array and place it in the 3rd array location:

| 2 - | 3 - | 9 | 5 | 7 |

5 < 9 so we swap the values in their respective array locations:

| 2 - | 3 - | 5 | 9 | 7 |

| 2 - | 3 - | 5 | 9 | 7 |

At the end of the 3rd pass, the next smallest data item has been placed in the sorted portion of the array:

2 -	3 -	5 -	9	7

We begin the 4th pass to find the next smallest data item in the unsorted portion of the array and place it in the 4th array location:

2 -	3 -	5 -	9	7

7 < 9 so we swap the values in their respective array locations:

2 -	3 -	5 -	7	9

At the end of the 4th pass, the next smallest data item has been placed in the sorted portion of the array:

2 -	3 -	5 -	7 -	9

There is no need to make an additional pass through the data items as the remaining data item is the largest in the array and is in its correct array location at the end of the array:

2 -	3 -	5 -	7 -	9 -

Note that each successive pass through the array guarantees that one more element is in its correct position. In general, an array containing n data items requires n-1 passes to sort the array.

Analysis
Bubble sort requires n-1 passes through the array with n comparisons and data movements in each pass. Thus, bubble sort is an $O(n^2)$ sort in its worst case, average case and best case.

The bubble sort has no redeeming characteristics. It is always very slow, no matter what data it is sorting. The algorithm is included here for the sake of completeness, not because of any merit.

```
// bubbleSort.java

public static void bubbleSort(int[] list, int max) {
    int temp;

    for (int i = 0; i < max-1; i++)
        for (int j = i+1; j < max; j++)
            if (list[i] > list[j]) {
                temp = list[i];
                list[i] = list[j];
                list[j] = temp;
            }

}
}
```

Time Complexity for Bubble Sort

Best Case	Average Case	Worst Case
$O(n^2)$	$O(n^2)$	$O(n^2)$

Quicksort

Quicksort is one of the simplest and fastest sorting algorithms. It works recursively using a divide-and-conquer strategy. Quicksort works on the principle that it is easier to sort two small arrays than it is to sort one large array. The essence of quicksort is to sort an array, `a(1)..a(n)`, by picking some key value in the array for comparison (as a pivot element) around which to rearrange the elements in the array into two parts:

- all elements < pivot element
- all elements > pivot element

All the smaller elements of the array should precede the pivot element and the larger ones should follow it. For some `j`, all the elements `< pivot` appear in `a(1)..a(j)` and all those elements `>= pivot` appear in `a(j+1)..a(n)`.

All that remains to be done is to sort the subarray of smaller elements and the subarray of larger elements. This is done by applying quicksort recursively to `a(1)...a(j)` and to `a(j+1) ... a(n)`. The array is thereby repeatedly divided until only arrays of 1 or 2 elements are considered. A one element array segment is certainly in order and nothing more need be done.

When quicksort returns from recursion, the two parts have been sorted and can simply be put together into one big sorted piece (because they were presorted before the recursion).

Most implementations of quicksort make use of the fact that you can partition the array by keeping two indices: one moving in from the left and a second moving in from the right. They are moved towards the center until the left index finds an element greater than the pivot and the right index finds an element less than the pivot. These two elements are then swapped. The indices are then moved inward again until they "cross over" and the partition is complete.

```java
// quickSort.java

public static void quicksort(int[] list, int first, int last) {
    int temp;

    int i = first;
    int j = last;
    int pivot = list[(first+last) / 2];
    do {
        while (list[i] < pivot)
            i++;
        while (list[j] > pivot)
            j--;
        if (i <= j) {
            temp = list[i];
            list[i] = list[j];
            list[j] = temp;
            i++;
            j--;
        }
    }
    while (i <= j);
    if (first < j)
        quicksort(list, first, j);
    if (i < last)
        quicksort(list, i, last);
}
```

Analysis of Quicksort

Assuming that the array breaks into two equal halves, we have two arrays of size $n/2$ to sort. In order for each half to be partitioned, $(n/2)+(n/2) = n$ comparisons are made. Also assuming that each of these arrays breaks into two equal sized subarrays, we can assume that there will be at the most $\log(n)$ splits. This will result in a best time estimate of $O(n \log n)$ for quicksort.

When is quicksort not fast? When we choose a bad pivot and the split of each section of the array is not in half. If pivot is chosen as the largest or smallest item of the array, then the number of items in the larger section of the array is $n-1$. So we end up with $n-1$ comparisons times n splits $= O(n^2)$. So the trick is to select a pivot that is well positioned towards the middle of the array.

In general, quicksort is a fast sorting algorithm. However, if a response time guarantee is required in our software, then quicksort's worst case of $O(n^2)$ should be considered. In mission-critical software, it is not acceptable to design based on average performance, you must always allow for the worst case, and thus treat quicksort as $O(n^2)$.

Time Complexity for Quicksort

Best Case	Average Case	Worst Case
O(n log n)	O(n log n)	$O(n^2)$

Linear Insertion Sort

Linear insertion sort works the same way we might add cards to a poker hand. We simply add one card at a time to the hand, placing the card into its correct position within the hand. We find the correct position for each card by comparing it with each of the cards already in the hand. When we locate the correct insertion point, we simply place the card in the hand at that location.

Insertion sort takes an item from an array and finds its correct position in the array by comparing it with previous items in the array. Given an array `list` containing n elements, we find the correct position for the ith element, `list[i]`, by comparing it with each of the elements `list[1]`, `list[2]`, `...`, `list[i-1]`. This ensures that at the ith pass of the algorithm, the first i elements in the array are sorted. By the nth stage, all n elements of the array are in order.

Insertion Sort Example

To sort an array, we simply move through the array from left to right and insert one item at a time into its proper position among the items to its left. Shown below is an array that will become sorted using insertion sort. The number in this shade is the number we're trying sort. The numbers in this shade are the sorted elements. The blank location in the array represents a possible insertion point. We begin with the assumption that the first element of the array is sorted:

5	3	8	2	9	4	6	7

The next element of the array to be sorted is 3:

We copy the data item to be sorted into a temporary location, thereby opening a possible insertion point in the sorted array for the data item:

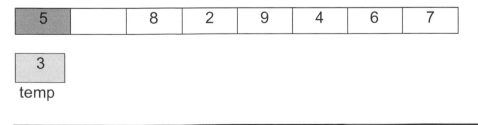

temp

---

3 < 5 so we must open a new insertion point. We shift 5 to the right one position opening a new insertion point:

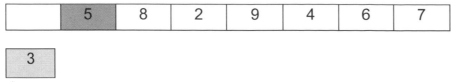

temp

Reaching the start of the array tells us that the current insertion point is valid as the new data item is the smallest data item seen so far. So we insert the data item into the insertion point:

| 3 | 5 | 8 | 2 | 9 | 4 | 6 | 7 |

temp

At the end of the 1st pass, the first 2 data items are sorted.

We begin the 2nd pass. The next data item to sort is 8:

| 3 | 5 | 8 | 2 | 9 | 4 | 6 | 7 |

temp

The data item 8 is placed into the temporary memory location, thus opening a possible insertion point:

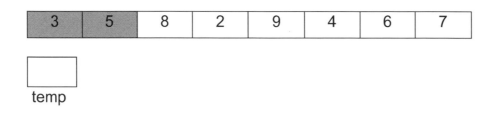

8
temp

8 > 5 so the 8 gets placed into the insertion point:

| 3 | 5 | 8 | 2 | 9 | 4 | 6 | 7 |

temp

At the end of the 2nd pass, the first 3 data items are sorted.

We begin the 3rd pass. The next data item to sort is 2:

| 3 | 5 | 8 | 2 | 9 | 4 | 6 | 7 |

temp

The data item 2 is placed into the temporary memory location, thus opening a possible insertion point:

| 3 | 5 | 8 | | 9 | 4 | 6 | 7 |

| 2 |
temp

2 < 8 so we must open a new insertion point. We shift 8 to the right one position opening a new insertion point:

| 3 | 5 | | 8 | 9 | 4 | 6 | 7 |

| 2 |
temp

2 < 5 so we must open a new insertion point. We shift 5 to the right one position opening a new insertion point:

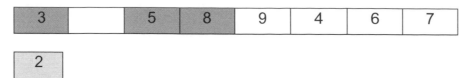

2
temp

2 < 3 so we must open a new insertion point. We shift 3 to the right one position opening a new insertion point:

| | 3 | 5 | 8 | 9 | 4 | 6 | 7 |

2
temp

Reaching the start of the array tells us that the current insertion point is valid as the new data item is the smallest data item seen so far. So we insert the data item into the insertion point:

temp

At the end of the 3rd pass, the first 4 data items are sorted.

We begin the 4th pass. The next data item to sort is 9:

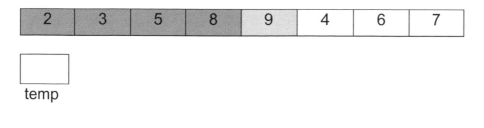

temp

The data item 9 is placed into the temporary memory location, thus opening a possible insertion point:

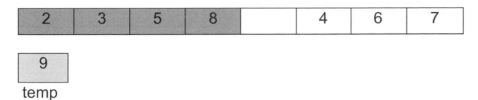

9 > 8 so 9 gets placed into the insertion point:

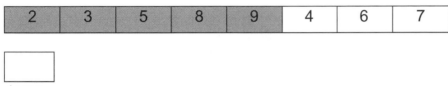

At the end of the 4th pass, the first 5 data items are sorted.

We begin the 5th pass. The next data item to sort is 4:

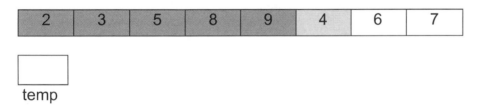

The data item 4 is placed into the temporary memory location, thus opening a possible insertion point:

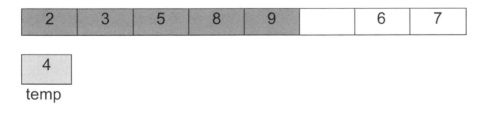

4 < 9 so we must open a new insertion point. We shift 9 to the right one position opening a new insertion point:

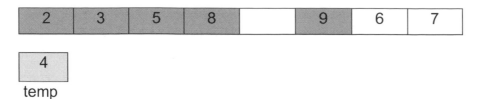

temp

4 < 8 so we must open a new insertion point. We shift 8 to the right one position opening a new insertion point:

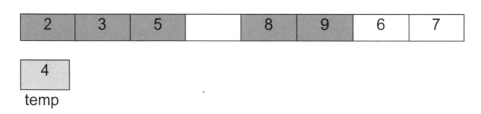

temp

4 < 5 so we must open a new insertion point. We shift 5 to the right one position opening a new insertion point:

temp

4 > 3 so 4 gets placed into the insertion point:

temp

At the end of the 5th pass, the first 6 data items are sorted.

We begin the 6th pass. The next data item to sort is 6:

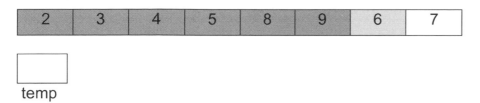

temp

The data item 6 is placed into the temporary memory location, thus opening a possible insertion point:

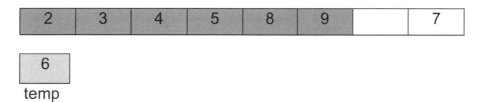

temp

6 < 9 so we must open a new insertion point. We shift 9 to the right one position opening a new insertion point:

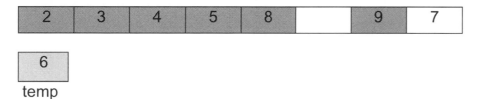

temp

6 < 8 so we must open a new insertion point. We shift 8 to the right one position opening a new insertion point:

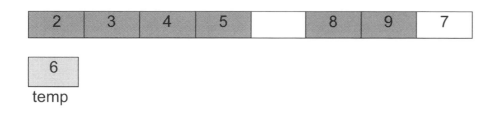

temp

6 > 5 so 6 gets placed into the insertion point:

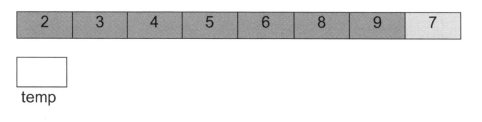

temp

At the end of the 6th pass, the first 7 data items are sorted.

We begin the 7th pass. The next data item to sort is 7:

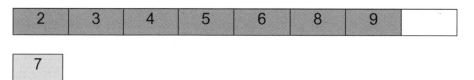

temp

The data item 7 is placed into the temporary memory location, thus opening a possible insertion point:

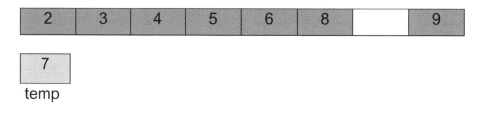

7 < 9 so we must open a new insertion point. We shift 9 to the right one position opening a new insertion point:

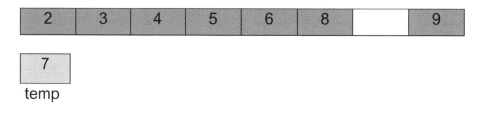

temp

7 < 8 so we must open a new insertion point. We shift 8 to the right one position opening a new insertion point:

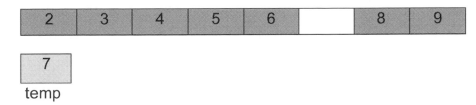

temp

7 > 6 so 7 gets placed into the insertion point:

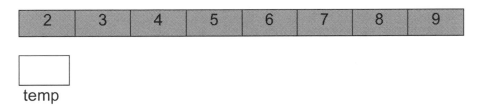

temp

At the end of the 7th pass, the array is sorted. In general, an array of `n` data items requires `n-1` passes to be sorted.

Analysis of Insertion Sort

With `n` data items, insertion sort makes approximately `n-1` passes over the data, each with $O(n)$ comparisons and data movements. Thus, insertion sort is an $O(n^2)$ sort in its average case.

Intuitively, the worst case for insertion sort is when the table is in reverse order, so that each element `list[i]` must be compared with `i-1` other elements (all the ones preceding it) before its correct position is found. Therefore, the worst case for insertion sort takes $O(n^2)$.

In its best case, if the numbers are almost sorted, the running time of insertion sort will be closer to $O(n)$, which makes it a very fast algorithm.

```
// insertionSort.java

public static void insertionSort(int[] list, int max) {
    for (int i = 1; i < max; i++) {
        int temp = list[i];
        int j = i - 1;
        while (j >= 0 && temp < list[j]) {
            list[j+1] = list[j];
            j = j - 1;
        }
        list[j+1] = temp;
    }
}
```

Time Complexity for Linear Insertion Sort

Best Case	Average Case	Worst Case
$O(n)$	$O(n^2)$	$O(n^2)$

Binary Insertion Sort

The linear insertion sort algorithm performs a linear search in order to find the position in which to do the insertion. However, since the element is inserted into a sequence that is already sorted, we can use a binary search instead of a linear search to determine the position at which to do the insertion. While a linear search requires $O(n)$ comparisons in the worst case, a binary search only requires $O(\log n)$ comparisons. Therefore, the binary search is often preferred.

```java
// binaryInsertionSort.java

public static void BinaryInsertionSort(int[] list, int max) {
    int left, right, middle, temp;

    for (int i = 1; i < max; i++) {
        temp = list[i];
        left = 0;
        right = i - 1;
        while (left <= right) {
            middle = (left + right) / 2;
            if (temp < list[middle])
                right = middle - 1;
            else
                left = middle + 1;
        }
        for (int j = i - 1; j >= left; j--)
            list[j + 1] = list[j];
        list[left] = temp;
    }
}
```

Time Complexity for Binary Insertion Sort

Best Case	Average Case	Worst Case
$O(n \log n)$	$O(n^2)$	$O(n^2)$

Shellsort

Shellsort is a simple extension of insertion sort that gains speed by allowing exchanges of array elements that are far apart. While insertion sort compares and exchanges only adjacent items, shellsort sorts an array by successively sorting larger and larger subarrays whose entries are non-contiguous in the array. The subarrays to be sorted are determined by a sequence of parameters, h, called increments. The final increment is 1.

For example, suppose the first increment is 7. Then the array is divided into 7 subarrays, each beginning with one of the first 7 data items and consisting of every 7th data item from there on. After the subarrays are sorted, the next increment (a smaller value) is used to separate the array again into subarrays and again the subarrays are sorted. The process is repeated for each increment until the increment = 1 and the entire array is sorted.

Shellsort Example

In our example below, note that when a comparison dictates a swap of two data items in a segment, this swap within a noncontiguous segment of the array moves an item a greater distance within the overall array than the swap of adjacent array entries in the usual insertion sort.

This means that one swap is more likely to place an element closer to its final location in the array with shellsort than with insertion sort. That is, a large-valued entry which appears near the front of the array will more quickly move to the tail end of the array because each swap moves it a greater distance in the array.

We begin with the following numbers to sort:

80	93	60	12	42	30	68	85	10	21	33	71	19	54	65	98	11	88	43	61	76

First we divide the array elements into 7 non-contiguous segments, labeled 1-7:

80	93	60	12	42	30	68	85	10	21	33	71	54	65	98	11	88	43	61	76
1	2	3	4	5	6	7	1	2	3	4	5	6	7	1	2	3	4	5	6	7

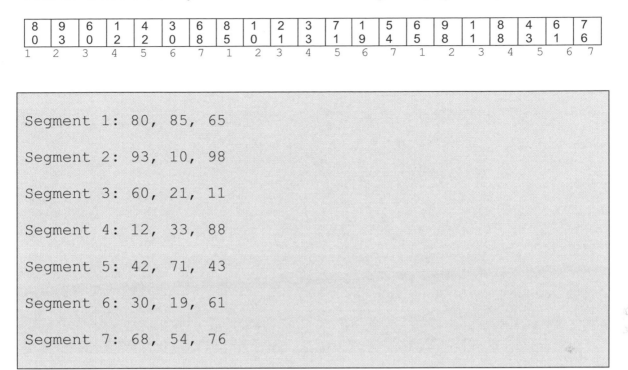

```
Segment 1: 80, 85, 65

Segment 2: 93, 10, 98

Segment 3: 60, 21, 11

Segment 4: 12, 33, 88

Segment 5: 42, 71, 43

Segment 6: 30, 19, 61

Segment 7: 68, 54, 76
```

Next we sort each segment (every 7th element):

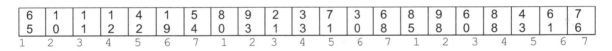

65	10	11	12	42	19	54	80	93	21	33	71	30	68	85	98	60	88	43	61	76
1	2	3	4	5	6	7	1	2	3	4	5	6	7	1	2	3	4	5	6	7

```
Segment 1: 65, 80, 85

Segment 2: 10, 93, 98

Segment 3: 11, 21, 60

Segment 4: 12, 33, 88

Segment 5: 42, 43, 71

Segment 6: 19, 30, 61

Segment 7: 54, 68, 76
```

Next, we divide the array elements into 3 segments:

6	1	1	1	4	1	5	8	9	2	3	7	3	6	8	9	6	8	4	6	7
5	0	1	2	2	9	4	0	3	1	9	1	0	8	5	8	0	8	3	1	6
1	2	3	1	2	3	1	2	3	1	2	3	1	2	3	1	2	3	1	2	3

Segment 1: 65, 12, 54, 21, 30, 98, 43

Segment 2: 10, 42, 80, 39, 68, 60, 61

Segment 3: 11, 19, 93, 71, 85, 88, 76

Next we sort each segment (every 3rd element):

1	1	1	2	3	1	3	4	9	4	6	7	5	6	8	6	6	8	9	8	7
2	0	1	1	3	9	0	2	3	3	0	1	4	1	5	5	8	8	0	0	6
1	2	3	1	2	3	1	2	3	1	2	3	1	2	3	1	2	3	1	2	3

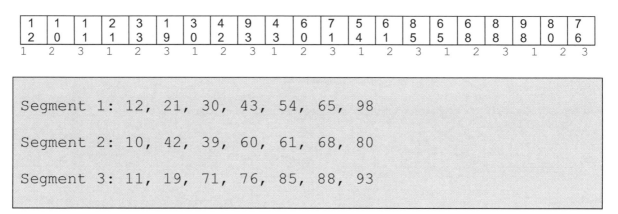

Segment 1: 12, 21, 30, 43, 54, 65, 98

Segment 2: 10, 42, 39, 60, 61, 68, 80

Segment 3: 11, 19, 71, 76, 85, 88, 93

Finally, we use an increment of 1 which produces only one segment (the entire array):

1	1	1	2	3	1	3	4	9	4	6	7	5	6	8	6	6	8	9	8	7
2	0	1	1	3	9	0	2	3	3	0	1	4	1	5	5	8	8	0	0	6
1	1	1	1	1	1	1	1	1	1	1	1	1	1	1	1	1	1	1	1	1

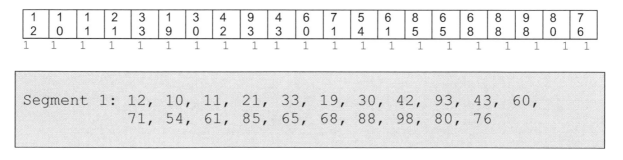

Segment 1: 12, 10, 11, 21, 33, 19, 30, 42, 93, 43, 60,
71, 54, 61, 85, 65, 68, 88, 98, 80, 76

And we do a final sort of the array (which is almost sorted):

1	1	1	1	2	3	3	4	4	5	6	6	6	6	7	7	8	8	8	9	9
0	1	2	9	1	0	3	2	3	4	0	1	5	8	1	6	0	5	8	3	8

So shellsort uses a series of increment sizes and performs insertion sort on the array using these increments. We can then think of the array as a series of interlaced subarrays, where we perform insertion sort on these subarrays concurrently.

Analysis of Shellsort

Shellsort is extremely simple to program and requires little overhead. It incorporates the logic of insertion sort to a certain extent. Instead of sorting the entire array at once, it first divides the array into smaller, noncontiguous segments that are then separately sorted using the insertion sort. Shellsort causes items to be moved across many others with the chance of eliminating many swaps for each comparison.

Shellsort is sometimes referred to as the diminishing increment sort because the value of `h` (the number of segments) continually decreases with each pass through the data. Knuth has recommended that the `(h + 1)`[th] incremental values be 2 times the `jth value + 1`. So typical incremental values are 1, 3, 7, 15, … .

So shellsort, like quicksort, divides a data set into subsets, sorts the subsets, and then recombines these sorted subsets. Shellsort's average performance is thought to be approximately $O(n^{3/2})$. The exact complexity of this algorithm is still being debated and is far too advanced for this class. Suffice to say that for mid-sized data sets it performs nearly as well, if not better, than the faster $O(n \log n)$ sorts.

Knuth has mathematically estimated that, with proper values of h, the shellsort will execute in average time proportional to $O(n (\log_2 n)^2)$. However, the sort will work for any values of `h`, as long as the last value of `h` is 1.

Shellsort, like insertion sort, is most efficient on arrays that are nearly sorted. In fact, the first chosen value of k is large to insure that the whole array is fragmented into smaller individual arrays, for which the insertion sort is highly effective. Each subsequent sort causes the entire array to be more nearly sorted, so that the efficiency of insertion sort as applied to larger partially sorted arrays is increased.

Shellsort Code

In the shellsort code shown below, the number of segments used for arranging the data in each step is in array `increment`. Thus, data are arranged in 1,391,376 segments in the first step and in one segment in the last step. Note that essentially nothing is done if the number of segments `h` is larger than the number of data elements `n`.

```
// Shellsort

public static void shellsort(int[] a, int l, int r) {
    int i, j, v;
    int increment[16] = { 1391376, 463792, 198768, 86961, 33936,
                          13776, 4592, 1968, 861, 336,
                          112, 48, 21, 7, 3, 1 };

    for (int k = 0; k < 16; k++) {
        for (int h = increment[k], i = l+h; i <= r; i++) {
            v = a[i];
            j = i;
            while (j > h && a[j-h] > v) {
                a[j] = a[j-h];
                j -= h;
            }
            a[j] = v;
        }
    }
}
```

Selection Sort

Selection sort starts by finding the smallest element in the array and interchanges it with the element in the first position of the array. After that it reexamines the remaining elements in the array to find the second smallest element. The element that is found is interchanged with the element in the second position of the array. This process continues until all of the array elements are placed in their proper order.

Selection Sort Example

Shown below is the selection sort in action. The number in angle brackets, <>, is the smallest element found so far. The shaded number is the number we are comparing with the smallest element found so far. The numbers with a dash after them are the sorted array elements.

Our initial array looks like this.

3	5	2	4	6	1

We are going to assume that the first array element is the smallest element seen so far.

< 3 >	5	2	4	6	1

Next we compare < 3 > with 5.

< 3 >	5	2	4	6	1

Next we compare < 3 > with 2.

< 3 >	5	2	4	6	1

2 < 3 so we hold on to 2 as the smallest element seen.

3	5	< 2 >	4	6	1

Next we compare < 2 > with 4.

3	5	< 2 >	4	6	1

Next we compare < 2 > with 6.

3	5	< 2 >	4	6	1

Next we compare < 2 > with 1.

3	5	< 2 >	4	6	1

1 < 2 so we hold on to 1 as the smallest element seen.

3	5	2	4	6	< 1 >

We've come to the end of the array. Therefore, 1 is the smallest array element and we swap it with the 1st array element.

1 -	5	2	4	6	3

At the end of the first pass the smallest array element is in the 1st array position and we no longer consider the first array element.

We continue the sort with the 2nd pass and now assume 5 is the smallest element seen so far:

1 -	< 5 >	2	4	6	3

Next we compare < 5 > with 2.

1 -	< 5 >	2	4	6	3

2 < 5 so we hold on to 2 as the smallest element seen.

1 -	5	< 2 >	4	6	3

Next we compare < 2 > with 4.

1 -	5	< 2 >	4	6	3

Next we compare < 2 > with 6.

| 1 - | 5 | < 2 > | 4 | 6 | 3 |

Next we compare < 2 > with 3.

| 1 - | 5 | < 2 > | 4 | 6 | 3 |

We've come to the end of the array. Therefore, 2 is the smallest array element and we swap it with 5.

| 1 - | 2 - | 5 | 4 | 6 | 3 |

At the end of the 2nd pass the 2nd smallest array element is in the 2nd array position and we no longer consider the 2nd array position.

We continue the sort with the 3rd pass and now assume 5 is the smallest element seen so far.

| 1 - | 2 - | < 5 > | 4 | 6 | 3 |

Next we compare < 5 > with 4.

| 1 - | 2 - | < 5 > | 4 | 6 | 3 |

4 < 5 so we hold on to 4 as the smallest element seen.

| 1 - | 2 - | 5 | < 4 > | 6 | 3 |

Next we compare < 4 > with 6.

| 1 - | 2 - | 5 | < 4 > | 6 | 3 |

Next we compare < 4 > with 3.

| 1 - | 2 - | 5 | < 4 > | 6 | 3 |

3 < 4 so we hold on to 3 as the smallest element seen.

| 1 - | 2 - | 5 | 4 | 6 | < 3 > |

We've come to the end of the array. Therefore, 3 is the smallest array element and we swap it with 5.

| 1 - | 2 - | 3 - | 4 | 6 | 5 |

At the end of the 3rd pass the 3rd smallest array element is in the 3rd array position and we no longer consider the 3rd array position.

We continue the sort with the 4th pass and now assume that < 4 > is the smallest element seen so far.

| 1 - | 2 - | 3 - | < 4 > | 6 | 5 |

Next we compare < 4 > with 6.

| 1 - | 2 - | 3 - | < 4 > | 6 | 5 |

Next we compare < 4 > with 5.

| 1 - | 2 - | 3 - | < 4 > | 6 | 5 |

We've come to the end of the array. Therefore, 4 is the smallest array element and we keep it in its current position.

| 1 - | 2 - | 3 - | 4 - | 6 | 5 |

At the end of the 4th pass the 4th smallest array element is in the 4th array position and we no longer consider the 4th array element.

We continue the sort with the 5th pass and now assume that < 6 > is the smallest element seen so far.

| 1 - | 2 - | 3 - | 4 - | < 6 > | 5 |

Next we compare < 6 > with 5.

1 -	2 -	3 -	4 -	< 6 >	5

5 < 6 so we hold onto 5 as the smallest element seen.

1 -	2 -	3 -	4 -	6	< 5 >

We've come to the end of the array. Therefore, 5 is the smallest array element and we swap it with 6.

1 -	2 -	3 -	4 -	5 -	6

With n data items we have made $n-1$ passes through the array. There is no need to make an nth pass as the remaining data item in the array must be the largest and it is in its correct position at the end of the array. Therefore the array is already sorted.

1 -	2 -	3 -	4 -	5 -	6 -

In general, if we have an array with n elements, we must make $n-1$ passes through the array.

Analysis of Selection Sort

For a given number of data items, selection sort always goes through a set number of comparisons and data movements (exchanges), so its performance is predictable. Selection sort makes $n-1$ passes through the data. There are approximately n comparisons during each pass. Thus, selection sort is an $O(n^2)$ sort for its best case, average case, and worst case.

One advantage of selection sort is that there are very few data exchanges. Unlike insertion sort, selection sort swaps elements only when it knows it is swapping one of them into its correct position within the array. Selection sort performs a maximum of $n-1$ data movements and, as a result, is preferred over insertion sort.

Finally, note that the insertion sort takes each successive piece of data and places it into the correct position relative to all previously considered items while selection sort searches through the entire sequence until the next smallest data item is found. Thus insertion sort starts out quickly and gets slower and slower as the number of items already considered grows. Selection sort starts out very slowly and speeds up as the number of items still to be considered shrinks.

```java
// selectionSort.java

public static void selectionSort(int[] list, int max) {
    for (int i = 0; i < max-1; i++) {
        int k = i;
        int temp = list[i];
        for (j = i+1; j < max; j++)
            if (list[j] < temp) {
                k = j;
                temp = list[j];
            }
        list[k] = list[i];
        list[i] = temp;
    }
}
```

Time Complexity for Selection Sort

Best Case	Average Case	Worst Case
$O(n^2)$	$O(n^2)$	$O(n^2)$

Heapsort

We have previously implemented binary heaps within arrays using canonical numbering of the nodes of the tree.

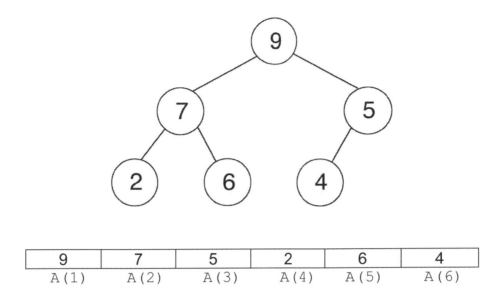

We defined the relationships between parent and child nodes of complete binary trees stored within arrays as follows:

- The left child of A(i) is at A(2i), if it exists.

- The right child of A(i) is at A(2i+1), if it exists.

- The canonical number of the parent of a left or right child at A(i) is A(i/2).

Our heapsort algorithm will utilize this implementation of binary heaps to sort the data in two steps:

- Create the initial heap.

- Sort the array.

Step 1: Create the Initial Heap
Given the binary tree below that is neither a heap nor an almost heap, we first work through the process of creating a heap:

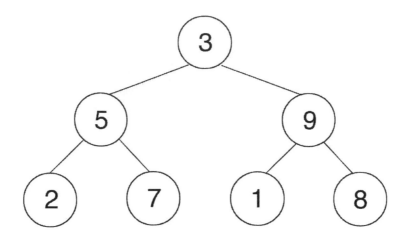

Note that the leaves are always considered heaps, as they have no children. So we look at the first internal node, i.e., the node with the next highest canonical number. In this case we look at the node with canonical number 3 that contains the value 9.

The tree rooted at 9 is a heap:

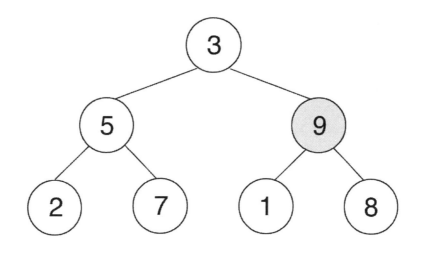

Next we look at the node with canonical number 2 that contains 5. The tree rooted at 5 is not a heap, but is an almost heap. So we must allow the node with 5 to sift down to its proper location in the tree.

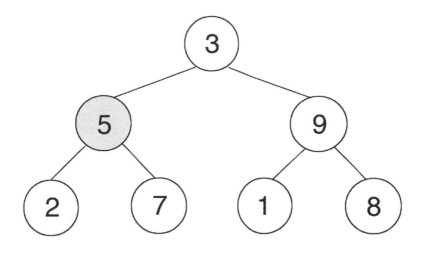

We swap the root of the subtree with its largest child:

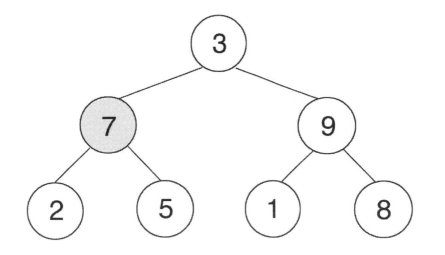

The tree rooted at 7 is now a heap.

Finally, we look at the node with canonical number 1, which contains the value 3 and is located at the root of the tree.

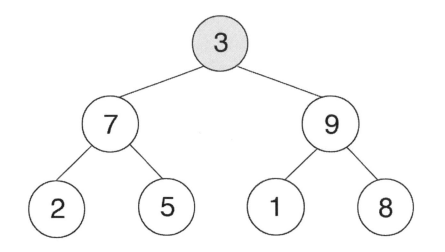

Once again we have an almost heap. So we must allow the root to sift down to its proper level. We swap the root with its largest child:

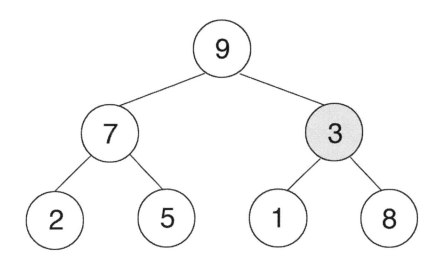

Once again, the tree rooted at 3 is an almost heap. So we must again swap it with its largest child:

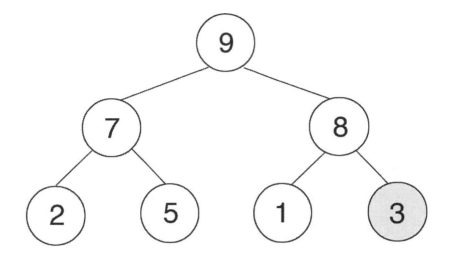

We now have a heap! Note that we had to work up the tree in reverse canonical number going from right to left, bottom to top, making subtrees into heaps.

Step 2: Sort the Array

Now that we have a heap, we can continue with the sorting part of the algorithm. Note that in a heap the root contains the largest value. We swap the root with the rightmost child at the lowest level:

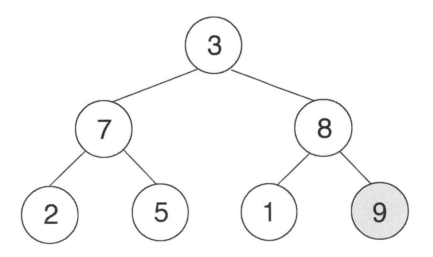

Remember we are implementing the binary tree using an array so the node containing the 9 has the highest canonical number, and therefore has been placed as the last element of the array. The value 9 is in its correct position within the array so we no longer need to consider that node.

We now have an almost heap that must be converted into a heap. Therefore, the root with value 3 must sift down to its lowest level. We swap it with its largest child, the node with value 8.

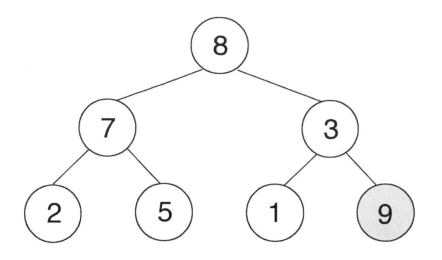

Once again we have a heap. Therefore we swap the root with the rightmost child at the lowest level:

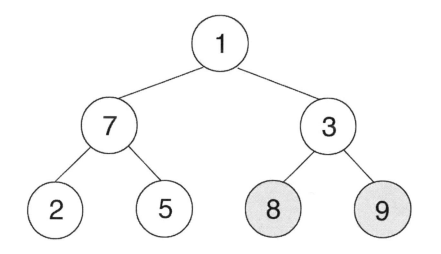

Again, we no longer need to consider the node with value 8 as it is now in its correct position within the array. However, we now have an almost heap. So we must allow the root to sift down to its proper level by swapping it with its largest child.

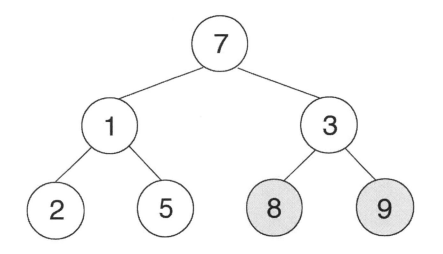

Once again the tree rooted at 1 is an almost heap so we must swap it with its largest child:

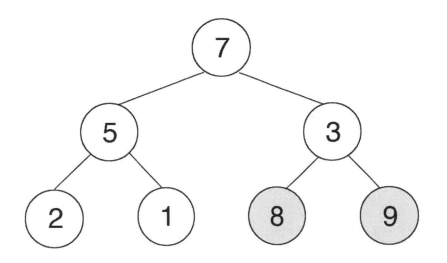

We now have a heap and we swap the root with the rightmost leaf at the lowest level.

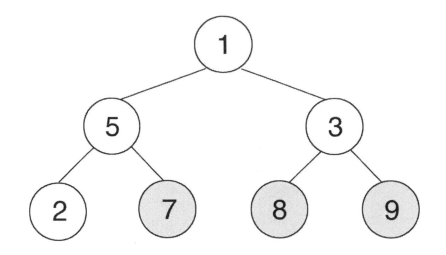

The node with value 7 is now in its correct position in the array and we no longer need to consider it. However, we now have an almost heap so we must allow the root to sift down to its proper level:

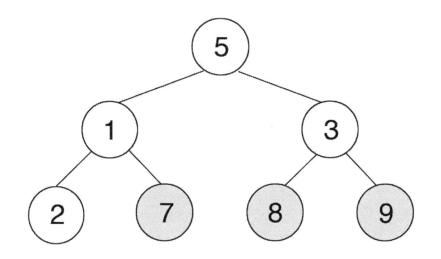

Again, the tree rooted at 1 is an almost heap and we must swap the root with its largest child:

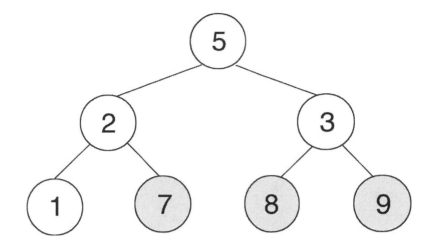

Once again we have a heap. Therefore let's swap the root with the rightmost child at the lowest level:

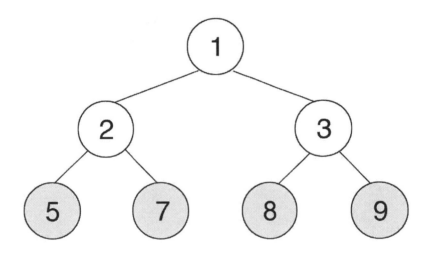

The node with value 5 is now in its correct position within the array. We now have an almost heap so we must allow the root to sift down to its proper level:

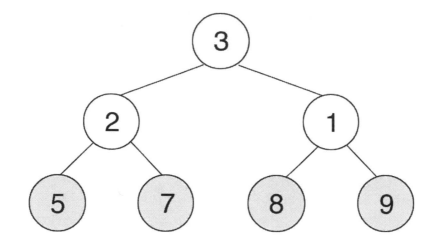

Once again we have a heap. Therefore we swap the root with the rightmost child at the lowest level:

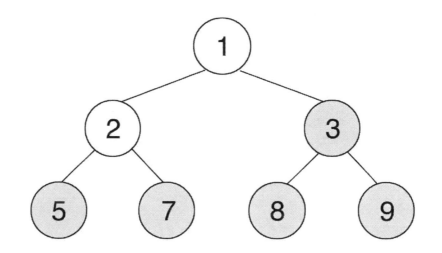

Once again, the node with value 3 is in its correct array location. However, we now have an almost heap. So we must allow the root to sift down to its proper level:

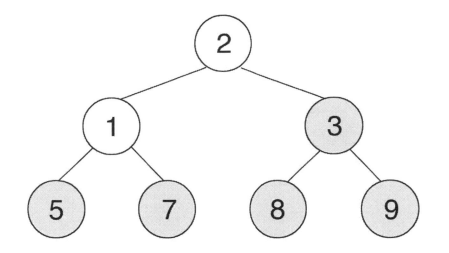

We now have a heap. Therefore we swap the root with the rightmost child at the lowest level:

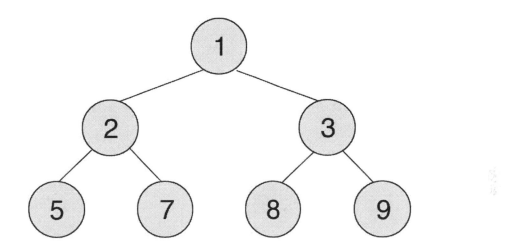

Keep in mind that the binary tree is implemented as an array. Therefore, if we iterate through the array we get the data values:

```
1 - 2 - 3 - 5 - 7 - 8 - 9
```

The data is sorted!

Analysis of Heapsort

The average case and worst case for heapsort is $O(n \log n)$, as there are n passes through the data with $O(\log n)$ comparisons each pass.

Heapsort is very efficient for large values of n, and is most efficient for data that is in reverse order. It is least efficient for data that is already in sorted order. Heapsort will, on average, take more time than quicksort by a small constant factor. However, unlike quicksort, it has no worst case scenario. It's the hardest of all algorithms to understand because the technique is counterintuitive since it involves sorting from the "other end".

```
// Heapsort - sorts count data items within array. Items to be sorted
// are at indices 1 - count.

public static void heapsort(int[] item, int count) {
    int i, temp;

    for (i = count/2; i >= 1; i--)
        buildHeap(item, i, count);
    for (i = count; i >= 1; i--) {
        temp = item[1];
        item[1] = item[i];
        item[i] = temp;
        buildHeap(item, 1, i - 1);
    }
}

public static void buildHeap(int[] item, int i, int count) {
    int max, temp;
    boolean isMaxHeap = false;

    while (i*2 <= count && !isMaxHeap) {
        if (i*2 == count || item[i*2] > item[i*2+1])
            max = i*2;
        else
            max = i*2+1;
        if (item[max] > item[i]) {
            temp = item[max];
            item[max] = item[i];
            item[i] = temp;
            i = max;
        }
        else
            isMaxHeap = true;
    }
}
```

Time Complexity for Heap Sort

Best Case	Average Case	Worst Case
O(n log n)	O(n log n)	O(n log n)

Java Program Style Guide
Java Reserved Words
Java Primitive Data Types
Precedence of Java Operators
Lifetime and Scope
Formatting Output Using printf()
NumberFormat Class
String Class
StringBuilder Class
Scanner Class
SuperOutput Class
Inheritance
ASCII Table

Java Program Style Guide

1. Naming
1.1 Use meaningful names.

Use descriptive names for all identifiers (names of classes, variables and methods). Avoid ambiguity. Avoid abbreviations. Simple mutator methods should be named `setSomething(...)`. Simple accessor methods should be named `getSomething(...)`. Accessor methods with boolean return values are often called `isSomething(...)`, for example, `isEmpty()`.

1.2 Class names start with a capital letter.

1.3 Class names are singular nouns.

1.4 Method and variable names start with lowercase letters.

All three - class, method and variable names - use capital letters in the middle to increase readability of compound identifiers, e.g. `numberOfItems`.

1.5 Constants are written in UPPERCASE.

Constants occasionally use underscores to indicate compound identifiers: `MAXIMUM_SIZE`

2. Layout
2.1 One level of indentation is four spaces (or one tab stop).

2.2 All statements within a block are indented one level.

2.3 Braces for classes and methods are alone on one line.

The braces for class and method blocks are on separate lines and are at the same indentation level, for example:

```
public int getAge()
{
    statements
}
```

2.4 For all other blocks, braces open at the end of a line.

All other blocks open with braces at the end of the line that contains the keyword defining the block. The closing brace is on a separate line, aligned under the keyword that defines the block. For example:

```
while(condition) {
    statements
}

if(condition) {
    statements
}
else {
    statements
}
```

2.5 Always use braces in control structures.

Braces are used in if-statements and loops even if the body is only a single statement.

2.6 Use a space before the opening brace of a control structure's block.

2.7 Use a space around operators.

2.8 Use a blank line between methods (and constructors).

Use blank lines to separate logical blocks of code. This means at least between methods, but also between logical parts within a method.

3. Documentation
3.1 Every class has a class comment at the top.

The class comment contains at least
- a general description of the class
- the author's name
- a version number

A version number can be a simple number, a date, or other formats. The important thing is that a reader must be able to recognize if two versions are not the same, and be able to determine which one is newer.

3.2 Every method has a method comment.

3.3 Comments are Javadoc-readable.

Class and method comments must be recognized by Javadoc. In other words they should start with the comment symbol /**.

3.4 Code comments (only) where necessary.

Comments in the code should be included where the code is not obvious or difficult to understand (while preference should be given to make the code obvious or easy to understand where possible), and where it helps understanding of a method. Do not comment obvious statements - assume your reader understands Java!

4. Language use restrictions

4.1 Order of declarations: class variables, constructors, methods.

The elements of a class definition appear (if present) in the following order: package statement; import statements; class comment; class header; class variable definitions; constructors; methods.

4.2 Class variables may not be public (except for final class variables).

4.3 Always use an access modifier.

Specify all class variables and methods as either private, public, or protected. Never use default (package private) access.

4.4 Import classes separately.

Import statements explicitly naming every class are preferred over importing whole packages. E.g.

```
import java.util.ArrayList;
import java.util.HashSet;
```

is better than

```
import java.util.*;
```

4.5 Always include a constructor (even if the body is empty).

4.6 Always include superclass constructor call.

In constructors of subclasses, do not rely on automatic insertion of a superclass call. Include the `super(...)` call explicitly, even if it would work without it.

4.7 Initialize all class variables in the constructor.

5. Code idioms
5.1 Use iterators with collections.

To iterate over a collection, use a for-each loop. When the collection must be changed during iteration use an Iterator, not an integer index.

Java Reserved Words

abstract	boolean	break	byte
case	catch	char	class
const	continue	default	do
double	else	extends	false
final	finally	float	for
goto	if	implements	import
instanceof	int	interface	long
native	new	null	package
private	protected	public	return
short	static	strictfp	super
switch	synchronized	this	throw
throws	transient	true	try
void	volatile	while	

Java Primitive Data Types

Data Type	Bits	Range
Integral numbers:		
byte	8	-128 to 127
short	16	-32,768 to 32,767
int	32	-2,147,438,648 to 2,147,483,647
long	64	-9,223,372,036,854,775,808 to 9,223,372,036,854,775,807
Floating point numbers:		
float	32	+/- about 10^{-45} to 10^{38}
double	64	+/- about 10^{-324} to 10^{308}
Boolean values:		
boolean	1	false - true
Characters:		
char	16	16-bit Unicode character: 0 to 65,535 For alphanumerics, these are the same as ASCII with the high byte set to 0: 0 to 255

Precedence of Java Operators

Precedence Level	Operator
Level 1	Unary +, Unary -
Level 2	*, /, %
Level 3	+, -
Level 4	<, <=, >, >=
Level 5	==, !=
Level 6	&
Level 7	|
Level 8	&&
Level 9	||
Level 10	?:
Level 11	=, +=, -=, /=, %=
Level 12	,

Lifetime and Scope

The **lifetime** of a variable is the period of time during the execution of a program when a variable exists. The **scope** of a variable is the portion of a program in which a variable is visible (defined, accessible). Different kinds of variables have different lifetimes and scopes, and are initialized differently.

Instance Variables

Lifetime: From the time the containing object is created until no other variable in the process has a reference to the object (after which time the object may be garbage collected).

Scope: If private, only in the methods of its own class; if public, at any point where the containing objects exists.

Initialization: Automatically initialized with a default value unless an initial value is specified, either in the declaration of the variable or in the class constructor.

Static (Class) Variables

Lifetime: From the time its class is first loaded until the class is unloaded (generally when the program terminates).

Scope: If private, only in the methods of its own class; if public, at any point in a file that imports the class (which, for classes in the package java.lang, is all files).

Initialization: Automatically initialized with a default value unless an initial value is specified.

Local Variables

Lifetime: From the time that the flow of control reaches the declaration of the local variable until the containing block is exited.

Scope: From the point of its declaration to the end of the enclosing block.

Initialization: Must be given a value prior to use, either in an initializer or by assignment.

Parameter Variables

Lifetime: From the time a method is called until the method returns.

Scope: The entire body of its method.

Initialization: Initialized with a copy of the corresponding actual parameter.

Formatting Output Using printf()

The syntax of the `printf()` output statement is shown below:

```
System.out.printf("format_control_string", arguments);
```

The format control string describes how the arguments to the `printf()` method are to be printed. For example we can add two integers and display the result:

```
int num1 = 50;
int num2 = 75;
int sum = num1 + num2;
System.out.printf("The sum of %d and %d is %d.%n", num1, num2, sum);
```

The output produced is:

```
The sum of 50 and 75 is 125.
```

Shown below is a table of control string formats:

```
%d     decimal integer (byte, short, int, long)

%f     floating point number (float, double)

%c     character (uppercase C outputs an uppercase character)

%e     scientific notation format

%o     octal format

%x     hexadecimal format

%n     generates a newline character (preferred over \n)

%s     String format (uppercase S outputs uppercase string)
```

We can also specify the field width for our outputted arguments by inserting a digit within the control string:

```
System.out.printf("%6d %6d%n", num1, num2);
```

This will allow 6 print positions for each output. Without the width specification, Java takes only as many positions as are needed to output the data.

We can also specify the number of digits of precision when outputting floating-point values.

```
double value = 123.456;
System.out.printf("Amount = %8.2f%n", value);
```

The field width of the output contains 8 columns (one of which is taken by the decimal point), two of which are to the right of the decimal place. Note that numbers are rounded to the specified precision.

```
Amount =    123.46
```

By default, numbers are output right justified. Preceding the field width with a dash will left justify the output in the field width:

```
double value = 123.456;
System.out.printf("Amount = %-8.2f%n", value);
```

The output produced is:

```
Amount = 123.46
```

String Class

Next to numbers, Strings are the most important data type that most programs use. A String is a sequence of characters, such as `"Hello, world."` In Java, Strings are enclosed in quotation marks, which are not part of the String. Note that unlike numbers, a String in Java is not a primitive type. It is an object that belongs to the `String` class. (You can tell that `String` is a class name because it starts with an upper case letter. The basic types `int` and `double` start with a lower case letter.)

String Literals

A String literal is a sequence (or string) of zero or more characters between double quotes:

```
""     "Hello"     "This is a String literal."
```

We have used String literals as arguments to the `System.out.println()` method. The `String` class is special in that it is the only class that has literal values. When a String literal is used, what is really happening is that:

• An instance of the `String` class (that is, a `String` object) is created.
• That `String` object is given the value of the String literal.
• A reference to that object is also created with the String literal representing the reference.

For example, the String literal:

```
"Hello"
```

creates the diagram below:

The new `String` object has the value `"Hello"` inside it and `"Hello"` is also thought of as the reference to that object.

Once we have a reference to an object, we can use that reference to call a method of that object. The only difference is that in the case of `"Hello"` the reference is not being held by a variable.

Constructing a String

You can construct a `String` by writing it as a literal:

```
String s1 = "Hello, World.";
```

This creates a `String` object containing the characters between quotation marks, just as before. A string created in this way is also called a String literal. All other objects are constructed by using the `new` operator.

Since a `String` is an object, you could construct it with `new`:

```
String s1 = new String("Hello, world.");
```

But using `new` for constructing a String is foolish, because you have to write the `String` as a literal to pass it on to the constructor. You're actually doing the same work twice!

The `null` Value

A reference variable can hold information about the location of an object, but does not hold the object itself. This following code:

```
String s;
```

declares a variable but does not construct any object. The following puts a reference in the variable:

```
s = "Good day sunshine.";
```

There is a special value called `null` that can be assigned to an object reference variable. The value `null` is a special value that means "no object." A reference variable is set to `null` when it is not referring to any object.

In most programs, objects come and objects go, depending on the data and on what is being computed. (Think of a computer game, where monsters show up, and monsters get killed). A reference variable sometimes does and sometimes does not refer to an object. You need a way to say that a variable does not now refer to an object. You do this by assigning `null` to the variable.

Consider the following code:

```
1.      String s1 = "Hello, world.";

2.      String s2 = null;

3.      String s3 = "";

4.      if (s1 != null)
             System.out.println(s1);

5.      if (s2 != null)
             System.out.println(s2);

6.      if (s3 != null)
             System.out.println(s3);
```

Note that variables `s1` and `s3` are initialized to object references. Variable `s2` is initialized to `null`.

A String object that contains no characters is still an object. It is similar to having a blank sheet of paper, versus having no paper at all. Let's look at the above code:

Line 1: An object is created and variable `s1` refers to it.

Line 2: Variable `s2` refers to no object.

Line 3: An object is created (containing no characters) and variable `s3` refers to it.

Line 4: `s1 != null` is `true`, so the `System.out.println(s1)` executes.

Line 5: `s2 != null` is `false`, so the `System.out.println(s2)` is skipped.

Line 6: `s3 != null` is `true`, so the `System.out.println(s3)` executes but it has no characters to print.

Note that the `System.out.println()` method expects a reference to a `String` object as a parameter. The example program tests that each variable contains a `String` reference before calling `System.out.println()` with it. Actually, `System.out.println()` will not crash if it gets a `null`. But some methods will. Usually you should insure that methods get the data they expect.

Strings Are Immutable

Java was designed after programmers had about 15 years' experience with object-oriented programming. One of the lessons learned in those years is that in robust code objects are seldom altered after they are constructed. So, for many Java classes, objects cannot be altered after construction. The class `String` is one of those.

We say that `String` objects are immutable. This means that after construction, they cannot be altered. <u>Once a String object has been constructed, the characters it contains will always be the same.</u> None of its methods will change those characters, and there is no way to change them. The characters can be used for various purposes (such as in constructing new `String` objects), and can be inspected, but never altered.

String Methods

There are about 48 methods that operate on `String` objects. It's not necessary to learn all 48 `String` methods unless you use them a lot. Instead, learn how to use the API. What follows is a sampling of `String` methods. All `String` methods are called as:

```
myString.method(params)
```

- `public char charAt (int index)`
Returns the character at the specified index, where index is between 0 and `length - 1`.

```
String s = "Hello";
System.out.println(s.charAt(0));
System.out.println(s.charAt(3));
System.out.println(s.charAt(4));
```

- `public int length()`

Returns the length of this `String`. The length is equal to the number of 16-bit Unicode characters in the `String`.

```
String s = "All you need is love.";
int size = s.length();
System.out.println("The length of the string is " + size);


String s = new String("Give peace a chance.");
System.out.println(s);
for (int i=0; i < s.length(); i++)
    System.out.print(s.charAt(i));

int len = "All the world's a stage".length();
```

Here's a method that returns the position of the first occurrence of the character ch in the String `str`: If character ch is not in the String, the method returns -1.

```
public int getPosition (String str, char ch) {
    for (int i = 0; i < str.length(); i++)
        if (str.charAt(i) == ch)
            return i;
    return -1;
}
```

- `public String concat(String str)`

Concatenates the specified String to the end of this String.

```
String s = "The colors of the flag are ";
s = s.concat("red, white, and blue");
```

Strings can also be concatenated with the + operator:

```
String name = "Samantha";
String message = "Hello, " + name;
```

The concatenation operator in Java is very powerful. If one of the expressions, either to the left or the right of a + operator, is a string, then the other one is automatically forced to become a string as well, and both strings are concatenated. For example, consider this code:

```
String s = "R2d";
int n = 2;
String robot = s + n;
```

Since `s` is a String, `n` is converted from the integer 2 to the String `"2"`. Then the two Strings, `"R2d"` and `"2"`, are concatenated to form the String `"R2d2"`.

This concatenation is very useful to reduce the number of `System.out.println()` instructions. For example, you can combine:

```
System.out.print("The total is ");
System.out.println(total);
```

to the single call:

```
System.out.println("The total is " + total);
```

The concatenation `"The total is" + total` computes a single string that consists of the string `"The total is "`, followed by the string equivalent of the number `total`.

- `public int indexOf(int ch)`
Returns the index within this String of the first occurrence of the specified character. If the character is not in this String, a value of -1 is returned.

```
String s = "Magical Mystery Tour";
int index = s.indexOf('g');
```

- `public int indexOf(int ch, int fromIndex)`

Returns the index within this String of the first occurrence of the specified character, starting the search at the specified index, `fromIndex`. If the character is not in this String, a value of -1 is returned.

```
String s = "Magical Mystery Tour";
int index = s.indexOf('a', 3);
```

- `public int indexOf(String str)`

Returns the index within this String of the first occurrence of the specified substring. If the character is not in this String, a value of -1 is returned.

```
String s = "the cat and the hat";
int index = s.indexOf("the");
```

- `public int indexOf(String str, int fromIndex)`

Returns the index within this String of the first occurrence of the specified substring, starting the search at the specified index. If the character is not in this String, a value of -1 is returned.

```
String s = "the cat and the hat. ";
int index = s.indexOf("the", 4);
```

- `public int lastIndexOf(int ch)`

Returns the index within this String of the last occurrence of the specified character. If the character is not in this String, a value of -1 is returned.

```
String s = "Magical Mystery Tour";
int index = s.lastIndexOf('a');
```

- `public int lastIndexOf(int ch, int fromIndex)`

Returns the index within this String of the last occurrence of the specified character, searching backwards starting at the specified String. If the character is not in this String, a value of -1 is returned.

```
String s = "Magical Mystery Tour";
int index = s.lastIndexOf('M', 7);
```

- `public int lastIndexOf(String str)`

Returns the index within this String of the rightmost occurrence of the specified substring. If the character is not in this String, a value of -1 is returned.

```
String s = "the cat and the hat";
int index = s.lastIndexOf("the");
```

- `public int lastIndexOf(String str, int fromIndex)`

Returns the index within this String of the last occurrence of the specified substring, starting the search at the specified index. If the character is not in this String, a value of -1 is returned.

```
String s = "the cat and the hat. ";
int index = s.lastIndexOf("the", 4);
```

What value is returned from each of the following?

```
String state = "Mississippi";
```

- `state.length()`
- `state.indexOf("is")`
- `state.substring(0, 4)`
- `state.substring(4, 6)`
- `state.substring(9, 11);`

- `public String toLowerCase(String str)`
- `public String toUpperCase(String str)`

Converts all of the characters in this String to lower case or upper case.

```
String greeting = "Hello";
System.out.println(greeting.toUpperCase());
System.out.println(greeting.toLowerCase());
```

This code segment prints:

```
HELLO
Hello
```

Note that the `toUpperCase()` and `toLowerCase()` methods do not change the original `String` object `greeting`. They return new `String` objects that contain the uppercase and lowercase versions of the original String. Remember, no String methods modify the `String` object on which they operate. Strings are immutable objects.

- `public String substring(int beginIndex)`

Returns a new String that is a substring of this String. The substring begins with the character at the specified index and extends to the end of the String. Note that as with all String methods, the original String remains unchanged.

```
"unhappy".substring(2) returns "happy"
```

- `public String substring(int beginIndex, int endIndex)`

Returns a new String that is a substring of this String. The substring begins at the specified `beginIndex` and extends to the character at index `endIndex-1`. Thus the length of the substring is `endIndex - beginIndex`.

```
"miles".substring(1, 4) returns "ile"

String name = "Haley Laurel";
String first = name.substring(0, 5);
```

The above code assigns the name "Haley" to String First.

A curious aspect of the substring operation is the numbering of the starting and ending positions. Starting position 0 means, "start at the beginning of the string". Note that Java string positions start at 0. The first string position is labeled 0, the second string position is labeled 1, etc.

H	a	l	e	y		L	a	u	r	e	l
0	1	2	3	4	5	6	7	8	9	10	11

Note that the position number of the last character (11 for the string "Haley Laurel") is always 1 less than the length of the string.

Let's figure out how to extract the substring "Laur". Count characters starting at 0, not 1. You find that L, the 7th, character has position number 6. The first character that you don't want, e, is the character at position 10. Therefore the appropriate substring command is:

```
String t = name.substring(6, 10);
```

It is curious that you must specify the position of the first character that you do want and then the first character that you don't want. There is one advantage to this setup. You can easily compute the length of the substring as:

```
endIndex - beginIndex
```

We can select the substring that contains the last name as follows:

```
String last = name.substring(6);
```

Note that if we omit the second parameter of the substring method, then all characters from the starting position to the end of the string are copied.

Give the output of the following program segment:

```
String s = "Hello";
For (int i=0; i < s.length(); i++)
    System.out.println(s.substring(0, i);
```

• `public String trim()`
Returns a new String that contains the same characters as the old one but has any whitespace characters (blanks, tabs, newlines, and several other non-printing characters) removed from both ends (but not from the middle). So, for example, after the last statement:

```
String userData = "      745    ";
String fixed = userData.trim();
```

The new String referenced by `fixed` will contain the characters `"745"` without the surrounding spaces. This is often useful in preparing user input data for conversion from character form to numeric form.

• `public int compareTo(String str)`
Compares two strings lexicographically based on the Unicode value of each character in the Strings. Returns negative number if this String object lexicographically precedes the argument String. Returns a positive number if this String object lexicographically follows the argument String. Returns zero if the strings are equal.

• `int compareToIgnoreCase(String str)`
Compares two strings lexicographically, ignoring case considerations, based on the Unicode value of each character in the String. Returns negative number if this String object lexicographically precedes the argument String. Returns a positive number if this String object lexicographically follows the argument String. Returns zero if the strings are equal.

- `public boolean equals(String str)`

Compares this String to the specified String. The result is `true` if the argument is not `null` and is a String object that represents the same sequence of characters as this subject.

```
String str1 = "Yellow";
String str2 = "Blue";

if (str1.equals(str2))
    System.out.println("Strings are equal. ");
else
    System.out.println("Strings are different. ");
```

Note the String referenced by `str1` has an `equals` method. That method is called with a parameter, a reference to `str2`. The method checks if both Strings contain identical characters and, if so, evaluates to `true` (returns `true`).

Note: the equality tests, `==` and `!=`, work just fine for primitives, but `==` and `!=` test for identity, not equality. As a result:

```
"abcde" != "abc" + "de"
```

Therefore, you should use:

```
str1.equals(str2)
```

instead of:

```
str1 == str2
```

- `public boolean equalsIgnoreCase(String str)`

Compares this String to the specified String, ignoring case considerations. The result is `true` if the argument is not `null` and is a String object that represents the same sequence of characters as this subject.

StringBuilder Class

The `String` class is used for strings that are not allowed to change. The `StringBuilder` class is used for strings that may be modified by the program. At any point in time, a `StringBuilder` may contain some particular sequence of characters, but the length and content of the sequence can be changed through certain method calls.

Constructing a StringBuilder Object

There are no `StringBuilder` literals. It is not possible to construct a `StringBuilder` object without the use of the `new` operator:

```
StringBuilder sb = "Hello, world.";          // invalid
```

However, it is possible to create a reference to a `StringBuilder` object:

```
StringBuilder sb;
```

But it is later necessary to use the `new` operator to actually instantiate an object:

```
sb = new StringBuilder("Hello, world.");
```

As with other objects in Java, we can declare, instantiate, and bind `StringBuilder` objects in a single statement:

```
StringBuilder sb = new StringBuilder ("Hello, world.");
```

A `StringBuilder` has a *capacity* (the number of characters it can hold) and a *length* (the number of characters it is currently holding). Here is the signature of the three defined constructors for the `StringBuilder` class:

- `public StringBuilder ()`

Constructs a `StringBuilder` with no characters in it and a default capacity of 16 characters.

- `public StringBuilder (int length)`

Constructs a `StringBuilder` with no characters in it and an initial capacity specified by the `length` argument.

- `public StringBuilder (String str)`

Constructs a `StringBuilder` containing the String `str`. The initial capacity of the `StringBuilder` is 16 plus the length of the String argument.

Here are additional methods for the `StringBuilder` class:

- `public int length()`

Returns the number of characters in this `StringBuilder`.

- `public int capacity()`

Returns the current capacity of this `StringBuilder`. The capacity is the amount of storage available for newly inserted characters; beyond which an allocation will occur. Note that the `String` class does not have a `capacity` method, because a String cannot change.

- `public void setLength()`

Sets the length of this `StringBuilder`.

- `public char charAt(int index)`

Returns the character located at the `index` argument.

- `public setCharAt(int index, char ch)`

The character at the specified index of the `StringBuilder` is set to `ch`. Note that here the `StringBuilder` is altered to represent a new character sequence that is identical to the old character sequence, except that it contains the character `ch` at position `index`.

- `public StringBuilder append(String str)`
Appends the `String` to this `StringBuilder`.

- `public StringBuilder append(StringBuilder sb)`
Appends the `StringBuilder` to this `StringBuilder`.

- `public StringBuilder delete(int start, int end)`
Removes the characters in a substring of this `StringBuilder`. The substring begins at the specified `start` and extends to the character at index `end – 1` or to the end of the `StringBuilder`.

- `public StringBuilder deleteCharAt(int index)`
Removes the character at the specified position in this `StringBuilder` (shortening the `StringBuilder` by one character).

- `public StringBuilder replace(int start, int end, String str)`
Replaces the characters in a substring of this `StringBuilder` with characters in the specified String.

- `public String substring(int start, int end)`
Returns a new `String` that contains a sub-sequence of characters currently contained in the `StringBuilder`. The substring begins at the specified `start` and extends to the character at index `end – 1`.

- `public StringBuilder insert(int offset, String str)`
Inserts the string into this `StringBuilder`.

- `public StringBuilder insert(int offset, char ch)`
Inserts the string representation of the `char` argument into this `StringBuilder`.

- `public StringBuilder reverse()`
The character sequence contained in this `StringBuilder` is replaced by the reverse of the sequence.

Here is some code to reverse the characters of a string, without using the `reverse` method:

```java
// reverseDemo.java

public static void main(String[] args) {
    String s = "The sky is blue.";
    int size = s.length();
    StringBuilder dest = new StringBuilder(size);
    for (int i = (size - 1); i >= 0; i--)
        dest.append(s.charAt(i));
    System.out.println(dest);
}
```

• `public String toString()`
Converts the data in the `StringBuilder` to a `String`. A new `String` object is allocated and initialized to contain the character sequence currently represented by this `StringBuilder`. The `String` is then returned.

It's interesting to note that `StringBuilder`s are used by the compiler to implement the binary string concatenation operator +. For example, the code:

```java
String s = "a" + 4 + "c";
```

is compiled to the equivalent of:

```java
s = new StringBuilder().append("a").append(4).append("c").toString();
```

which creates a new `StringBuilder` (initially empty), appends the `String` representation of each operand to the `StringBuilder` in turn, and then converts the contents of the `StringBuilder` to a `String`. Overall, this avoids creating many temporary `String`s.

When to Use StringBuilders

If you make a lot of changes or additions to a `String`, it is much more efficient to use a `StringBuilder`. If you are simply examining the contents of a `String`, then a `String` is at least as efficient as a `StringBuilder`. For incidental use (such as creating output lines), use `String`s, they are more convenient.

Note, if you are making a lot of changes to `String`s, use `StringBuilder`s instead:

```
StringBuilder buf = new StringBuilder(myString);
```

Make your changes to `buf` and then convert back to a `String`;

```
String str = buf.toString();
```

Use the API!

Keep in mind that Java is huge and no one knows it all. There's complete documentation online at:

```
http://docs.oracle.com/javase/8/docs/api/index.html
```

It's smart to keep this open in a browser as you are programming. It's even smarter to download it onto your hard drive first.

Scanner Class

The `Scanner` class, which is part of the standard Java class library, provides convenient methods for reading input values of various types. The input could come from various sources, including data typed interactively by the user or data stored in a file. The following declaration creates a `Scanner` object that reads input from the keyboard:

```
Scanner scan = new Scanner(System.in);
```

The `System.in` object represents the standard input stream, which by default is the keyboard.

Unless specified otherwise, a `Scanner` object assumes that white space characters (space, tab, newline) are used to separate the input tokens from each other. These characters are called the input delimiters and can be changed if the input tokens are separated by characters other than white space.

The `next` method of the `Scanner` class reads the next input token as a string and returns it. Therefore, if the input consisted of a series of words separated by spaces, each call to next would return the next word. The `nextLine` method reads all of the input until the end of the line is found, and returns it as one string.

The following code simply reads a line of text typed by the user, stores it in a variable that holds a character string, then echoes it back to the screen:

```
import java.util.Scanner;

public class Echo {
    public static void main(String[] args) {
        String msg;
        Scanner scan = new Scanner(System.in);
        System.out.println("Enter a line of text: ");
        msg = scan.nextLine();
        System.out.println("You entered: " + msg);
    }
}


Output:
Enter a line of text: Hello, world.
You entered: Hello, world.
```

Constructors

`Scanner(InputStream source)`
Constructs a new `Scanner` that produces values scanned from the specified input stream.

`Scanner(File source)`
Constructs a new `Scanner` that produces values scanned from the specified file.

`Scanner(String source)`
  Constructs a new `Scanner` that produces values scanned from the specified
    string.

Methods

`String next()`
  Returns the next input token as a character string.

`String nextLine()`
  Returns all input remaining on the current line as a character string.

`boolean nextBoolean()`
Returns the next input token as a boolean.

`byte nextByte()`
Returns the next input token as a byte.

`double nextDouble()`
Returns the next input token as a double.

`float nextFloat()`
Returns the next input token as a float.

`int nextInt()`
Returns the next input token as an int.

`long nextLong()`
Returns the next input token as a long.

`Short nextShort()`
Returns the next input token as a short.

`Boolean hasNext()`
Returns true if the scanner has another token in its input.

```java
import java.io.*;
import java.util.*;

public class ScanTest {
    public static void main (String arg[]) {
        Scanner scan = new Scanner(System.in);
        try {
            System.out.print("Enter integer: ");
            int i = scan.nextInt();
            System.out.println("Integer = " + i + "\n");

            System.out.printf("Enter float: ");
            float f = scan.nextFloat();
            System.out.println("Float = " + f + "\n");

            System.out.printf("Enter double: ");
            double d = scan.nextDouble();
            System.out.println("Double = " + d + "\n");

            System.out.printf("Enter string: ");
            String s = scan.next();
            System.out.println("String = \"" + s + "\"" + "\n");
            s = scan.nextLine();

            System.out.printf("Enter text: ");
            String t = scan.nextLine();
            System.out.println("String = \"" + t + "\"" + "\n");
        }
        catch  (InputMismatchException e) {
            System.out.println ("Mismatch exception:" + e );
        }
    }
}
```

Here's the program output:

```
Enter integer: 123
Integer = 123

Enter float: 123.456
Float = 123.456

Enter double: 123.45678987654
Double = 123.45678987654

Enter string: Hello
String = "Hello"

Enter text: Hello, world.
String = "Hello, world."
```

The program below uses a scanner to read from a file:

```
import java.util.Scanner;
import java.io.*;

public class EchoFile {
    public static void main(String[] args) throws IOException{
        Scanner fileScan = new Scanner(new File("getty.txt"));
        while (fileScan.hasNext()) {
            String buf = fileScan.nextLine();
            System.out.println(buf);
        }
    }
}
```

Here's the program output:

```
Four score and seven years ago our fathers brought forth, upon this
continent, a new nation, conceived in liberty, and dedicated to the
proposition that all men are created equal. Now we are engaged in a
great civil war, testing whether that nation, or any nation, so
conceived, and so dedicated, can long endure. We are met here on a
great battlefield of that war. We have come to dedicate a portion of
it as a final resting place for those who here gave their lives that
that nation might live. It is altogether fitting and proper that we
should do this. But in a larger sense we can not dedicate - we can not
consecrate - we can not hallow this ground. The brave men, living and
dead, who struggled here, have consecrated it far above our poor power
to add or detract. The world will little note, nor long remember, what
we say here, but can never forget what they did here. It is for us, the
living, rather to be dedicated here to the unfinished work which they
have, thus far, so nobly carried on. It is rather for us to be here
dedicated to the great task remaining before us that from these honored
dead we take increased devotion to that cause for which they here gave
the last full measure of devotion - that we here highly resolve that
these dead shall not have died in vain; that this nation shall have a
new birth of freedom; and that this government of the people, by the
people, for the people, shall not perish from the earth.
```

The `Scanner` class can also be used to parse a character string into separate pieces.

`Scanner useDelimiter(String pattern)`
Sets the scanner's delimiting pattern to the specified String.

`Scanner useDelimiter(Pattern pattern)`
Sets this scanner's delimiting pattern to the specified Pattern.

`Pattern delimiter()`
Returns the Pattern this Scanner is currently using to match delimiters.

```java
import java.util.Scanner;
import java.io.*;

public class Delimiter {
    public static void main(String[] args) throws IOException{
        Scanner fileScan = new Scanner(new File("url.txt"));
        while (fileScan.hasNext()) {
            String url = fileScan.nextLine();
            System.out.println("URL: " +  url);

            Scanner urlScan = new Scanner(url);
            urlScan.useDelimiter("/");

            while (urlScan.hasNext())
                System.out.println("      " + urlScan.next());
            System.out.println();
        }
    }
}
```

Here's the program output:

```
URL: www.palomar.edu/csit
    www.palomar.edu
    csit

URL:
www.dilbert.com/comics/dilbert/archive/images/dilbert2813970050926.gif
    www.dilbert.com
    comics
    dilbert
    archive
    images
    dilbert2813970050926.gif
```

Inheritance

Inheritance is one of the best things about Java. After classes, inheritance is probably the most powerful feature of object-oriented programming. It's the feature that sets object-oriented programming apart from traditional programming because it allows us to extend and reuse existing code without having to rewrite the code.

So far most of the classes we've created have been built from scratch, which is probably the way you've been working when you want to add new features to a program, since it's usually just as easy to write new code as it is to change existing code, debug it, etc. What we want to do is to be able to add new features to a program without changing the original code, and that's what inheritance lets you do!

In non-object-oriented languages, if you have a library of code and its source, which isn't always the case, you can make changes. But first you have to have a copy of the source code. As you make modifications, you need to understand the internals of the functions that someone else may have written. As you do this, it is a given that you're going to introduce some bugs, which may or may not be easy to find. So you end up with 2 bodies of code:

> • the old debugged body
>
> • your new body of code which contains the old code in some form, plus additions and changes, and of course new bugs.

Future changes mean more copies and the amount of code you need to maintain increases, but without an equivalent increase in functionality.

Creating new classes is the fundamental activity in Java, since we use classes to model the problem being solved. When we think about changing or extending code in Java, it's natural that we think not in terms of instance variables or methods, but in terms of classes. Thus, reusing code in Java means reusing classes.

It's very common that an existing class that you or someone else has written or debugged doesn't quite do what you want. In Java, you can make a new class from an old one using inheritance. When you inherit, you say:

> "This new class is just like that old one plus some additional data and methods."

With inheritance, you don't make a copy of the existing methods. You just use the ones that are already there:

> • You can add new instance variables and methods.
>
> • You can also change the meaning of existing methods by redefining them so they have a different behavior for your new class.

You don't even need the source code for the method definitions, just the `.class` files containing the class definitions that must always be available to use the class in any case. This means you can inherit from any vendor's class library, whether they provide source code or not!!

Derivation

Java implements inheritance through the mechanism of *derivation*. A *subclass* is derived from a *superclass* and inherits all the instance variables and methods of the superclass.

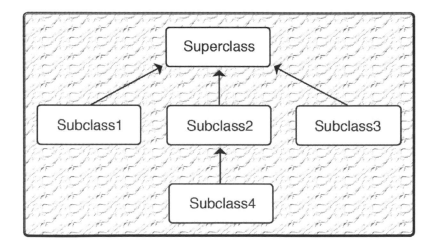

• Many subclasses might be derived from a single superclass.

• A subclass class may itself be a superclass from which additional classes are derived.

Thus, we can build up a class hierarchy where each class can serve as a parent or root for a new set of classes.

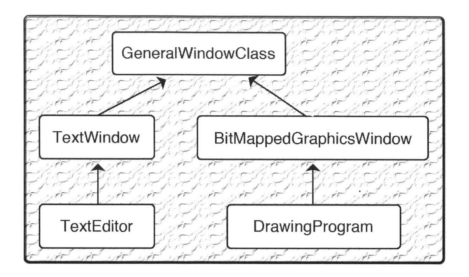

Note that there is no set limit on the number of classes that may be derived from one another.

So inheritance allows us to collect related classes into a hierarchy with the classes at the top serving as abstractions for those below. This implies that a subclass class is a specialization of its parent class, i.e., the subclass "is a" type of superclass, but with more detail added. For this reason, the relationship between a subclass and its superclass is called an *is-a* relationship.

Note that the superclass remains unchanged by this process of inheritance regardless of the number of classes that are derived from it. Therefore a subclass is always at least as big as its parent class so that an instance of the derived class always contains all of the members of its parent class.

Note that you cannot subtract or remove anything from a parent class. However, accessing the inherited members is a different matter we'll look at later, i.e., just because you happen to subclass does not mean that you are automatically granted complete and unlimited access privileges to the instance variables and methods of the superclass.

Inheritance is commonly used in two ways:

• In one role it can be thought of as a reuse mechanism, a way to create a new class that strongly resembles an existing one.

- In another role, it can be thought of as an abstraction mechanism, a tool to organize classes into hierarchies of specializations.

In both cases, you can think of it as a way for one class to subcontract or delegate some of its tasks to another.

`Counter` Class Example

We could define a `Counter` class that includes a general-purpose counter variable, `count`, which could be:

- initialized to 0 with the default ctor
- initialized to some other value with an one-arg ctor
- incremented with the `inc` method
- returned with the `getCount` operator

The class is shown below:

```
// Counter.java

public class Counter {
    private int count;

    public Counter() {
        count = 0;
    }

    public Counter(int c) {
        count = c;
    }

    public int getCount() {
        return count;
    }

    public void inc() {
        ++count;
    }
}
```

Here's the driver program to test the `Counter` class:

```
// testCounter.java

import java.io.*;

public class testCounter {
    public static void main(String[] args) {
        Counter c1 = new Counter(5);
        System.out.println(c1.getCount());
        c1.inc();
        System.out.println(c1.getCount());
    }
}
```

Here's a look at the class diagram that shows the relationship between the two classes:

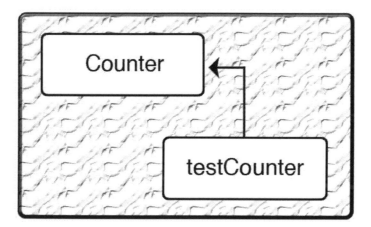

Suppose we've worked long and hard to make the `Counter` class operate just the way we want and we're pleased with the results, except for one thing. We really need a way to decrement the count. Perhaps we're counting people entering a bank and we want to increment the count when they come in and decrement the count when they go out. So the count represents the number of people in the bank at any moment.

We could insert a decrement routine directly into the source code of the `Counter` class, but there are several reasons why we might not want to do this:

- The `Counter` class works very well and has undergone many hours of testing and debugging. (While this is an exaggeration in this case, it might be true in a larger and more complex class.)

- If we start fooling around with the source code for `Counter`, the testing process will need to be carried out again and we may foul something up and spend hours debugging code that worked fine before we modified it.

- Another reason for not modifying the `Counter` class is that we might not have access to its source code, especially if it has been distributed as part of a class library.

To avoid these problems, we can use inheritance to create a new class based on `Counter`, without modifying `Counter` itself. We can derive a new subclass, `CountDn`, which adds a decrement method to the `Counter` class:

The classes are shown below. Note the access specifier changes from `private` to `protected`.

```java
// counter2.java
public class Counter2 {

    protected int count;

    public Counter2() {
        count = 0;
    }

    public Counter2(int c) {
        count = c;
    }

    int getCount() {
        return count;
    }

    public void inc() {
        ++count;
    }
}
```

```
// countDn.java

public class CountDn extends Counter2 {
    public void dec() {
        --count;
    }
}
```

Here's a breakdown of the syntax:

• The `private` access specifier in the `Counter2` class has been replaced with the `protected` access specifier. More on this later.

• `CountDn` is the subclass name
• `extends Counter2` specifies that `CountDn` is derived from class `Counter2`
• `Counter2` is the name of the superclass

Note that the new `CountDn` class inherits all the features of the `Counter2` class. `CountDn` doesn't need a constructor, it doesn't need the `getCount()` method, and it doesn't need the `inc()` method because they already exist in the superclass `Counter2`. Keep in mind that the `public` methods of a superclass remain public in the subclass.

Here's the driver program to test the `CountDn` class:

```
// testCountDn.java

import java.io.*;

public class testCountDn {
    public static void main(String[] args) {
    CountDn c = new CountDn();
    System.out.println(c.getCount());
    c.inc();
    System.out.println(c.getCount());
    c.dec();
    System.out.println(c.getCount());
    }
}
```

Here's a look at the class diagram that shows the relationship among the three classes:

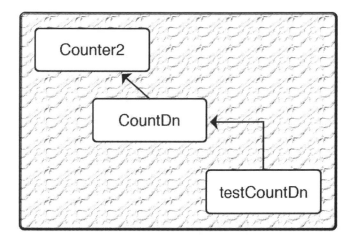

The output produced is:

```
0
1
0
```

Accessing Base Class Members

An important part to inheritance is to know when a method in the superclass can be used by objects of the subclass. This is called *accessibility*. For example, in `main()`, we created an object of class `CountDn`:

```
CountDn c = new CountDn();
```

that caused `c` to be created as an object of class `CountDn` and be initialized to 0. But wait! How is this possible? There is no constructor in the `CountDn` class specifier. So what entity carries out the initialization?

It turns out that under certain circumstances, if you don't specify a constructor, the subclass will use an appropriate constructor from the superclass. Here, there's no constructor in `CountDn`, so the compiler uses the default constructor from the superclass, `Counter2`.

Note that object `c` of the `CountDn` class also uses the `inc()` and `getCount()` methods from the `Counter2` class. If the compiler doesn't find these methods in the class of which `c` is a member, it uses methods from the superclass.

Subclass Ctors

There's a potential glitch in our program. What if we want to initialize a `CountDn` object to a value? Can the one-arg constructor in `Counter2` be used? No it cannot! Although the compiler will substitute a default constructor from the superclass, it draws the line at more complex constructors. Therefore we must write a new set of constructors for the subclass:

```
// countDn2.java

public class CountDn2 extends Counter2 {

    public CountDn2() {
        super();
    }

    public CountDn2(int c) {
        super(c);
    }

    public void dec() {
        --count;
    }
}


// testCountDn2

public static void main(String[] args) {
    CountDn2 c = new CountDn2(5);
    System.out.println(c.getCount());
    c.inc();
    System.out.println(c.getCount());
    c.dec();
    System.out.println(c.getCount());
}
```

Here's a look at the class diagram that shows the relationship among the three classes:

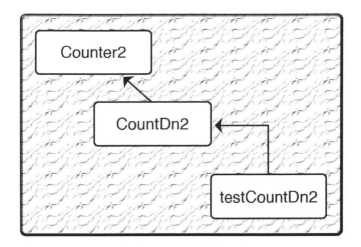

The output produced is:

```
5
6
5
```

Here,

```
    super();
```

causes the `CountDn2` default constructor to call the `Counter2` default constructor in the superclass and

```
    super(c);
```

causes the `CountDn2` one-arg constructor to call the `Counter2` one-arg constructor in the superclass.

Note that the `CountDn2` constructor could add additional statements of its own, but in this case is doesn't need to. So there are no additional statements within the braces. But if it defined a new data member, it could initialize it here and then call the superclass constructor to initialize the rest of the object. More on this later.

The Protected Access Specifier

- Methods of a class can access both private and public members.

- Objects of a class can access only public members.

- Private members are private.

This is all we need to know if we don't use inheritance. With inheritance, there are new possibilities. The question that concerns us at the moment is this:

Can methods of the subclass access instance variables of the superclass? That is, can `dec` in `CountDn2` access `count` in `Counter2`?

The answer is that methods can access instance variables of the superclass if the instance variables are *public* or *protected*. They can't access *private* instance variables.

We don't want to make `count` public since that would allow it to be accessed by any method anywhere in the program and eliminate the advantages of encapsulation. A protected member, on the other hand, can be accessed by methods in its own class, or in any class derived from its own class. It can't be accessed from methods outside the class, such as `main()`, which is just what we want!

So a protected instance variable is a cross between a private and a public instance variable.

- Like private instance variables, protected instance variables are accessible only to other class methods. Outside of the class, protected instance variables are invisible.

- Like public instance variables, protected instance variables are inherited by the subclass and are accessible to methods in the subclass.

Keep the following rules in mind when deciding whether to make instance variables private, protected, or public:

- A private instance variable is accessible only to members of the class in which the private member is declared.

- A protected member is accessible to members of its own class and to any members in a subclass.

- A public member is accessible to the class's own members, to a subclass's members, and to all other users of the class.

Access Specifier	Accessible From Own Class	Accessible From Subclass	Accessible From Objects Outside Class
private	yes	no	no
protected	yes	yes	no
public	yes	yes	yes

The moral is that if you are writing a class that you suspect might be used, at any point in the future, as a superclass for other classes, then any instance variable that the subclass class might need to access should be made protected rather than private. This ensures that the class is "inheritance ready."

Note that inheritance doesn't work in reverse. The superclass and its objects don't know anything about any classes derived from the superclass. For instance, in the declaration:

```
Counter2 c;
```

object c cannot use the dec-- method defined in CountDn2. If you want a counter that you can decrement, it must be of class CountDn2 and not class Counter2.

The Employee Class
Consider the `Employee` superclass below:

```java
// Employee.java

public class Employee {
    protected String name;
    protected String address;
    protected int age;
    protected int dependent;
    protected int jobClass;

    public Employee(String name, String address, int age,
                            int dependent, int jobClass) {
        this.name = name;
        this.address = address;
        this.age = age;
        this.dependent = dependent;
        this.jobClass = jobClass;
    }

    public void display() {
        System.out.println("Name: " + name);
        System.out.println("Address: " + address);
        System.out.println("Age: " + age);
        System.out.println("Dependent: " + dependent);
        System.out.println("jobClass: " + jobClass);
    }

    public int getAge() {
        return age;
    }

    public int getDependent() {
        return dependent;
    }

    public int getJobClass() {
        return jobClass;
    }
}
```

The superclass `Employee` is set up like any other class. However, because we intend that this class have a class derived from it, we put the instance variables in the `protected` access region because we want the subclass methods to have direct access to these instance variables. Note that this class has a constructor, output method, and three access methods.

Occasionally very little is done with a superclass. We may not even declare any objects of a superclass because a superclass object is not required to declare a subclass object. Superclasses can be created to provide instance variables and methods that will be shared by a variety of different subclass definitions. The subclass looks like this:

```java
// WorkData.java

public class WorkData extends Employee {
    private String occupation;

    public WorkData(String name, String address,
                        String occupation, int age, int dependent,
                        int jobClass) {
        super(name, address, age, dependent, jobClass);
        this.occupation = occupation;
    }

    public String getOccupation() {
        return occupation;
    }

    public void display() {
        super.display();
        System.out.println("Occupation: " + occupation);
    }
}
```

Class `WorkData` is a subclass that inherits from the superclass `Employee`.

A subclass will inherit all the instance variables and methods of its superclass and can declare some of its own. The methods of the subclass can see the public and protected instance variables of the superclass, but not the private instance variables.

The superclass methods cannot see the instance variables of any of its subclasses. How could it? The superclass has no idea what classes may be derived from it. The subclass can only indirectly access the private instance variables of the superclass by using the protected or public methods of the super class.

Note that the subclass has a constructor with 6 arguments, although the class has only declared one instance variable of its own:

```java
private String occupation;
```

One argument is used to give `occupation` a value, while the remaining five arguments are used to initialize the memory inherited from the superclass. So the constructor for `WorkData` is responsible for initializing the superclass portion of a subclass object as well as its own instance variable.

The subclass inherits the ability to use the following methods of the superclass:

```
public void display()

public int getAge()

public int getDependent()

public int getJobClass()
```

In addition, the subclass has added a new method called:

```
public String getOccupation()
```

and redefines the method:

```
display()
```

for the derived class.

Note that this redefined method is not an example of method name overloading because both the superclass and subclass methods have identical signatures. The subclass can actually use both `display()` methods, i.e., those defined in `Employee` and the others defined in `Workdata`.

```
// testWorkData.java

public static void main(String[] args) {
    WorkData w = new WorkData("Haley Laurel", "Austin, Texas",
                                        "Physician", 35, 2, 5);
    w.display();
}
```

Here's a look at the class diagram that shows the relationship among the three classes:

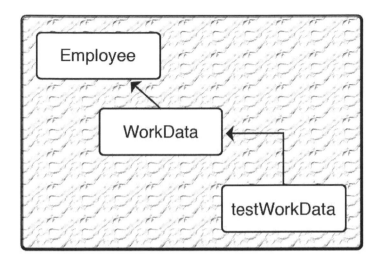

The output produced is:

```
Name: Haley Laurel
Address: Austin, Texas
Age: 35
Dependent: 2
jobClass: 5
Occupation: Physician
```

Note that the `display` method that is invoked is the one defined in the `WorkData` class. A subclass object can access the display method of the superclass by using the form:

```
super.display();
```

Note that `super` is required when methods in the superclass and the subclass have the same signature. Also note that a subclass can act as a superclass for classes derived from it allowing you to create a hierarchy of subclasses.

Class Hierarchies

In the examples so far, inheritance has been used to add functionality to an existing class. Let's look at an example where inheritance is used for a different purpose, as part of the original design of a program.

Our example models a database of employees of a widget company. In this company, there are three kinds of employee's:

- managers – manage other employee's

- scientists - perform research to develop better widgets

- laborers - operate the dangerous widget-stamping presses

The database stores a name and an employee id number for all employee's, no matter what category they are. For managers, it also stores their title and golf club dues. For scientists is stores the number of scholarly articles they have published. Laborers need no additional data beyond their names and id numbers.

So our program design will start with a base class `Employee` that handles the employee's last name and id number. From this class, three other classes will be derived: `Manager`, `Scientist`, and `Laborer`.

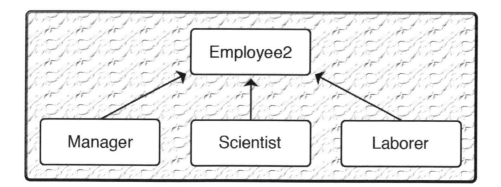

The Manager and Scientist classes contain additional information about these categories of employee as well as methods to handle this information.

```java
// Employee2.java

import java.util.Scanner;
import java.io.*;

public class Employee2 {
    private String name;
    private long id;

    public void getData() {
        Scanner scan = new Scanner(System.in);
        System.out.print("Enter name: ");
        String name = scan.next();
        System.out.print("Enter ID: ");
        long id = scan.nextLong();
    }

    public void putData() {
        System.out.println("Name: " + name);
        System.out.println("ID:    " + id);
    }
}

// Manager.java

import java.util.Scanner;
import java.io.*;

public class Manager extends Employee2 {
    private String title;
    private double dues;

    public void getData() {
        Scanner scan = new Scanner(System.in);
        super.getData();
        System.out.print("Title: ");
        String title = scan.next();
        System.out.print("Golf Club Dues: ");
        dues = scan.nextDouble();
    }

    public void putData() {
        super.putData();
        System.out.println("Title: " + title);
        System.out.println("Golf Club dues: " + dues);
    }
}
```

```
// Scientist.java

import java.util.Scanner;
import java.io.*;

public class Scientist extends Employee2 {
    private int pubs;

    public void getData() {
        Scanner scan = new Scanner(System.in);
        super.getData();
        System.out.print("Number of Publications: ");
        pubs = scan.nextInt();
    }

    public void putData() {
        super.putData();
        System.out.println("Number of Publications: " + pubs);
    }
}

// laborer.java

public class Laborer extends Employee2 {
}
```

Once again, here's a look at the class diagram that shows the relationship among the four classes:

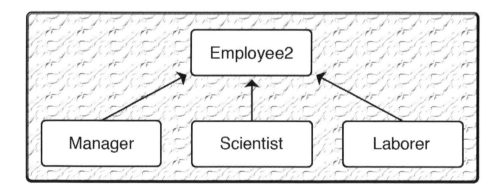

Note that the `Laborer` class operates identically to the `Employee2` class since it contains no additional instance variables or methods. It may seem that the `Laborer` class is unnecessary, but by making it a separate class, we emphasize that all classes are derived from the same source, `Employee2`.

Another reason for creating an apparently empty `Laborer` class concerns the issues of maintenance. In the future, if we decide to modify the `Laborer` class, we would not need to change the specifier for `Employee2`.

Classes used only for deriving other classes, i.e. `Employee2`, are sometimes called *abstract classes*, meaning that no actual instances (objects) of this class are created. The term abstract has a more precise definition connected with polymorphism that we'll come across later.

Levels of Inheritance

Classes can be derived from classes that are themselves derived classes. Consider the class hierarchy below:

```
public class A {
}

public class B extends A {
}

public class C extends B {
}
```

Here, class `B` is derived from class `A`, and class `C` is derived from class `B`. This process can be extended to an arbitrary number of levels.

In this way, we can extend our `Employee2` class program to add a special kind of laborer called a foreman. Since a foreman is a kind of laborer, the `Foreman` class will be derived from the `Laborer` class.

Foremen oversee the widget-stamping operation, supervising groups of laborers. They are responsible for the widget production quota for their group. A foreman's ability is measured by the percentage of production quotas successfully met. So we'll have a quota data item in the `Foreman` class that represents this percentage:

```
// Foreman.java

public class Foreman extends Laborer {
    private float quotas;

    public void getData() {
        super.getData();
        System.out.print("Enter quotas: ");
        quotas = IO.readFloat();
    }

    public void putData() {
        super.putData();
        System.out.println("Quotas: " + quotas);
    }
}
```

Here's a look at the class diagram that shows the relationship among the four classes:

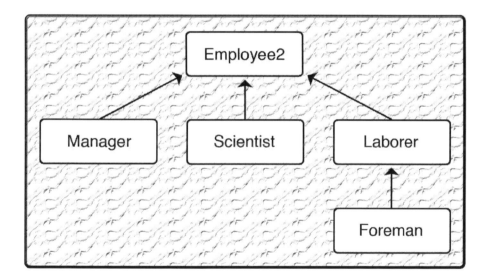

Notice that a class hierarchy is not the same as an organizational chart. An organization chart shows lines of commands. A class hierarchy results from generalizing common characteristics. The more general the class, the higher it is on the chart! Thus, a `Laborer` is more general than a `Foreman`, who is a specialized kind of `Laborer`. So `Laborer` is shown above `Foreman` in the class hierarchy.

Made in the USA
Middletown, DE
02 September 2020